THE WISDOM OF
ANCIENT EGYPT

THE WISDOM OF ANCIENT EGYPT

*Writings from
the Time of the Pharoahs*

Translated and edited
by Joseph Kaster

BARNES
&NOBLE
BOOKS
NEW YORK

Note: The following texts have been revised and modernized from
the translations in *The Literature of the Ancient Egyptians* by
Adolf Erman, translated by Aylward M. Blackman, London, Methuen,
1927. While this volume was not copyrighted, acknowledgments are
hereby gratefully made.

     The Instruction of Ptah-Hotep
     The Instruction of Ka-Gemni
     The Instruction of Amen-em-Hat
     Advice to Schoolboys
     The Prophecy of Nefer-Rohu
     King Cheops and the Magicians

Originally published as *The Wings of the Falcon*

This edition published by Barnes & Noble, Inc.,
by arrangement with Henry Holt and Company.

1993 Barnes & Noble Books

ISBN 1-56619-224-2

Printed and bound in the United States of America

M 9 8 7 6 5 4 3 2 1

Contents

Foreword

Ancient Egypt is like one of those darkly beautiful women who seem to exude an aura of deep and awesome mystery and in whose languid eyes there lurk nameless secrets and desires. She is sometimes radiant with splendid majesty, sometimes shimmering with undulating gleams of languorous sensuality, always glamorous, always entrancing men with the unearthly magic of her fascination. Some men approach her in hesitating awe, and then, fearful of the eventual frustration of their hopes of penetrating the dark and solemn mystery, make a hurried and confused retreat. Others, with a brash confidence engendered of their self-esteem as men of experience, who thereby obviate the expenditure of time, effort, and love necessary for an understanding of her, unhesitatingly proceed to create an elaborate picture of the intricacies of her personality, complete with all the details of her "mysteries," and all founded on nothing but the wooly fancies of their fertile imaginations. They have never actually conversed with her, but of course they hasten to inform all and sundry of their intimate knowledge. Most men do not approach her at all.

Only a few indeed have taken the time and the pains to get to know her as a person, the first necessity being, of course, to learn her language; and of these few how many have, or are capable of, the love? The result is that our dark lady is a very lonely lady indeed—very famous and glamorous, but very lonely.

However, those who have approached her as one mature individual to another, and have succeeded in cultivating her as a human being, find that she is neither as formidable nor as distant as she seemed. They find that she is a person of great warmth and charm, with a mature and always wide-awake intelligence, possessed of a refined and delicate and always sophisticated artistic sense with a flair all her own; all of this balanced and complemented with an excellent sense of humor. True, a great deal of the mystery is gone (most of it due, in the first place, to our initial ignorance), but does not this make for our greater pleasure in her many-faceted personality?

It is the purpose of this book, as presented by one who has managed to establish communication, to allow ancient Egypt to speak in her own words and tell the modern reader what her men and women felt and thought: some of their attitudes toward life and love, toward the world and its realities, toward the overwhelming powers of what we would call the unseen but what to them was quite visible and apparent, toward death and the life of eternity beyond.

It should be remembered that the number of texts discovered during almost a century and a half of exploration and excavation in Egypt is vast, and that only a selection can be presented here. An important purpose in selection has been to present what was typical of the culture. Another has been to offer the reader a sampling of the various genres of writing in which the ancient Egyptians expressed themselves. A most important purpose has been to acquaint him with their essential humanity; in many respects, the ancient Egyptians will turn out to have been startlingly modern. It will also be seen that Egyptian culture, Egyptian ways of thought and expression, exerted a profound influence upon the writers and thinkers of ancient Israel whose works we read in the Old Testament.

The translations, for the most part, have been made by the present writer, and when he has taken advantage of the labors of his predecessors, the translations have been collated with the published editions of the original hieroglyphic texts and thoroughly revised both in the light of more recent scholarship, and with the purpose of presenting the material in such a form as would make for ease in reading, eliminating such scholarly but distracting apparatus as brackets, dots, and italics for surmised renderings.

It is hoped that many readers will be stimulated to consult the translations and discussions by the renowned scholars in the field listed in the Appendix, in which publications such apparatus is supplied.

As for the language, we have studiously avoided the tendency of many scholars, who feel that they ought to translate ancient texts into sixteenth-century English as exemplified by the King James version of the Bible. The ancient Egyptians were in many respects much more modern in their outlook than the translators who produced the Authorized Version of 1611. For this reason, and because it seems rather silly to translate into a language that is not used, we have avoided the *thee*'s and *thou*'s and the sundry other characteristics of "Biblical" English. On the other hand, we have eschewed as abhorrent language that is cute or slangy, such as may be found in some modern versions of ancient classics.

The notes are intended as elucidations for the general reader, and they have been kept as brief as possible to avoid loss of continuity in the reading of the text. They have, however, been placed in their proper position at the bottom of the page, for all too often this writer has had to leaf hurriedly to the back of the book or of the chapter in search of the footnote, frequently losing both the place and the trend of thought in the process and roundly cursing author, editor, and publisher of the wretched volume. For those interested in further study of the matters touched upon in the notes, additional readings have been indicated in the Appendix on How to Become an Amateur Egyptologist. It is the fervent hope of this writer that these recommended readings will also serve to guide the interested reader away from the fantastic nonsense put out by self-important ignoramuses—what book dealers call "squirrel food" and much of which gluts the shelves of bookshops dealing in the occult.

The obligations of one who publishes translations and/or interpretations of ancient texts are many. Generations of scholars and investigators have all contributed to the understanding and interpretation not only of the literature but of the life of a vigorous ancient people such as were the Egyptians, and neither literature nor life can be understood without the other. Even the greatest scholars are deeply indebted both to their predecessors and to their contemporaries in the field, and productive scholarship is always the result of a co-operative endeavor, whether scholars are working as an official "team" or alone. To make a list of acknowledgments in the present case would therefore be gratuitous. It is with the very greatest pleasure, however, that the author avails himself of this opportunity to express his gratitude to two men *sine quibus non:* to Professor Cyrus H. Gordon of Brandeis University, under whom he earned his doctorate in Egyptology, Assyriology, and Ugaritic studies when at Dropsie College, who helped him in innumerable ways and who has always been a continuing source of inspiration and encouragement; and to Mr. Arthur A. Cohen of Holt, Rinehart and Winston, who welcomed the project at its inception and who has exercised profound understanding and heroic patience.

JOSEPH KASTER

A Note on Proper Nouns and Spelling

Much sympathy is to be extended to the many interested persons who, in their various readings in Egyptian history, religion, and related subjects have been utterly confused by the wide disparity in the transliteration of Egyptian words and proper nouns. When a reader has encountered such variant forms as *Ra* and *Re, Amenemhat* and *Amenemmes, Tahutimes, Thothmes, Thutmose, Tuthmosis* and *Thutmosis, Amenhotep* and *Amenophis, Akhenaten, Akhenaton,* and *Ikhnaton,* he is justifiably entitled to his confusion. A few words on the reasons for these different renderings and on the

xii

nature of the written language of ancient Egypt as we have it are in order.

All forms of Egyptian, with the exclusion of Coptic, were written with the consonants only. There are no vowels as such in the signs used in the writing. Egyptian shares this orthographic peculiarity with other Semitic languages such as Hebrew and Arabic. We can pronounce Hebrew and Arabic with more or less accuracy because during the Middle Ages a series of little marks were devised to designate the different vowels and were written over or under the consonants with which they were to be pronounced. This was not done with ancient Egyptian, as Coptic, the last stage of the language, was written with an adaptation of the Greek alphabet, in which the vowels are part of the alphabet itself. It is important to remember, however, that Coptic differs from classical Egyptian as much as, say, current vernacular English differs from Old English or even Anglo-Saxon, and it seems only logical that it is as incorrect to pronounce classical Egyptian according to derived words in Coptic as it would be to pronounce the language of King Alfred like modern English. It has become the fashion, however, among some modern scholars to try to work back the pronunciation *à la* Coptic, but

to this writer it seems rather futile, for the reason just given.

It was long ago decided among Egyptologists that since we do not know the vowels, the only thing to do in order to pronounce the words is to insert a short *e* (the vowel of greatest frequency in the European languages) between the consonants—a most logical and sober procedure. Thus, the word for "good" or "beautiful," which is spelled in Egyptian with the consonants *n, f,* and *r*, we transliterate *nfr* and we pronounce *nefer*. For all we know, it may have been pronounced *nofar, nifur, nufar,* or even *nefer*. The fact that in Coptic the word has become *noufe* (pronounced noo-feh) has given rise to such renderings of proper nouns of which the word is a part as *Nofretiti*.

We have a number of royal names rendered into Greek in various Greek writings dating from the late period. The Greeks had quite a cavalier attitude to all foreign names and absolutely "murdered" them. Thus the name of the Egyptian deity who was the scribe of the gods and the patron of learning, which reads, in Egyptian, something like *Djehwty*, the Greeks rendered variously as *Thoth, Thouth, Thout,* and in theophoric (god-bearing) names introduced further corruption plus the ornament of a

Greek ending, with the result that in the name of a king such as *Djhwty-ms,* "Born of the god Djehwty," we get such specimens of wild misrenderings as *Tethmosis* and *Thmosis.* Again, it has become fashionable among some modern scholars to use the Greek renderings of Egyptian names in their translations, which accounts for *Ammenemes, Sesostris, Tuthmosis,* and so on. To this writer, at least, it seems not only affected but barbarous and recalls the old-fashioned eighteenth- and nineteenth-century custom of using the Roman names of the gods when translating from the Greek: Zeus was "Englished" as Jupiter, Athena as Minerva, and so forth.

It has seemed most sensible to us to use the following guiding principles with regard to names and other proper nouns:

1 When the Greek version of an Egyptian name has become so familiar with usage through the centuries that another version would be strange or confusing to the general reader, we will use the Greek: *Cheops, Memphis, Thoth.*

2 When the traditional and familiar Greek version is part of a name it will be used, but we will not pedantically use the entire Greek rendering of the name. Thus the reader will find *Cheops,* and *Thothmes* but not *Tuthmosis.* This method was followed by some of the older Egyptologists and seems a reasonable compromise.

3 In other proper nouns, we will give the closest approximation to the transliteration, except in some cases where a slightly differing version may be more familar; for example, we will use *Amenhotep* and not *Yemenhetep,* but certainly not *Amenophis!*

4 With regard to the Semitic consonants *aleph* and *ayin,* for which no equivalents exist in the Indo-European languages, we will render them as *a* as pronounced in "father." Thus we will read, for example, *Ra* instead of the Coptic *Re.* In cuneiform diplomatic correspondence of the Empire period the *Ra* element in royal names is rendered as *riya,* but again we cannot be guided by the pronunciation of foreigners.

Please note: Capitals in a translated text indicate that those words are written in red ink on the original papyrus.

1
Introduction

1 What Was Ancient Egypt? Egypt's Place in the History of Civilization

Like the dark and mysterious enchantress of our Foreword, Egypt has always intrigued anyone who came in contact with her, even in ancient times. Perhaps it was because men could not help but be powerfully impressed by her huge stone pyramids and temples, awesome, majestic, overpowering monuments to the genius of man, and seemingly as ancient and venerable as time itself. Perhaps it was because of the high sophistication of her art—sculptured figures varying from the grandly monumental to the tiniest masterpieces of *kleinkunst*, brilliantly cut in granite, marble, and sandstone, in gold, silver, and bronze, and in every kind and color of precious jewel and gem; reliefs and mural paintings in brilliant colors and of fascinating interest—all masterfully fashioned in clean economy of line and with an unerring and exquisite refinement of taste.

Or one might say that they were intrigued by her enigmatic hieroglyphic writing that they saw everywhere, carved on monuments, obelisks, and statuary, and on the walls of temples and tombs. Surely all these rows and columns of little marching birds, animals, and human figures in a variety of postures, and the heads, hands, wings, and a host of objects of nature unknown, engraved and colored with the same consummate artistry and verve that is displayed in their painting and sculpture, surely these must have important meaning; since the meaning is unknown to us, it is mysterious, and what is mysterious is intriguing.

Actually, it was all of these factors combined that made Egypt such a land of fascination and interest to all who visited it and left us their impressions of their travels. Herodotus was there in the fifth century B.C. and buttonholed every priest he met for answers to his insistent questions (many answered him quite accurately, but many also, with typical Egyptian canny humor, told him some howling cock-and-bull stories); and the famous travelers and geographers of Hellenistic and Roman times, the Middle Ages, the Renaissance, and the beginnings of the modern period in the seventeenth and eighteenth centuries, all recounted the wonders of that ancient, mysterious, and highly civilized land, many repeating and compounding the errors of their predecessors.

It was not until the beginning of the nineteenth century that Egypt began to be explored and studied by anything like a scientific method. The decipherment of the language of the hieroglyphics by Champollion and Young in the early part of the century, together with the tremendous progress of objective science during the 1800's, opened wide the avenues to serious exploration and study of ancient Egypt. The development of scientific methods in archaeology and philology as important aids in the study of civilizations placed our ever-increasing knowledge of ancient Egypt on solid foundations. Egyptology thus became a scholarly discipline, and in concert with analogous developments in the study of the ancient Mesopotamian and classical worlds, revolutionized our concepts of the development of Western civilization and extended immeasurably the boundaries of our knowledge.

By the end of the nineteenth century, the main developments and periods of Egyptian history were known; great collections of objects yielded by archaeological excavation were established in museums in Europe, in America, and in Egypt itself; quite a number of hieroglyphic texts from the papri and the monuments had been published; and a large body of both scholarly and popular exposition was accumulating. During the twentieth century our knowledge has been vastly increased. There have been spectacular discoveries resulting from the brilliantly conducted excavations of the period immediately preceding World War I, and of the twenties and thirties, the most widely popularized of which has been the discovery of the only tomb of an Egyptian king that had not been thoroughly robbed in antiquity, that of Tut-Ankh-Amen (the "old King Tut" of newspaper literature, though he was all of eighteen when he died).

But what has been perhaps the most important development in Egyptology in this century has been the great advances in our knowledge of the Egyptian language. During the past forty years the great studies of Egyptian grammar and syntax have been published by such brilliant scholars as Battiscombe Gunn, Adolf Erman, Sir Alan H. Gardiner, and Gustave Lefebvre, to mention only a few—researches that have made possible for us a control of hieroglyphic Egyptian comparable to that of the classical and Semitic languages. These advances, in turn, have enabled Egyptologists to publish scholarly, well-considered, and annotated editions and renditions of the texts, and to present Egyptian literature to the intelligent lay reader in reliable and accurate translations, such as *The Literature of the Ancient Egyptians,* published in German during the twenties and translated into English by Aylward M. Blackman; Gustave Lefebvre's excellent *Romans et Contes Égyptiens de l'Époque Pharaonique,* published in 1949 (and, alas, still not translated into English); and most valuable of all for its variety and excellence as the work of one of the foremost contemporary scholars in the field, the translations of the Egyptian texts by Professor John A. Wilson of the University of Chicago in *Ancient Near Eastern Texts Relating to the Old Testament,* published in 1950, with a second edition in 1955, by Princeton University Press. It is only fair to add that there are still some difficulties and obscurities to challenge us, with consequent divergence of opinion among scholars in the matter of translation and interpretation, but the same is true of classical texts and certainly of the Bible, even today.

The reduction of the methods of archaeological excavation to a science—greatly aided recently by the discovery of ingenious electronic detection devices activated by subatomic radiation from buried objects[1]—plus our intimate knowledge of the language and the accessibility of most of the discovered writings and inscriptions in good scholarly editions, have enabled us to make an intelligent comparative evaluation of the civilization of ancient Egypt, and to determine its place in the political and cultural development of mankind. We find, as a result, that the debt of Western civilization to ancient Egypt is far greater than one might be inclined to imagine. In a work intended as a general reader's introduction to Egyptian literature, we can attempt to indicate Egypt's contributions to civilization only in broad outline. The following are only some of what the writer believes to be the salient factors involved, quite concisely stated of necessity.

Development of the Calendar   The solar calendar of twelve months, which governs our lives and our movements, is Egyptian. By the beginning of recorded history, the Egyptians were already using a yearly cycle of twelve months, which began in midsummer, when the Nile annually overflowed its banks. A precise astronomical point of determination had already been discovered in prehistoric times: the day on which the brightest of the fixed stars, that which we call Sirius, rose on the horizon together with the sun and remained visible for

---

[1] Radiation methods of dating, such as the carbon-14 test, are usually accurate within a range no narrower than four hundred years. Although this range of accuracy is not of prime importance for the broad periods of prehistory, it obviously has little value in dealing with historic periods where dating must be pinpointed as accurately as possible.

a few moments until it faded with the advance of dawn. We refer to this as the "heliacal" rising of Sirius (from Greek *helios*, "the sun"). Each of the twelve months consisted of thirty days. They were quite aware, however, that the year consisted of 365 days, and the extra five days were intercalated at the end of the year as the birthdays of the great gods and observed as festivals during which no work was done or business conducted. It is not to be presumed that the Egyptians were unaware that they were still missing a quarter of a day (the actual duration of the year being $365\frac{1}{4}$ days), as they made allowances for it even if they did not do anything about it. For instance, we know that they knew the exact length of a year from autumn equinox to autumn equinox within two minutes. They knew also that it would take Sirius 1,460 years (365 × 4) to get back exactly to the same point on the horizon. We refer to this as the "Sothic Cycle," Sothis being the Greek name for Sirius. And it is this ancient Egyptian calendrical system, as modified by Julius Caesar (the "Julian" calendar) and refined with further accuracy by Pope Gregory XIII in A.D. 1582 (the "Gregorian" calendar, which we use today).

Development of the Alphabet   The "Roman" alphabet, which is used today by us and an increasingly large number of peoples throughout the world, may seem rather far removed from Egyptian hieroglyphics. It is common knowledge that the letters of our alphabet have come to us from the Romans who adapted them from the Greek alphabet. The ancient Greeks have informed us that they received their alphabet from the Phoenicians. The Phoenicians, the Hebrews, and the other peoples of the lands at the eastern end of the Mediterranean all spoke dialects of the same Semitic language and used the same consonantal alphabet in their script, which they transmitted to the Ionian Greeks who colonized the Aegean islands and the western shores of Asia Minor. The word "alphabet" itself is made up of the Greek names of the first two letters, *alpha* and *beta*, which were their versions of the names of the same letters (and in the same order throughout) in the Semitic languages: *aleph, bet.* One could go on with *gamma = gimel, delta = dalet,* and so forth to the end, *tau = tav,* each name having meaning in the Semitic but not in the Greek. However, the Greeks had to add a few signs for Greek consonant sounds which did not appear in the Semitic: *phi, chi, psi.*[2] But what, in turn, was the origin of the Semitic alphabet?

In 1906 Sir William Flinders Petrie, one of the great pioneers in scientific archaeology, was digging at Serabit el-Khadim, a site in the middle of the Sinai Peninsula where the Pharaohs had operated turquoise mines for centuries.[3] Among his discoveries were the remains of a temple to the Egyptian goddess Hathor, "Lady of Turquoise," and statues and stelae with hieroglyphic inscriptions dedicated to the goddess by the Egyptian officials. Also discovered were ten tablets of rock, inscribed with characters of a different sort and much simpler and cruder in form. It was Sir Alan Gardiner who succeeded in proving these signs to be a connecting link between Egyptian hieroglyphic writing and the Semitic alphabetic script.

In the "proto-Sinaitic" inscriptions, as they were called, there were no more than thirty-two different characters in all, indicating that this was an alphabetic script. Also, there was a group of characters that were often repeated in the same sequence. The first letter in this group looked very much like the Egyptian sign for "house." Other characters were similar to those in the Semitic alphabet, the names of whose letters are actual words, the sound of the letter being that of the first

[2] *Omega* simply means "large (long) *o*," as *omicron* means "small (short) *o*."
[3] It is quite possible that the Israelites of the Exodus had to pursue their very devious and circuitous route, which took them "forty" years (forty being a round number indicating "quite a few") around the edge of the inverted triangle of the Sinai Peninsula, in order to avoid both the Egyptian fortresses along the coastwise route to Palestine and the heavily guarded turquoise mines in the central portion.

letter of the word, as if we were to draw a picture of a leaf and use it for the sound *l* (the "acrophonic" principle). It occurred to Gardiner to try applying the same principle to the Egyptian-looking characters, with the hypothesis that they were borrowed by Semitic-speaking workers from Canaan, whom the Egyptians were known to have employed. Thus, he tried using what looked like the Egyptian "house" sign for *b*, as the Semitic word for "house" is *bet*. Proceeding on this principle, he read the repeated group of characters as *baalat*, which means in Semitic, "the lady," or "the mistress" (the feminine form of *baal*, which means "the lord," "the master") and which was the regular Semitic epithet of the Great Goddess. Obviously these proto-Sinaitic texts were the votive inscriptions of the Semitic-speaking Canaanite laborers, their own dedication to Hathor, Lady of Turquoise. Subsequently a few alphabetic inscriptions with similar types of characters were discovered in Palestine itself, offering corroboration of Gardiner's theory of the derivation and adaptation of the Semitic letters from the Egyptian. We still cannot produce a complete translation of the proto-Sinaitic inscriptions since we have not as yet enough texts to work with, but we have sufficient evidence to indicate that we owe the origin of our alphabet to ancient Egypt.

Development of Art and Architecture It was Egypt's art and architecture that were the immediate and striking objects of perception to the other Mediterranean peoples who came in contact with it and were of the most immediate influence. Fortunately, within recent years, many beautifully illustrated books dealing with Egyptian art have been published, which can give the reader a rather good idea of Egyptian genius with respect to this all-important criterion of human culture. During one of the earliest periods of its history—the Old Kingdom, which lasted for about five hundred years (about 2700 to about 2200 B.C.)—the Egyptians created some of the finest masterpieces of sculpture and architecture that are the cherished possessions of the Western world. It was this era which the Egyptians regarded as the "classical" period of their art, and two thousand years later, during their brief revival of national consciousness and pride before the end, they went back to the classical purity of Old Kingdom forms, which we can discern in the masterpieces from the Twenty-sixth Dynasty (about 660–525 B.C.). Already at the earliest period of the Old Kingdom, in the great pyramid-temple complex of King Zoser, we find the tall, graceful, fluted columns and the clean, soaring lines strikingly similar in style and feeling to those of the Greek temples of almost two and a half millennia later. Columns and their capitals and the technical methods of architectural construction based upon sound engineering principles, aesthetic canons, and artistic techniques in sculpture, relief, and painting (and particularly portraiture in these media), styles and techniques in metalworking, cabinetry, and the art of the lapidary, can all be traced back in a direct line of development from the achievements of classical Greece to their origins in ancient Egypt. As one of the great authorities on Egyptian art has put it: "Our final conclusion may be that Egypt reveals to us the knowledge of one of the sources—perhaps the source— from which the great river of beauty has flowed continuously through the world."[4]

Development of Law   One of the most important criteria of the advancement of a culture is the nature of its ethical values, usually reflected in its law codes and/or religious writings and in its literature. Unlike most ancient peoples, Egypt has left us no formal codes of law (at least, no such codes have as yet been discovered), and it is most probable that they had none. We do know that they had courts of law, and we have countless refer-

[4] Jean Capart in *The Legacy of Egypt*, S. R. K. Glanville, ed. (New York, Oxford University Press, 1942).

ences to legal arbitrations and decisions. What, then, was the basis for the innumerable legal decisions handed down by magistrates and their councils?

We find permeating all Egyptian writings, from the earliest times and throughout Egyptian history, the concept of a certain standard by which not only men but also the very gods themselves were governed, namely, the concept of *maat*. Like "justice," which is one of the varied implications of the word, *maat* is not easily translated or defined by one word. Basically, we might say that it means "that which, of right, should be; that which is according to the proper order and harmony of the cosmos and of gods and men, who are part of it." In context, *maat* variously denotes "truth," "righteousness," "justice," "divine harmony." The gods order the affairs, not only of men but of their very selves, by the principles of *maat*. The divine king is to govern according to *maat*, and his vizier is strictly enjoined to do likewise. When the deceased justifies his life on earth before the gods of the Other World, he states that he has not treated his fellow man unjustly, that he has not caused weeping or pain, that he has not robbed or stolen, that he has given bread to the hungry and clothing to the naked, and so on (see The Negative Confession); he sums it up by saying that he has followed *maat*. As a result, he is declared *maa kheru*, "true of voice," "justified." In the many didactic texts, which had a direct influence upon the didactic writings of the Old Testament, the continual injunction of the preceptor to his "son" is to follow *maat*. The opposite of *maat* is injustice, falsehood, and deceit, injury to one's fellow man.

Maat was also personified as a goddess, and her symbol was the Feather of Truth, called *shu*, which she wore on her head. It was the *shu*-feather which was weighed against the heart of the deceased at his judgment before Osiris in the Other World. *Shu* means "air," and as an adjective, "free of, empty," as we would say, "free and clear," with the obvious implications of "free of evil, simple and uncontaminated." To the ancient Egyptian, the principles of *maat* had been handed down from the beginning of time, and contributed all the elements of precedence in judgment. *Maat* is the unwritten law of mankind, the inner sense of right and justice which is the common heritage of humanity, and according to those principles both gods and men should be governed, for the ongoing order of the cosmos. Evidently the Egyptians felt that they did not need codifications of the law, that man had a vivid awareness of his inner sense of human justice. It was not until a relatively late stage in the development of the culture of the ancient world that this humanistic ethic was formulated by Socrates, after the Egyptians had been governing themselves by its principles for over two thousand years.

The foregoing are only a few of some of the basic contributions of ancient Egypt, possibly too briefly stated, to human civilization as we know it. One could go on, for example, to discuss such important factors as political organization, the beginnings of technology and engineering, mathematics, astronomy, and other sciences. An extremely important factor in human history was the discovery and extensive development of the principles of medicine and pharmacology; our earliest pharmacopoeias and medical treatises come from ancient Egypt. In short, it is to Egypt that we may look for the very mainsprings of human civilization.

2 Decipherment of the Hieroglyphics and the Progress of Egyptology

The Egyptian language and its hieroglyphic writing had been kept alive by the scribes and priests of ancient Egypt almost until the collapse of the entire ancient world with the spread of Christianity and the later invasion of Egypt by the Arabs in the seventh century A.D., although the language began to be used less and less by the majority of the population beginning with the conquest of the country by Alexander the Great toward the end of the fourth century B.C.

With the establishment of the dynasty of Ptolemy, who was one of Alexander's generals and a pure-blooded Macedonian Greek, began the Hellenization of Egypt and the use of Greek gradually percolated downward through the various levels of the population. The masses of the people had been using a late vernacular stage of Egyptian called demotic, written in a rather crabbed script far removed from the hieroglyphic and the hieratic (the latter was analogous to our longhand) of the Empire period. Demotic, in turn, like all vernaculars, developed further and further away from the old language, even more than, say, modern English has developed away from Old and Middle English. As Christianity spread through Egypt, an adaptation of the Greek characters was used to write the last stages of the vernacular, known as Coptic. Fortunately for the decipherment of hieroglyphic Egyptian, about a dozen centuries later there arose a fairly large body of Coptic writings, a Christian ecclesiastical literature dealing mostly with the legends

13

and sayings of the Coptic church fathers, and piously preserved by the Coptic Church for centuries after the Copts (the Egyptian Christians) had become a small and degraded minority under Moslem rule. The study of Coptic, which had practically died out as a spoken language (although used a little longer in the church liturgy), was revived among a few European scholars during the seventeenth century, notably Athanasius Kircher. Kircher also tried, as others had before him, to decipher the language of the hieroglyphics (some rather miserable copies of ancient Egyptian inscriptions had been circulating about Europe for quite a while), but proceeded according to wildly fantastic allegorical theories of their meaning, as some half-educated "mystical" ignoramuses try to do today. To quote Sir Alan H. Gardiner: ". . . the theories of Kircher as to the content of the hieroglyphic inscriptions exceed all bounds in their imaginative folly."

It was not until the very end of the eighteenth century that the key to the true reading of the hieroglyphic writing and the language of ancient Egypt was found. In 1799, Napoleon (then still General Bonaparte) was in Egypt with his army. His entourage included a corps of French savants who went along to record the antiquities of the country, and it was these savants who initiated the opening of the Nile Valley and its monuments to scientific study. While some repair work was being done at a French fort near Rosetta, a small port on one of the mouths of the Nile in the western Delta, an officer of engineers, Bouchard by name, found a broken stone stele, which had been re-used as masonry and thus imbedded in a wall. Many fragments of Egyptian reliefs and inscriptions had been found reduced to such uses, but what was interesting and unique about this one was that it contained an inscription in three scripts: The first was obviously hieroglyphic; the second turned out to be in demotic; and what was most important for decipherment, the third was in Greek and so could easily be read.

The value of this "Rosetta Stone" was immediately recognized, as no inscription both in hieroglyphic and a known language had yet been found. It proved to be a decree issued in 196 B.C., promulgating various honorary observances to be accorded to the young king, Ptolemy V, and to his mother, his wife, and other female relatives. The names Ptolemy, Arsinoë, Berenice, Irene, Demetria, and their positions in the Greek inscription proved later to be of primary importance in the decipherment of the Egyptian.

The stone was removed and brought to Cairo, where Napoleon examined it with keen interest and ordered that both casts and ink impressions be made of the inscriptions and sent immediately to the various learned societies of Paris and the rest of Europe. The stone itself went on a distant voyage not long after: The French army in Egypt was defeated by the British in 1801, and the stone was appropriated as spoils of war, together with other antiquities that had been gathered by the French, and carried off by the victors to London and deposited in the British Museum, where it remains to this day.

The first progress in the decipherment, by a comparison of the Greek with the other inscriptions, was made by J. D. Akerblad, a Swedish diplomat and orientalist with a knowledge of Coptic. He carefully compared the Greek and the demotic texts, and working with the proper names, he was able to identify and publish a list of some of the alphabetical demotic signs corresponding to the Greek letters in those names, as well as a few words and grammatical suffixes through the Coptic. However, he kept working on the presumption that all the Egyptian signs were alphabetical, and his further attempts broke down. But a good beginning had been made, and many of his readings were adopted by Young and Champollion.

A much more successful attempt was made by Thomas Young, a remarkably brilliant English scholar, physician, and scientist who had discovered the wave theory of light. Like all

15

men of science in those days, he had a good background in the humanities and had acquired a familiarity with the various ancient and oriental languages, including Coptic. Utilizing the discoveries of Akerblad and de Sacy (a French scholar with whom Akerblad had worked), Young subjected the three texts to a thorough scientific comparison and analysis. As a result of his scientific method, plus a series of educated guesses, he came to some far-reaching conclusions. One was that most of the Egyptian signs were phonetic, and that only a limited number were alphabetic, a discovery without which further progress would have been impossible. Also, he established the fact that the hieroglyphic and the demotic inscriptions were closely related. Furthermore, by checking with other texts besides the Rosetta Stone, he demonstrated that the "cartouches," the rectangles with rounded corners and a bar at one end drawn around certain groups of hieroglyphic characters,[1] actually enclosed the names of kings and queens. This had been guessed previously, but it was Young who conclusively proved it and went on to identify some of them. In his hieroglyphic list, he assigned the correct or nearly correct values to nine signs. The results of all his researches were incorporated in his article "Egypt," written for a supplement to the Encyclopaedia Britannica published in 1819. After the publication of this article he abandoned his hieroglyphic studies, probably because he felt that he was primarily a physicist and not a philologian.

It was the young French scholar Jean François Champollion who was to be celebrated as having laid the successful foundations for the decipherment of the hieroglyphics. Since his early teens, he had been fired with an enthusiasm for all things oriental, particularly ancient Egypt, and became a serious student of ancient history and the Semitic languages—Hebrew, Aramaic, Syriac, and Arabic—with a thorough study of Coptic. During

[1] *Cartouche* is the French word for "cartridge," and it does look something like a shotgun shell.

16

the various vicissitudes of his twenties (he was born in 1790), which included branching off into other interests, as many scholars do, and a professorship at his university of Grenoble at the age of eighteen, which he lost a few years later because of his republican sympathies, he continued to maintain his all-absorbing interest in ancient Egypt, gathering all the materials available at the time, and new Egyptian inscriptions that had come to light, including some more from the Ptolemaic period in both Greek and hieroglyphic. These additional bilingual inscriptions were of primary value for his further work on the Rosetta Stone.

We still do not know exactly how much Champollion was indebted to the researches of Young, if he was familiar with them at all. The name of Ptolemy, in Greek, *Ptolemaios,* transliterated in the hieroglyphic as *Ptolmiis,* had already been read alphabetically in its demotic cartouche by Akerblad. At any rate, Champollion immediately recognized the cartouche of Ptolemy on an inscription from Philae in southern Egypt, which also had another cartouche. From the Greek inscription he knew that the second cartouche should be that of Cleo-patra. He then proceeded as follows: Transliterating the known hieroglyphic alphabetic signs common to both names, and leaving blanks for the unknowns, he got $x + L + O + P + x_1 + x + x + x_1 + x$ (our x_1 is the same Egyptian sign repeated). Filling in the name Cleopatra, he obtained the values of the unknown Egyptian signs: $K + L + E + O + P + A + T + R + A + T$. The first *t* sign was different from the one at the end, which was the same as that in Ptolemy, but he knew that it must be a variant, which is found in all languages; it sub-sequently proved to be a *d*, making the Egyptian transliteration of the Greek name *Kleopadrat* (actually there is no *l* in Egyptian, and they used another form of the *r* for *l* when it occurred in foreign words, but this was not known until later). The seemingly superfluous *t* at the end of the name did not bother

17

him, as he knew that it was the regular feminine ending in the Semitic languages. Working on the same principles with more material, he soon made out the Egyptian alphabet and then proceeded to attack other royal names in earlier texts, which of course had no parallel Greek inscriptions.

However, he soon had a problem. There were many more and varied characters than his alphabet contained, and they could not all be variants. For instance, in one royal name there was a group consisting of a little circle, another unknown sign, and then two s's, which we might attempt to show as O + x + S + S. Most previous scholars had concluded that Coptic and the ancient hieroglyphic language were related, and so he played a hunch and guessed that the circle might denote the word "sun," which in Coptic is *re*. And so he read Re + x + S + S. What could this name be but that of Ramesses? Thus the unknown x becomes the syllable *mes*. This was double-checked by another cartouche which contained an ibis-bird, then the *mes* sign, and then an *S*. From his Egyptological studies, he knew that the ibis was the bird of the god Thoth. Obviously, then, this was the royal name Thothmes, rendered in the Greek as Tuthmosis. Thus he knew that the hieroglyphics include not only an alphabet but also syllables.

Continuing along these lines, which entailed, of course, much painstaking effort and time, Champollion was able eventually to build up not only an alphabet, but also a list of syllables which were actually groups of two or more consonants, which we call biliterals, triliterals, and so on, as Egyptian, like all Semitic languages, has properly speaking no written vowels. In addition, he made a list of two other kinds of signs which make up the hieroglyphic system: ideograms, which are signs for an entire word, the original "picture-writing," and determinatives. These last have no phonetic values, but are placed at the end of many words to denote the general class or type of action to which the word belongs: a little man after names of men or after their professions (the word for *scribe* will have a little man at the end), an eye after verbs of seeing or other actions of the eye, and so on; they are very helpful in ascertaining the meaning of unknown words.

The result of all this was that Champollion was enabled to produce an *Egyptian Grammar* and an *Egyptian Dictionary*, leaving his great contribution, one of the outstanding achievements of modern scientific method, to be published after his early death at the age of forty-one. Fortunately he had published his preliminary researches in the 1820's, and they made him famous, but he could not have achieved his great discoveries without his great devotion to his study and the gathering of information and materials. To quote the greatest modern authority on the language of ancient Egypt, Champollion "was constantly adding to his store of Egyptian and Coptic knowledge, ever and again trying new solutions to the problem; when at last the truth was borne in upon him with all the vividness of a revelation, his complete mastery of the available materials enabled him to extend his discoveries with a speed and a sureness far beyond the scope of any of his contemporaries."[2]

Champollion's achievement, brilliantly pioneering, was certainly not perfect, but his excellent foundation imparted a tremendous impetus to further studies, and upon it was built the great edifice of Egyptology that grew by leaps and bounds during the nineteenth century. Trained scholars from all over Europe came to Egypt, gathered antiquities and inscriptions, worked on them, and published their results and added to our knowledge. From Germany came Richard Lepsius, who published the huge compendium of engravings of monuments and inscriptions in colossal elephant folios—the great *Denkmäler aus Ägypten und Nubien*—the successor to the huge volumes, equally elephantine, in which were published the results of

[2] Sir Alan H. Gardiner, *Egyptian Grammar*, 3rd ed. (New York, Oxford University Press, 1957).

Napoleon's Egyptian expedition of 1799, and also Brugsch, who published monumental researches on hieroglyphic and demotic. From England came Samuel Birch, who published much material on Egyptology and many editions and translations of Egyptian texts. From France came de Rougé and Chabas who furthered our knowledge of the language, and Maspéro and Mariette, two of the great pioneers in Egyptology, both in philology and in archaeology.

Toward the end of the century, archaeological method was developed into a strict science by Sir William Flinders Petrie, of England, and further improved and refined during the early decades of the twentieth century by our great American Egyptologists, James H. Breasted, George A. Reisner, Herbert E. Winlock, and William F. Albright. These are only a few of the names in the procession of brilliant men of genius and devotion who have afforded us the fascinating picture we have today of the splendor of the high civilization that was ancient Egypt.

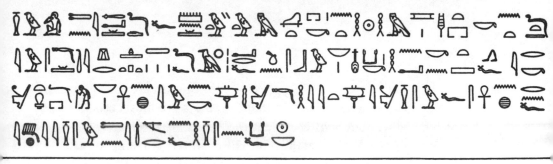

3 The Course of Egyptian History

One of the popular misconceptions about Egypt is that its history has continued in one unbroken chain during the past five thousand years, and that the present inhabitants of the country are the direct descendants of the ancient Egyptians. This is certainly not the case. The last remaining vestiges of ancient Egypt as an area of distinctive civilization disappeared with the Arab invasions and conquest under the Caliph Omar in A.D. 639–642. Already for several centuries its culture had assumed a predominantly Hellenistic-Roman aspect, and this, with its heavy overlay of Coptic Christianity during the years of Byzantine rule, had reduced Egyptian civilization to a tasteless travesty. With the invasions of the Arab hordes even this caricature was obliterated, and to every intent and purpose Egypt became an Arab country ethnically, with a liberal admixture that was contributed later by the various Turkish invasions of the medieval period. Religiously and culturally Egypt became thoroughly Moslem, and its language Arabic, which was and is spoken by all, including the tiny minority of Copts (the Christians in Egypt), Coptic having become a dead language centuries before. Today Egypt is a purely geographical term, designating the Valley of the Nile from the northern boundary of the Sudan to the Mediterranean. Politically, at present it includes this area plus a portion of the northeastern Sahara, and has been correctly renamed by the current regime as United Arab Republic. It should be kept

21

in mind, therefore, that the present inhabitants are Egyptian in a geographic sense only, and that the rulers are most certainly not "the descendants of the Pharaohs"!

Ages ago nature divided the Nile Valley into two distinct parts: 1) the very narrow strip of fertile land on either side of the river (never more than ten miles wide) down to where the Nile branches to begin the formation of its Delta, not far from where Cairo is today (it is well to remember that the Nile flows *northward,* and that what is actually downstream is *up* on the map); 2) the inverted triangle of the Delta itself, comprising the various arms of the Nile that flow into the Mediterranean. The first region, the southern, is at a higher level above the sea, and hence was always called Upper Egypt, whereas the marshy lowlands of the Delta were always known as Lower Egypt. Upper and Lower Egypt differ from each other in many respects, among them being the smaller breadth of cultivable land along the narrow strip of fertile land in Upper Egypt, contrasted with the broad and fertile marshy plains of the Delta; Upper Egypt with its hot, dry climate versus the moist and cooler region of Lower Egypt; and the constricted area of Upper Egypt with its close proximity to the desert and its limited contacts vis-à-vis the broad scope of the Delta, facing toward the Mediterranean and naturally with more cosmopolitan contacts. In prehistoric times the two areas were inhabited by two different peoples, who probably spoke different dialects. The differences were always felt in ancient times, and Egypt was referred to as the "Two Lands" all through its history. One of the official titles of the king was "Lord of the Two Lands," and he wore the Double Crown, the low red crown of Lower Egypt and the tall white crown of Upper Egypt. This strong impression of duality was reflected throughout: The king's dwelling was "the Double Palace," which had double gates, each with a name of its own; the Royal Granary was double; each of the Two Lands had its own symbols and tutelary deity; and so forth. Interestingly, this duality is reflected in the Hebrew name of Egypt throughout the Old Testament, *Mitzrayim, -ayim* being the regular dual ending of nouns, denoting things double or a pair. The concept of the duality of Egypt is important to remember for an understanding of many of the expressions used in the literature.

In the prehistoric period immediately prior to the beginning of Egyptian history, the two lands existed as separate political entities, each with its own rulers, frequently warring with each other and making incursions into each other's territory. The beginnings of Egyptian history are shrouded in considerable obscurity because of our lack of detailed information such as we have for later periods, but the evidence seems to indicate that at about 3100 B.C. the king of Upper Egypt conquered Lower Egypt and unified the Two Lands under his sole rule. According to the most reliable archaeological evidence, his name was *Nar-Mer* and was identical with the *Menes* of the king-lists, who is the first king of the First Dynasty.[1]

The following is an outline of the main periods of Egyptian history. Such terms as "Old Kingdom," "First Intermediate period," are used by modern scholars as a convenient way of classifying the periods into which Egyptian history resolves itself and were not used in ancient times. Dates given are approximate, particularly for the earlier periods. Only some of the more well-known kings are mentioned. The dates are those of their actual rule.

---

[1] The ancient Egyptians did not reckon in dynasties. This we owe to Manetho, a Hellenized Egyptian scribe of the Ptolemaic period who compiled in Greek a list of the kings of Egypt through the Persian conquest of 525 B.C. Manetho divided his list into thirty dynasties (some add a thirty-first), giving the first king of the First Dynasty as Menes. This checks with the name of Meni given as the first king in hieroglyphic king-lists of the Empire period. Even though the ancient Egyptians did not reckon by the dynastic system, it has been universally adopted by historians as a convenient handle to use in the chronology.

Proto-Dynastic, or Archaic, Period
First and Second Dynasties   3100–2700 B.C.

This is the period of the unification of the two kingdoms under Narmer-Menes of Upper Egypt, who became the first king of the First Dynasty. We have relatively few archaeological remains from this period, including some brief inscriptions with royal names. The art is rather crude and rough (with the notable exception of the famous Palette of Narmer) and seems to show a degree of influence from contemporary Mesopotamia, but one can discern, particularly in the Narmer Palette, the general tendency and feeling of the distinctive Egyptian style.

The Old Kingdom
Third Through Sixth Dynasties   2700–2200 B.C.

This period, of about five hundred years, was the formative period of Egyptian civilization. Enjoying a long era of security, isolation, and relative peace, Egyptian genius produced some of its greatest achievements in political organization, in engineering, in art, particularly in sculpture, and in architecture. Some of the classic works of Egyptian literature, which we have in copies from later times, were ascribed to this period. The capital of the Old Kingdom was located at Memphis, near the juncture of the Two Lands, not far from where Cairo is today, but on the western side of the Nile.

The great king of the Third Dynasty (2700–2650) was Zoser (more correctly Djeser), the probable founder of the dynasty. He built the first monumental stone structure in the world, the famous Step Pyramid and its temple-complex at Sakkarah. The large pyramids which distinguish the following dynasty are developments of Zoser's Step Pyramid. The design and en-

gineering of the pyramid were attributed to Zoser's vizier, Imhotep, who was also known as a great physician and as the
author of a book of proverbs. He was the Leonardo da Vinci
of his time, and his fame as an outstanding genius left such a
powerful impression on succeeding generations that he was
later deified, the only mortal to be so honored in Egypt (the
king was never considered a mortal, but a god reigning upon
earth).

The Fourth Dynasty (2650–2500) was the age of the great pyramid builders, in whose times were constructed the three huge
pyramids at Gizeh, which have become the "trademark" of Egypt.
Other and smaller pyramids were built by lesser monarchs of this
and the succeeding two dynasties, but they were not as well built,
and most of them have fallen into ruin.

Seneferu, the founder of the dynasty (about 2650) was followed by Cheops—his correct Egyptian name, *Khufu,* is gradually becoming better known—who flourished about 2600. He
was the builder of the Great Pyramid, which was regarded
as one of the seven wonders of the ancient world and remains
one of the most remarkable structures erected by man to this
day. Without the use of mortar, the huge granite blocks were
put into place with perfect accuracy to a height of 481 feet, all
this by means of only the rope, the lever, the inclined plane
(the Egyptians apparently were unacquainted with the principle
of the pulley), and manpower, of which there was no lack.
This towering achievement, as well as their other works of
genius and taste during the next two thousand years, they
could not have accomplished without their great "magic," the
powerful "secret wisdom of the Egyptians": tenacity of purpose,
keen and brilliant intelligence, and unerring aesthetic taste.

The other two large pyramids at Gizeh were built, in de-
scending order of chronology and size, by two other monarchs
of the Fourth Dynasty, Chephren (*Khaf-Ra,* about 2560) and
Mycerinus (*Men-Kau-Ra,* about 2525).

The important contribution left us by the Fifth and Sixth dynasties (2500–2200) is the large number of religious texts we have found carved on the corridors and chamber walls of their pyramids, much smaller and inferior in construction to those of the Fourth Dynasty, with the result that they are now rather unglamorous heaps of ruins. The large and well-preserved pyramids of the Fourth Dynasty have no inscriptions whatsoever. Of immense importance for an understanding of the ancient Egyptian systems of religion, the *Pyramid Texts* of the Fifth and Sixth dynasties throw much light on the social, economic, and cultural life of the times. These texts, which make up a large literature by themselves, are found in the tombs of Unis (about 2425), the last king of the Fifth Dynasty, and of four of his successors of the Sixth Dynasty.

The First Intermediate Period
Seventh Through Eleventh Dynasties
2200–2050 B.C.

After the death of Pepi II, one of the last of the Sixth Dynasty kings, who reigned for ninety years (2275–2185), we find that the strong central authority of the king that obtained during the Old Kingdom breaks down completely, and Egypt resolves itself into its constituent districts or provinces, called *nomes,* with the power wielded by the various nome chiefs, each the authority in his own petty domain. We have lists of royal names of the Seventh to Eleventh dynasties, but these kings are quite shadowy figures with, apparently, merely nominal rule. The situation seems to have been very similar to that which obtained during the Middle Ages in Western Europe, where the actual power was exercised by the local lords and barons, acknowledging only nominal fealty to king or emperor.

26

The Middle Kingdom
Twelfth Dynasty   2050–1780 B.C.

About 2060, the leader of a family of ruling nobles in Thebes (up the Nile, deep in Upper Egypt) emerged victorious in a series of struggles with the chieftains of other cities and seized control of the entire kingdom. The consolidation of Egypt was effected by Neb-Hepet-Ra Mentu-Hotep (2060–2010), one of the later kings of the Eleventh Dynasty, and the capital was henceforth at Thebes. The succeeding Twelfth Dynasty produced some energetic kings, under whom Egypt first expanded commercially to the shores of the eastern Mediterranean, and Egyptian spheres of influence were established in the various city-states along the Phoenician coast.

Domestically, the Middle Kingdom was characterized by a strong central government at Thebes, under the Amenemhats and the Senusrets, with a new burgeoning of all aspects of Egyptian culture, particularly in literature.

The Second Intermediate Period
(The Hyksos Invasion)
Thirteenth Through Seventeenth Dynasties
1800–1500 B.C.

With the passing of the strong Twelfth Dynasty, Egypt relapsed once more into a period of disintegration and chaos, leaving the country wide open to invasion by the chieftains of the various peoples of Canaan and Syria, who had gradually become powerful during the past few generations, and looking for *lebensraum,* had been casting eyes at Egypt. The Egyptians called them *Hekau Khasut,* "rulers of foreign lands," and this term the Greek writers of later times rendered as *Hyksos.* The Hyksos expansion into

Egypt was not a sudden one, but probably occurred as a series of heavy infiltrations, ending in the seizure of power by the strongest of the Hyksos leaders, who ruled from Tanis, or Avaris, in the eastern Delta. We have very few remains from this period, documentary or otherwise, for after the last kings of the Seventeenth Dynasty and the first kings of the Eighteenth finally expelled the Hyksos, they obliterated whatever traces they could of the hated foreign rulers. The Thirteenth and Fourteenth dynasties (1780–1680) embrace the period of political disintegration, and the Fifteenth and Sixteenth dynasties (1730–1570) are those of the Hyksos kings. The Hyksos rulers allowed some of the Egyptian dynastic kings to reign nominally as vassals at Thebes; hence the overlapping in dates. These Theban rulers subject to the Hyksos comprise the Seventeenth Dynasty.

The New Kingdom and the Empire
Eighteenth Through Twentieth Dynasties
1570–1090 B.C.

Under the leadership of the last two of the vassal kings of the Seventeenth Dynasty the Egyptians succeeded, with much heroic self-sacrifice, in expelling the Hyksos rulers. The first kings of the Eighteenth Dynasty, beginning with Aahmes (1570–1545), completed the work of expulsion, pursuing the Hyksos back to Syria-Palestine, seizing the territories which they overran in the process and making them tributary to Egypt. This was the beginning of the Egyptian empire in Syria.

The building of the empire and the far-reaching consequences resulting therefrom was the distinguishing feature of the New Kingdom. Among those consequences was the great enrichment of Egypt with the spoils and tribute of the conquered Syrian territory and the growth of international commerce, which is always accompanied by interchange of ideas, the spread of cosmopolitanism, and the broadening of cultural contacts. The great increase in the prosperity of the country, which filtered down through all classes of the population, resulted in a taste for luxuries and the various refinements of civilization, all of which is reflected in the literature and in the arts and in the generally highly sophisticated outlook of the period.

With the Eighteenth Dynasty (1570–1320), the capital was once more established at Thebes, which was tremendously enriched with the flow of tribute and commercial prosperity. This was reflected particularly in the construction of the vast temple-complexes of Amen, the local god of Thebes and its rulers, who was now elevated to a position of supremacy, equated with the ancient supreme god of Egypt, Ra, and henceforth always designated as Amen-Ra. The kings of this and the following Nineteenth Dynasty vied with each other in constructing huge and sprawling additions to the Amen temples at what are now Luxor and Karnak, and neither the ravages of time over three thousand years nor the spoliation and vandalism under Christian and Arab rule have been able to obliterate their awesome impression of hugeness and complexity.

The Eighteenth Dynasty produced some rulers of powerful strength of personality and intelligence, who exercised an excellent capacity for administration. The great conquerors were Amenhotep I (1545–1525) and Thothmes III (1468–1436). Queen Hatshepsut (1486–1468) was an intelligent and determined woman who declared herself the daughter of Amen and ruled as Pharaoh, having herself represented in many of her statues wearing the square beard of the king. Her reign was a peaceable one, distinguished by the expansion of trade and the building of her magnificently beautiful tomb and temple-complex at Deir el-Bahri. The height of artistic luxuriance, sumptuous prosperity, and busy international relations was reached during the reign of Amenhotep III, who was the *grand monarque,* the Louis XIV of his time. It was his son, who ascended the throne as Amenhotep IV (later Akhenaten, 1375–1362), whose queen was the beautiful and determined Nefertiti, who broke away from the domination of the wealthy and powerful Amen priesthood and established the *Aten,* the sun-disk itself, as the predominant deity, and to whom he composed some hymns distinguished by their beauty and sensitivity. Significantly, he changed his name to *Akh-en-Aten,* "the glory of the Aten." The religious and cultural revolution of Akhenaten, which incidentally produced an interestingly modern type of art, was short-lived and he neglected the business of empire; but he has justifiably earned Breasted's accolade, "the first individual in history."

Akhenaten was succeeded by his young and insignificant son-in-law, Tut-Ankh-Amen (1362–1352), who fell completely under the domination of the Amen priesthood, and has become famous in modern times only because his was the only tomb of an Egyptian king which had not been thoroughly rifled in antiquity or later. The Eighteenth Dynasty petered out not long after his early death, but the imperial rule was fortunately consolidated once more under the efficient Hor-em-Heb (1349–1319), who paved the way for the Nineteenth Dynasty.

Most of the activities of the principal monarchs of the Nineteenth Dynasty (1320–1205), Seti I (1318–1301) and Ramesses II (1301–1234), were concerned with the recapture of the empire in Syria and with the conflicts and complexities of international relations with the rulers of the various peoples of Asia Minor, Syria, and Mesopotamia in an increasingly complex world. A new political capital was established at Tanis-Avaris in the eastern Delta, which had been the old Hyksos capital four hundred years earlier, and strategically close to the Asian sphere of operations, Thebes remaining the religious capital. Culturally, we see the beginnings of the decline of artistic and literary taste, and an increasingly ostentatious vul-

garity in the architecture and sculpture, particularly under
Ramesses II. The great glory of Egypt is now definitely on the
wane.

The Post-Empire Period of Decline
Twenty-first Through Twenty-fifth Dynasties
1100–660 B.C.

These five hundred years saw the long, slow period of decline, politically and culturally. It was mostly a period of petty
intrigues, both domestic and foreign, of spasms of inflation and
hard times; and Egypt gradually became a second-rate power
with the rise of the various new empires in Mesopotamia,
Syria, and Asia Minor. Finally, Egypt was invaded and sacked
by the Assyrians, 671–663.

The Saïte Period
Twenty-sixth Dynasty   663–525 B.C.

The power of Assyria was broken by the Neo-Babylonian
Empire, with the result that Egypt enjoyed a temporary respite
from foreign interference and was governed by the vigorous
rulers of the Twenty-sixth Dynasty, who established their capital
at Saïs, in the central portion of the Delta. An attempt was
made to re-establish the authority of Egypt on the international
scene, but it was brief and unsuccessful. In its efforts at escape
from the current despair, Egypt went back to dwell on its pris-
tine glories, when the world was young and Egypt enjoyed its
long and idyllic period of isolated security and cultural vigor,
the "good old days" of the Old Kingdom. We see a vigorous
revival of the arts, particularly in sculpture, which displays a
consciously archaizing tendency faithfully to follow Old King-

dom forms and techniques. A great deal of the sculpture of the Saïte period is of the finest quality, and difficult to distinguish stylistically from Old Kingdom pieces of two thousand years previously. This brief revival, however, was only the beginning of the end, and the Persian conquest of 525 B.C. brought about the end of native Egyptian rule. Henceforth Egypt is to be governed by foreign rulers until the complete eclipse of its identity with the Arab conquest.

Foreign Domination   525 B.C.–A.D. 640

The Persian period (525–332 B.C.) lasted from the Twenty-seventh through the Thirtieth dynasties (some add a Thirty-first). The Ptolemaic period (332–30 B.C.) began with Alexander the Great, who put an end to the broadly spread Persian Empire. He had left his general, Ptolemy, who was one of his own Macedonian Greeks, to control Egypt while he himself pressed on farther to the east. After Alexander's death in 323, Ptolemy made himself king of Egypt, and his descendants, all Greeks and rather intensively inbred, ruled Egypt, down to the famous Cleopatra (the sixth of her name), when Egypt became a province of the Roman Empire.

Alexandria, on the western coast of the Delta, was the capital under the Ptolemies and soon became the largest and most cosmopolitan city in the ancient Mediterranean world. There was quite a bit of important literary and cultural activity in Egypt during the Ptolemaic period, mostly in Alexandria, but it was all Greek. The Museum at Alexandria contained the largest collection of Greek and Latin manuscripts in the world when it was destroyed after the Arab conquest. Artistically, we have a good deal of sculpture and painting from Hellenistic Egypt, but whatever is not purely Greek in inspiration and technique is a rather tasteless bastardization of Egyptian and Greek styles, and a great deal of it is ridiculously hideous.

The defeat of Cleopatra and Antony at the hands of Octavian
(the later Emperor Augustus) ushered in the Roman period, during which Egypt was ruled by Roman provincial governors (30
B.C.–A.D. 324). During this time, the last stages of whatever
remained of the old Egyptian civilization were speedily brought
to an end by the spread of Christianity and the rise of the
Coptic Church. We have quite a bit of Coptic art from this
period, particularly in figured textiles, showing a remarkable
childlike crudity very similar to the art of the Christian Middle
Ages which it foreshadowed.

The Byzantine period (A.D. 324–640) began with the accession
of Constantine as eastern Roman emperor and the establishment
of Christianity as the official state religion. Egypt became Byzantine in most respects, the use of the hieroglyphic writing was
abandoned and lost, and Coptic now became the language of the
people. Egypt's history in this period is marked by a series of petty
political intrigues and violent factional strife between the various
Christian sects, all characterized by much barbarity and bloodshed, until with the Arab invasions of 640, Egypt became an Arab
and Moslem state.

4 Religion

Since the reader will find some of the basic concepts of ancient Egyptian religion set forth in the first texts in this volume, and in the introductions and notes to them, with many further details discussed throughout the book, we will not present here an exposition of the Egyptian system, or to speak correctly, systems of religion, but will attempt to explain certain fundamental religious attitudes of mythopoeic man, particularly in ancient Egypt, which do not seem logical to the monotheist of today (or to Western man in general, for that matter) and may constitute a perplexing obstacle to understanding. We will also touch upon some uniquely Egyptian aspects of religious thought.

As in any of the naturally evolved (in contrast to revealed) religions of mankind, there was not one religious system in Egypt, but several. The reader will soon discover that Ra first created himself and then the gods and the phenomena of life. Shortly thereafter he will learn that all this was really Ptah. Ptah was not only Ra and his acts of creation, but he was also the primeval waters out of which Ra came in the first place. Again, in other texts we find mention of the demiurgic power as being exercised by neither Ra nor Ptah, but by Thoth. Which, or whose, cosmogony did the intelligent Egyptians believe? Another example: In some texts the goddess Hathor is referred to as the consort of Ra, and in others as his daughter. In an important ritual at Thebes, she is the consort of Amen. Which was she? What, actually, did the Egyptians believe?

Actually, they believed everything. A fundamental tenet, whether expressed or implied, of all religious belief, monotheistic as well as polytheistic, is that deity exists and acts on a plane totally different from that of mortals. To deity there is no such thing as finite time, for instance, since deity is ageless and immortal. Deity has none of the corporeal and mundane limitations of mortal man. Limitations of space, time, and the nature of the physical world simply do not apply to deity. In Egypt, every mortal, by means of magic words spoken and magic things done, becomes the god Osiris after his death. This is not illogical at all, since it happens in the Other World, which exists on an entirely different plane than this. It is a different dimension entirely, or rather a different set of dimensions. The other plane is neither above nor below that of us who are still mortal—it is *different*. Thus the Other World, although frequently mentioned as being in the West, is also mentioned as being below. It really makes no difference, and if you are still mortal, no matter how far you journey westward (or downward) you will never find it anyhow. It is *different*. Then why say it is in the West? As the March Hare answered Alice, "Why not?"

Another reason for the seeming confusion stems from the fact that originally, in early prehistoric times, Egypt was not one political entity, nor even two, but consisted of many small, isolated settlements strung along the Nile and strewn about the Delta. Each settlement or village would have its own god or goddess. Some might be similar in their attributes and/or their totems, and thus at a later period become fused and take their places among the great gods, although with special attachment to their original localities. A case in point is that of Horus, who was most strongly connected with the sun and totemically was the falcon, but still specially the patron deity of several towns in ancient Egypt. Other deities, such as Thoth, Hathor, and Osiris, although very important in the national pantheon, were always considered as hailing from one specific town, which enjoyed their particular protection and where their great sanctuaries were located.

On the other hand, many deities always remained local and minor, their home towns never amounting to any prominence. They were none the less important, however, to those who came under their jurisdiction: in many texts we have reference to one's "local god" (literally, "the god of the town"), whose protection and approval it behooves one to obtain. An interesting and most important exception is that of the god Amen, who was only the local god of Thebes until the Middle Kingdom, when that city was made the capital. As a result, he was elevated to the supreme rank and later equated with the great god Ra himself, being known from the Empire period on as Amen-Ra.

An important aspect of Egyptian religious thought, but sometimes exaggerated out of all proportion in some popular journalistic reading matter, is the attitude of the ancient Egyptians toward life after death and the nature of the other World. The details are discussed in our introduction and notes to the selections from *The Book of the Dead*. It is well to point out here, however, the remarkable difference in attitude toward death and the afterlife between the ancient Egyptians and the other peoples of Mediterranean antiquity. Pervading the literature of ancient Mesopotamia, Syria-Canaan, Anatolia (the Hittites)— and the Homeric epics, be it noted—we find, expressed or implied, the view that it is just no good to be dead, and that the other world is not a good place in which to find yourself. The deceased dwell in a place gloomy and dark; they move about, vague and dim shades, in constant fear of hunger and thirst should their survivors neglect their offerings, and are governed by cruel and malignant deities. Although the *Sheol*

of the Old Testament has had its polytheistic elements edited
out, it is still a vague and gloomy region where it is not good
to be, and like the domain of the dead in other Eastern Mediterranean texts, everyone goes there, both bad and good, for
example, the prophet Samuel (I Samuel 28:3). We find the
very same concept prevailing in Homer (*Odyssey*, Book XI).

In ancient Egypt we find a difference as between night and
day. Both the texts and the lively and varied paintings in the
tombs show us an Other World of gaiety and good living, of
quite a real and happy existence of busy activity, in which the
deceased enjoys eternal banquets complete with music and
lovely dancing girls and "every good thing." In the world of
eternity he continues all the activities he performed in this
world—overseeing his estates, yachting on the Nile, fowling,
and spearfishing in the marshes, attending gay dinner parties,
or what you will—but without any of the sorrows, pains, and
various unpleasantnesses to which all humans are subject during
their sojourn in mortality. And for all eternity the deceased
rejoices in the beneficent rule of the great Osiris, "the good
and beautiful Being," in fact, the deceased *is* Osiris.

This fortunate existence is, of course, to be attained only by
those who have deserved it: those who during their lives have
exercised justice and right, who have aided the poor and the
hungry, who have given the gods their due by the appropriate
temple-offerings, who have been far from anger and free of
evil. These necessary qualifications for eternal felicity are
acquired with relative ease, by the method of magic ritual. If
the various ceremonies attendant upon the preparation of the
mummy of the deceased are observed, if the complicated
funerary rituals are scrupulously performed, and extremely
important, if the deceased takes along the book of efficacious
magic spells and declarations that ensure his passing safely
through the various perils on the way to the Other World (we
refer to this book of spells as *The Book of the Dead,* but the

37

Egyptians called it *The Chapters of Coming Forth by Day,* which shows a completely different point of view), his heart will favorably balance with the Feather of Truth on the scales of Thoth, and he will be justified before Osiris. The fact that anyone could have these requisite ceremonials performed and have a copy of *The Book of the Dead* placed in his mummy case should not lead us to assume that the generality of the ancient Egyptians regarded the ethical values of humanity with any cynicism. The same ethical precepts are constantly repeated, again and again, in all the didactic writings—in the instructions to viziers, in the many collections of proverbs and maxims for right living, in the exhortations to schoolboys, all assiduously copied as classroom exercises through the centuries by the schoolboys themselves—and are reflected throughout all the other genres of ancient Egyptian literature, and so we have excellent reason for concluding that they took these values seriously.

This strikingly different attitude of the ancient Egyptians to the afterlife indicates quite an interesting difference in psychological makeup between the Egyptians and their contemporaries, which also seems to account for many of the unique factors in their culture. A people who regard death as merely a transition to eternal life, who so intensely enjoy this life that they look forward to living in ongoing felicity on the divine plane, doing all the good and happy things they enjoyed doing upon earth, must have been a people of buoyant spirits and great optimism, particularly when we know the gay, sensual, and concrete type of pleasures they enjoyed, so much so that they projected them into all eternity. Perhaps this factor in the Egyptian psyche is a most important one in accounting for the extraordinary vitality, optimism, and verve of much of the art and literature and of Egyptian genius in general, which leaves us with the impression that to the human spirit all things are possible.

The reader who constantly keeps these points in mind will
find it much easier to understand the religious texts and many
allusions and points of view in Egyptian literature and art in
general, inured and predisposed as our culture has been to a
rather different attitude over the past two thousand years and
more.

5 Literature

The total corpus of ancient Egyptian literature available to us is quite a large one, despite the fact that a good deal of it has been destroyed, both by the ravages of time and the vandalism of man. It is also quite possible that some texts may yet be discovered, even though practically all of Egypt has been gone over with the proverbial fine-toothed comb. One never can know but some unexpected discovery may take place, such as that of Tutankhamen's tomb in 1923, in which, however, no manuscripts or new texts were found.[1] We still have enough texts from ancient Egypt to fill many volumes, and only a small sampling of them can be given here in an introductory anthology. We have also attempted to indicate, in our choice of texts, something of the variety of genres in which the ancient Egyptians wrote.

The following is an outline of the development of Egyptian literature, mentioning by name only some of the highlights among the texts.

The largest body of texts from the Old Kingdom period are the *Pyramid Texts,* the nature and significance of which we discuss with our first selections. The first contributions to Didactic literature, a genre that assumed great importance among the peoples of the ancient eastern Mediterranean, date from the Old Kingdom;

[1] The shrines enclosing the triple mummy case of the king were covered with inscriptions made up mostly of extracts from various religious and funerary texts previously known to us. See A. Piankoff and N. Rambova, *The Shrines of Tut-Ankh-Amon* (New York, Harper Torchbooks, 1962).

they are collections of proverbs and precepts for correct living, which the Egyptians called "instructions," such as those of Ptah-Hotep and Ka-Gemni.

The disintegration of the Old Kingdom and the ensuing period of chaos and confusion are reflected in the small but incisive group of texts from the First Intermediate period. This, the pessimistic literature, is exemplified by such expressions of cynicism and despair as *The Dispute of a Man with His Soul, The Admonitions of Ipuwer,* and *The Prophecy of Nefer-Rohu.*

The assumption by many of the nobles of the prerogatives of sovereignty during this period of feudalism is illustrated by the *Coffin Texts* found in painted and decorated wooden coffins containing the mummies of the nobles of the Ninth through the Eleventh dynasties—texts taken from the *Pyramid Texts* of the Old Kingdom monarchs, which were for the benefit of the king only and adapted for the use of the nobles, who also arrogated to themselves the privilege of becoming Osiris.

The Middle Kingdom is regarded as the classic period of the Egyptian language, and from this period we have some of the best examples of belles-lettres. The famous tales and stories date from the Middle Kingdom: *The Tale of Sinuhe, The Shipwrecked Sailor, The Story of the Eloquent Peasant,* and *King Cheops and the Magicians.* Poetry is represented by several religious hymns, by some work songs, and by a special type of poetry celebrating the goodness of life, such as *The Songs of the Harper.*

The confusion and destruction attendant upon the Hyksos incursions of the Second Intermediate period and their later expulsion have left us little from this period besides one or two woefully incomplete fragments.

In quantity, the largest body of our texts date from the quite busy and cosmopolitan times of the New Kingdom period. Of the religious literature, we have the long and sometimes beautifully illustrated papyri containing the series of spells known as *The Book of the Dead,* which were the further adaptation of the

Coffin Texts for the use now of everyone who could afford it. From the New Kingdom also date other collections of spells, such as *The Book of What Is in the Other World* and *The Book of Gates*. We also have many hymns to the various gods; of particular interest are the *Hymns to Amen* and the *Hymns to the Aten*. There is also quite a bit of magical literature, such as the *Incantations* and *The Interpretation of Dreams*.

Poetry and belles-lettres flourished during this prosperous period, and we have the various collections of love lyrics and banquet songs, as well as the complicated tales of intrigue and satire, such as *The Tale of the Two Brothers* and *The Contendings of Horus and Set*.

Another feature of the New Kingdom is the schoolboy literature, which we would call didactic, which also incidentally tells us much of the social life of the time. In formal didactic literature we have such important long works as *The Proverbs of Amen-em-Ope*.

An important series of texts are the medical papyri, which give us an idea of the vast body of information which the ancient Egyptians accumulated in the sciences of anatomy, pathology, and pharmacology. Invaluable for our knowledge of the history are the many annals and historical texts and inscriptions. Like the medical papyri, however, these would not be classified as literature.

II
Gods and
Kings

6 The Creation

The overwhelming influence of the Bible upon the development of Western civilization has made all of us familiar with the creation as described in the opening chapter of the Book of Genesis. In the Genesis narrative, the deity brings order out of the primeval watery chaos, divides the waters of the abyss, and causes dry land to appear. Then, by his utterance, he causes the various forms of life, in orderly progression from the simpler forms to the more complex, to come into being. The last form of life to appear is man, who is endowed by the Creator with the spirit of life and the power to rule over all the creatures of the earth who are below his intellectual and spiritual level. Man is then given certain basic conditions regarding his obligations to deity, to the world of creation about him, and to the human society of which he is a part. These conditions are the governing factors of his existence, and determine the nature of the necessary relationship of the *I* of the individual man to the *Thou* of that which is above him and which brought him into being.

To attain to the sublimity of such a simple theory of the origin of the cosmos and of the relationship between man and God, one which, moreover, evinces the perception of an ordered progression in the complexity of living organisms (which required the advances in natural science of the nineteenth century A.D. to be reduced to the theory of evolution) man had to have reached a rather highly advanced stage in the development of

45

his thought. This necessitated a long period, not only of intellectual development and of acute observation of the phenomena of nature itself, but also of thorough familiarity with the various crosscurrents of culture flowing between Egypt and Mesopotamia, the two great centers of ancient Near Eastern civilization, and where man first emerged into civilized life. The Hebrew concept of creation as embodied in Genesis could not have emerged much before about 1000 B.C.

The earliest Egyptian and Mesopotamian civilizations, which appeared about 3000 B.C., show no such simplicity of conception in their theories of the origins of the universe. Rather, the further back we penetrate into the beginnings of human thought, the more complex do we find creation stories to be, and anthropologists have found the same to be true of primitive cultures existing today. In both early Egypt and in the Mesopotamian civilizations of Sumer and Akkad, we have a very ancient and primeval god who in turn creates other deities representing various cosmic and societal forces. In much of the mythology, the god is quite old at the beginning of earthly history, and sometimes even weak and ineffectual. The only human being with whom the gods are concerned is the king, who in Egypt is officially the incarnation of one of the deities (Horus), and after his death assumes the identity of Horus's father, Osiris, his heir on the throne in turn becoming Horus, and so on. The rest of humanity is, according to one of the two great schools of early Egyptian theology to be described below, in rather a sorry state, being incidentally derived from tears shed by the original creating deity. And so, ordinary man is nothing. He is completely overwhelmed by the cosmic forces represented by the gods. It is the king who continually performs the necessary rituals for proper relationship and communication with the gods, in order to maintain the welfare of the state and to insure the fertility of the earth, that it may bring forth sustenance. The priests are only the officially delegated subordinates of the king and are responsible to his divine authority. Any equilibrium between the mass of humanity and the deity is thus maintained only through the divine offices of the Pharaoh, who is himself one of the company of the gods, the great and powerful Horus come to earth to order the welfare of Egypt. There is no *I* of the individual man in continual relationship to the *Thou* of the deity. There is only one *I*, which is the company of the gods, and the king is one of them.

The two great systems or schools of Egyptian theology are those of Heliopolis and Memphis. Both of these names were given to these cities by the Greeks, who did not enter Egypt until her civilization was almost three thousand years old. For some reason most Egyptologists always use these Greek names today, although the Greeks were notorious for slaughtering foreign names. Some Egyptologists are purists even to the extent of using the Greek names for the Pharaohs, such as Tuthmosis for Thothmes, Amenophis for Amenhotep, and Ramose for Ramesses. In order to understand why the deities of these cities developed into high gods, let us see how, among the hundreds of gods of primitive Egypt, a dozen or so emerged to the fore, with Ra-Atum of Heliopolis and Ptah of Memphis as creators of the universe.

The various supreme gods in Egyptian mythology arrived at their supremacy through the political prominence of the cities of which they were originally the local deities. Ancient Egypt was divided since predynastic times into some forty petty states, or local communities, called *nomes* (again a Greek word). Before the First Dynasty, the nomes of the region comprising, roughly, the Delta of the Nile in the north had been unified as a result of a long period of internecine warfare. The petty chief of the nome that had proved strongest became king of the entire region, which was henceforth known as the Land of the North, or as we call it today, Lower Egypt (since it comprises the Nile Delta which is at sea level, and at Egypt's lower point geographically speaking). The same process took place in the region beyond the Delta and up the Nile, and called, of course, Upper Egypt, or the Land of the South. Then came the final struggle between the kings of Lower and Upper Egypt for the mastery of the entire land. This war, which must have been quite a long and bloody one, was won by Narmer (in some king-lists called Menes), the king of Upper Egypt. Narmer established himself on the throne of a united Egypt, and is known as the first king of the First Dynasty. The memory of the original Two Egypts persisted, however, to the very end, and one of the titles of the king was always "Lord of the Two Lands." The double nature of the Egyptian state was preserved in the Biblical name for Egypt, *Mitzrayim,* the *-ayim* suffix denoting a dual noun in Hebrew.

In these prehistoric struggles for supremacy between the various petty principalities, the local nome-god, who probably had a totemic origin, would naturally become more prominent or less, according to the fortunes of his nome. The gods of the most powerful and victorious nomes would become the most important deities, whereas the gods of the lesser nomes would either be assimilated to the more powerful gods, or would come to occupy a relatively minor position in the pantheon. Thus we see Horus, originally the falcon-god of Narmer's nome in Upper Egypt, becoming a major deity through identification with the king himself. Osiris, originally the vegetation and fertility deity of Abydos, another nome capital in Upper Egypt, in like manner became the Lord of the Netherworld, the embodiment of the king after his decease, and father of Horus, the new, living king.

To the ancient Egyptian, as an inhabitant of a practically rainless country, the foremost and most ancient deity was, quite logically, the sun-god which, in its daily journey across the sky, brought life and warmth to the world and fructified the earth, made fertile by the waters of the Nile. Many of the local nome-gods were identified with the sun, but in prehistoric times one center of sun worship in particular came into prominence. This was the city of Ionu, near the bottom of the Delta, where a shrine of Ra, the sun-god, had been established in remote antiquity, and which became the huge and wealthy seat of the priesthood and temples of Ra, prime god of Egypt. The Greeks called the city Heliopolis, "the city of the sun." In the Bible Ionu is referred to as On, and it will be recalled that Pharaoh gave the daughter of a priest of On to Joseph as a wife (Genesis 41:45).

The theory of creation evolved by the priesthood of Ra at Heliopolis dates from very early times, since we have several references to it in the *Pyramid Texts,* which date from about 2500 B.C., but which must have been very old at the time they were inscribed within the pyramids. According to the Heliopolitan Theology, the sun-god Ra has two other names: *Atum,* which means "he who completes, or perfects," and *Khepri,* or *Kheprer,* which means "he who comes into being," or "he who brings into being." (The Hebrew name of the deity, *Yahweh,* means exactly the same thing.) Ra-Atum-Khepri is self-created and emerges from *Nun,* the Primordial Waters of chaos. He has no place upon which to stand and so causes to come into being a hillock to support him. This Primeval Hill, the first mound of dry land, named the *benben,* occupied an important position in Egyptian mythology. It is the symbolical benben-hill in the form of the pyramid, as symbolizing Ra-Atum-Khepri, which became the tomb of the kings of the Old Kingdom; it is also a miniature benben that we see, set on lofty supporting pillars, as the pyramidal points of the Egyptian obelisks. Standing upon the benben, Ra-Atum-Khepri then proceeded to create the other cosmic deities, and since he had no mate, he fashioned his first pair of gods, *Shu* ("air"), and *Tefnut* ("moisture"), from his own semen. It should be borne in mind that to early man bringing forth seed was the creative act, the direct workings and results of which he discerned among his fellow men, in the animal world, and in the planting and growth of vegetation. Once Shu and Tefnut had been created, from their union in turn were born *Geb* (the earth-god) and *Nut* (the sky-goddess). Geb and Nut in turn bore two gods and two goddesses: Osiris, Isis, Set, and Nephthys. Thus we have the group of nine gods, which is

49

referred to as the *Ennead* (another Greek word which means "a group of nine"). The last two pairs of the Ennead then brought forth the multitude of the gods of Egypt.

As for man, far from being the crowning achievement of creation, he comes into being only incidentally, from the tears shed by Ra. After Shu and Tefnut had been created, they had been left in the happy care of Nun, the Primordial Waters, possibly until they should mature. But Ra's Eye (the sun itself) left his head to follow and look after them. Naturally Ra had to make another one to take its place. When the original Eye of the Universal Lord finally returned and saw that it had been replaced, it reproached its master angrily, and Ra wept. From these tears men came into being. Ra-Atum appeased his Eye by transforming it into the uraeus-serpent on his brow, where it may be seen on every representation of a king of Egypt, eternally vigilant in protecting the Pharaoh from all enemies of the Lord of the Two Lands. When all was calm once more, Ra-Atum created vegetation and animal life.

Memphis, also at the lower end of the Delta, but somewhat farther down from Heliopolis and on the western side of the Nile, was the capital of Egypt throughout the period of the Old Kingdom (about 2800–2200 B.C.). The local god of this city was another ancient deity named Ptah. With the city's rise to prominence, we find the Memphite priesthood of Ptah evolving another theology, in which its own god is the creator. This theology, however, presents a remarkable advance over that of Heliopolis. It is Ptah alone, Ptah, whose name literally means "the opener," who himself was the primordial watery chaos, and who then brought Atum and the entire Ennead into being. What is more, Ptah began the process of creation by no such physical method as masturbation, but by conceiving in his mind and by uttering with his tongue. The texts state specifically that this is what is meant in the old myths by "the semen and the hands of Atum." All created things—gods, men, and animals—are but manifestations of the heart and tongue of Ptah. It should be noted that in the

50

ancient Near East, the seat of the intellect was regarded as being in the heart, and the term was always used for what we call "mind." This ascription by the Memphite theology of the creation of all things to the conception and commands of Ptah is the closest the Egyptians came to the intellectual theory of the Logos, or the creative divine word which we find in Genesis.

The Theology of Heliopolis

Our principal sources for the Heliopolitan Theology are two: the *Pyramid Texts* and *The Book of Smiting Down Apophis,* in the Bremner-Rhind Papyrus.

The pyramids of Egypt, the first image that comes to the minds of most of us when we think of that fascinating land, were all built during the early period of Egypt's history, the last of them constructed at least five hundred years before the time of Abraham. We call this age the period of the Old Kingdom, which lasted for approximately five hundred years, roughly between 2700 and 2200 B.C., and during which Egypt was ruled by the Pharaohs of the Third, Fourth, Fifth, and Sixth dynasties. These monarchs, at huge expense of manpower, built the pyramids to serve as their tombs in which their embalmed bodies, decked in the most beautiful ornaments of gold and precious jewels and surrounded by the exquisitely carved furniture of their private chambers, inlaid with ivory and gold, would enjoy life everlasting. Their queens and high nobles lay in much smaller pyramids clustered about that of their divine master, and an important part of the entire complex of structures was the pyramid-temple in which food offerings and sacrifices to the royal personages were regularly made. These pyramids and their surrounding buildings were intended to stand unto all eternity, and some of the largest have indeed survived for five thousand years, awesome monuments to the ingenuity of man.

Unfortunately, however, the main purpose of the early

Pharaohs in building their pyramids was frustrated also by the ingenuity of man, for, alas, all of the pyramids, large and small, were quite thoroughly and efficiently robbed in antiquity. The most elaborate and sinister precautions, such as corridors sealed off with a series of huge, sliding blocks of stone and deceptive passages intended to lead the thief to a deep well into which he would fall to a miserable death, were all to no avail. The first-class cracksman was just as ingenious fifty centuries ago as he is today, and without the various aids put at his disposal by modern technology. The result is that we have absolutely nothing of the bodies or the treasures of the occupants of the pyramids, except for a few pitiful things from the arm of a queen, torn from her mummy and apparently dropped in haste by some butter-fingered member of the gang. The Pharaohs succeeding the Sixth Dynasty must have given up in despair. Realizing that their tremendous expenditure in human resources was all in vain, they built no more pyramids. Recently there was discovered the tomb-chamber of one of the pyramids that had crumbled to pieces in ancient times. Surely this one had not been rifled! The archaeologists, after much labor, dug out a beautiful alabaster sarcophagus and, tense with anticipation, finally removed the heavy lid. The sarcophagus was empty.

Most fortunately, however, the pyramids have yielded us a far greater treasure than all the gold and jewelry of the Pharaohs and their queens. These treasures, which have proven to be a most valuable source for our understanding of the culture and intellectual outlook of the earliest civilization of Egypt, consist of thousands of lines of inscriptions carved on the walls of the galleries and chambers of the pyramids of five kings of the Fifth and Sixth dynasties. These inscriptions, incised in beautiful hieroglyphics inlaid with brilliant color, consist of spells and ritual formulas designed to accompany the deceased in his journey to the company of the gods in the other world, and to insure his felicity in the hereafter. These *Pyramid Texts,* as they are called, are not a uniform work. They are a collection of various rituals of mortuary offerings, hymns, and utterances addressed to the gods; magical charms, prayers, petitions, and fragments of myths, all concerning the entry of the departed king into life eternal, and his assumption of the godhead of Osiris, with whom the king after his death was always identified, just as in this life he was identified with Horus, Osiris's son. The spells were, no doubt, pronounced in the pyramid-temples to the accompaniment of the designated rituals, but their mere presence within the pyramid assured the accomplishment of their purpose. Many, if not most, of the texts go back to the earliest predynastic times, and their extreme value for us lies in the insight they provide into the thought and experience of the men who produced them.

Imbedded within the *Pyramid Texts* are several utterances which reveal the oldest of the Egyptian concepts of creation. There is no connected narrative as in the Memphite theology or in the Apophis ritual since, as mentioned above, the *Pyramid Texts* are not a connected work. The selection below is a compilation of several spells that mention the role of Ra-Atum-Khepri in the creation. It will be noted that in the *Pyramid Texts* the story of creation is according to the Heliopolitan Theology, which shows it to be more ancient than that of Memphis.

Ra-Atum-Kheprer, Sun-God and Creator

They [the gods] recite for thee this spell which they recited for Ra-Atum
    who shines every day.
They cause thee to come into being as Ra, in his name of Kheprer.
Thou ascendest unto them like Ra, in his name of Ra.
Thou turnest back from their presence like Ra, in his name of Atum.[1]

---

[1] Kheprer as the rising sun who is "coming into being," Ra as the sun high in the heavens, and Atum as the "completing" or setting sun.

Hail to thee, O Atum,
Hail to thee, O Kheprer, who brought himself into being.
Thou art on high, in this thy name of High One.[2]
Thou comest into being, in this thy name of Kheprer, He-Who-
    Comes-Into-Being.
Atum is he who indeed created by his masturbation in Ionu;
He placed his phallus in his fist
And aroused desire therewith.
Then were born the twins, Shu and Tefnut.
O Atum-Kheprer, thou didst mount high on the Primeval Hill;
Thou didst spit out what was Shu, thou didst spurt out what was
    Tefnut;
Thou didst put thine arms about them as the arms of a Divine
    Essence,[3] that thy Divine Essence might be in them.
O great Ennead which is in Ionu:
Atum, Shu, Tefnut, Geb, Nut, Osiris, Isis, Set, Nephthys,
Whom Atum begot, his heart is joyful in that which he has begotten,
    in your name of Nine Bows![4]
Thou [the king] art standing upon it, this earth, which came forth
    from Atum, the sputum which has come forth from Kheprer.

The Book of Smiting Down Apophis is from a portion of a large papyrus now in the British Museum. The Bremner-Rhind Papyrus, as it is known, is a relatively late one, dating from about 312 B.C., the beginning of the Hellenistic period. The entire papyrus contains four distinct works of a ritual nature and was apparently written for a temple library. The titles of these rituals are *The Songs of Isis and Nephthys, The Ritual of Bringing in Sokar, The Book of Smiting Down Apophis,* and *The Names of Apophis, Which Shall Not Exist.* The Heliopolitan story of creation is found in the third book, that dealing with bringing

---

[2] As having mounted upon the benben, the Primeval Hill of creation.
[3] The Egyptian hieroglyphic *ka*, which means "divine essence," is in the form of a pair of arms raised on high.
[4] "Nine" is, of course, the Ennead. The "Bows" may possibly be a group of stars.

about the overthrow of Apophis, the ancient serpent who is the enemy of Ra and of the divine king. Apophis (*Apep* in Egyptian) was sometimes represented as a crocodile, but usually as a huge, coiling serpent who lay beneath the earth to destroy the sun during its subterranean journey at night, and whom Ra, the sun, defeated daily as he emerged again on the eastern horizon. Apophis, then, represented the hostile and hated forces of darkness and the eternal enemy of Ra. The Apophis portion of the Bremner-Rhind Papyrus contains, for the most part, detailed spells and incantations to be uttered and rituals to be performed daily, by which the utter destruction of the ancient serpent might be accomplished. In the midst of the book there occurs the following section, in which Ra-Atum-Khepri describes his work of creation. It will be seen that in this very late papyrus the same processes of creation by Ra-Atum are detailed which are first found in the *Pyramid Texts,* witnessing the persistence of the motif for a period of at least three thousand years.

The Creation According to Ra

The Book of Knowing the Creations of Ra and of Smiting Down Apophis. The words to be spoken:

Thus said the Universal Lord after he had come into being: I am the one who came into being as Khepri.[5] When I came into being, being [itself] came into being. All beings came into being after I came into being. Manifold were the beings from that which came forth from my mouth. Not yet had the heaven come into being; not yet had the earth come into being; not yet had the ground been created or creeping things in this place. I raised some creatures in the Primordial Waters as [still] inert things, when I had not yet found

---

[5] Throughout this text, as well as in the *Pyramid Texts,* there is a continual play on the verb *kheper,* "come, or bring into being," and *Khepri-Kheprer,* "he who comes into being, or brings into being."

a place upon which I could stand.[6] I found it favorable in my heart, I conceived with my sight. I made all forms, I being all alone. Not yet had I spat out what was Shu, not yet had I emitted what was Tefnut, not yet had there come into being one who could act together with me.

I conceived in my own heart; there came into being a vast number of forms of divine beings, as the forms of children and the forms of their children.[7]

I it was who aroused desire with my fist; I masturbated with my hand, and I spat it from my own mouth. I spat it out as Shu; I spewed it out as Tefnut. By my father Nun, the Primordial Waters, were they brought up, my Eye[8] watching after them since the aeons when they were distant from me.

After I had come into being as the only god, there were three gods aside from me.[9] I came into being in this earth, but Shu and Tefnut rejoiced in Nun, the Primordial Waters, in which they existed. They brought back to me my Eye which had followed after them. After I had united my members, I wept over them, and that was the coming into being of mankind, from the tears which came forth from my Eye.[10] It was wroth against me after it came back and found that I had made another in its place, having replaced it with the Glorious Eye.[11] And so I advanced its place onto my brow,[12] and when it was exercising rule over this entire land, its wrath fell away completely, for I had replaced that which had been taken from it.

I came forth from among the roots,[13] and I created all creeping things, and all that exists among them. Then by Shu and Tefnut were Geb and Nut begotten, and by Geb and Nut were begotten Osiris,

[6] Before he raised the benben, the Primeval Hill.

[7] Note here the theme of creation by the intellectual conception of the god, which is the central feature of the Memphite theology. Evidently the theme, with its philosophical appeal, was syncretized with the theology of Heliopolis during the intervening millennia.

[8] See introduction to this section.

[9] Nun, Shu, and Tefnut.

[10] The Egyptians loved puns. The word for "mankind" is *remet*, and the word for "tears" is *remyt*.

[11] The sun in its course.

[12] As the uraeus-serpent, which became one of the main emblems of royalty, protecting the king from all enemies. It can be seen on the diadems, crowns, and helmets of all the rulers of Egypt.

[13] Namely, "which I had created." This refers, no doubt, to the creation of vegetation.

Horus, Set, Isis, and Nephthys from the womb, one after the other, and they begot their multitudes in this land.[14]

The Theology of Memphis

The text upon which our knowledge of the Memphite theology is based is on a black stone in the British Museum. The stone was inscribed by the Pharaoh Shabaka, an Ethiopian who ruled during the eighth century B.C., in the long period of Egypt's decline, which began about 1200. At the beginning of the inscription, Shabaka states that he found the text on a very old document, eaten by worms and barely legible, and in order to preserve it, had it written out anew on stone. When discovered, the stele had been used for years by Arab villagers as a nether millstone, and a large hole with channels radiating from it had been cut in its center. Years of grinding by the upper millstone had all but obliterated the text, and it was read with great difficulty. The reading, study, and interpretation of this important text is a tribute to a generation of scholars, led by the great American Egyptologist, James H. Breasted.

The document deals with a series of mythological incidents, and was probably read by a lector-priest assisted by other priests in the character of the various gods, since the text is in the form of a narrative interspersed with dialogues carried on by the gods. It was thus a sort of sacred drama or "mystery play." This is the portion dealing with the creation by Ptah.

Ptah and the Divine Logos

The gods who came into being from Ptah:
Ptah on the Great Throne . . . who created the gods;
Ptah-Nun, the father who created Atum;

[14] The third and fourth generations of the gods were begotten in normal manner from the womb, differentiating them from Shu and Tefnut, who were begotten from Ra-Atum himself.

57

Ptah-Nunet, the mother who bore Atum;[15]

The Great Ptah, who is the heart and tongue[16] of the Ennead.

There came into being as the heart, and there came into being as the tongue, the form of Atum.

Ptah is the Great and Mighty One, who has given the bounty of his power to all the gods and to their divine essences through this heart and this tongue.

Horus and Thoth[17] came into being through them as Ptah.

And it came to pass that the heart and the tongue exercised power over every limb, through teaching that he is within every body [as the heart] and within every mouth [as the tongue] of all the gods, of all mankind, of all cattle, of all creeping things and of all living things, in that he thinks [as heart] and commands [as tongue] everything which he desires.

His Ennead is before him as teeth and lips, which are the same as the semen and hand of Atum.[18] The Ennead of Atum, indeed, came into being through his semen and his fingers, but the Ennead [of Ptah] is the teeth and the lips of this mouth, which proclaimed the names of all things, and from which Shu and Tefnut came forth, and which created the Ennead.

The seeing of the eyes, the hearing of the ears, the nose smelling the air, they transmit to the heart. Thus [the heart] causes all perceptions to come forth, and by the tongue is the thought of the heart proclaimed.

And thus were begotten all the gods, and his Ennead was completed, and indeed all divine utterances came into being from that which the heart thought and the tongue proclaimed.

Thus were fashioned the Divine Essences, which furnish all food and nourishment by means of this word.

---

[15] Here a feminine form of Nun is devised. Ptah is both the masculine and feminine form of the Primeval Waters out of which Ra-Atum came. Note that Ptah is even the primeval watery chaos which existed before the gods and all creation.

[16] The heart as the conceiving mind, and the tongue as the divine creative utterance.

[17] Thoth is the god of scribes and of all wisdom. All the gods are merely various forms of Ptah, as is, indeed, all creation.

[18] Interpreting the cruder Heliopolitan Theology as an allegory of Ptah's creation by divine utterance.

As for him who does what is loved and him who does what is hated,
   so life is given to him who is peaceful, but death is given to the
   lawbreaker.[19]
And thus was made every work and every craft, the action of the
   arms and the going of the legs, the movement of every bodily
   member, according to what is ordered by what the heart thought
   and which the tongue brought forth, and which brings about the
   useful qualities of every thing.
It came to pass that it was said with respect to Ptah:
He created Atum and caused the gods to come into being.
He is Ta-Tjenen,[20] who begot the gods. Everything came forth from
   him, nourishment and food, the nourishment of the gods and
   every good thing.
Thus it was discovered and perceived that his power is greater than
   that of the other gods, and thus was Ptah content after he had
   created all things and all the divine utterances.[21]
He had begotten the gods, he fashioned cities, he founded nomes, he
   placed the gods in their shrines, he firmly established their
   sacrificial revenues, he founded their holy places, he modeled
   their bodies as their hearts desired.[22]
And so the gods entered into their bodies, in the form of every sort
   of wood, of every sort of mineral, as every sort of clay, as everything which grows upon him,[23] in which they had come into
   being and assumed form.[24]
Thus there gathered to him all the gods and their Divine Essences,
   content and joined with the Lord of the Two Lands.[25]

---

[19] Note the coupling of ethical concepts with creation.
[20] Literally, "the risen land," another ancient name for Ptah in the Memphite
Theology, and alluding to the Primeval Hill, which was the first earth to appear.
[21] Compare with Genesis 1:31.
[22] He allowed the gods to choose in which forms they wished their images to be
represented.
[23] Ptah, as earth-god (Ta-Tjenen).
[24] The gods entered into the images and statues of whatever material they were made.
[25] The king of Egypt.

7 Ra, Isis, and
the Mystery of the Divine Name

In all theologies, particularly those prevailing among early peoples and among primitive societies today, the name of the deity is an important aspect of his nature. Not only is the name symbolic of the deity and his power, but the solemn enunciation of his name can bring forth his dynamic essence to work that power. Just so, on the human level, an individual's name is considered to be a vital part of him and identified with his essence and/or soul. Thus the name can be used magically to work an influence upon him, for good or for evil.[1] For this reason, a man will have at least two names: one by which he is generally known, and another, his "real" name, which he keeps a close secret lest it become known to his enemies and he fall into their power. In relation to the divine plane, whoever knows the god's real name, secret and ineffable and taboo, has control over him in the sense that he can evoke his power. In all ceremonial magic, the essential portion of the spell is the calling forth of the spirit or deity by *name;* when he is evoked by his real name, he must work the desire of the magician who "controls" him. This is "a name to conjure with."

The great gods had many names, most of them being not actual names but epithets denoting some aspect of their nature and power. In our text, quoted below, Ra tells Isis some of his many and well-known names in an attempt to evade her demand for his

[1] On this concept in general, see J. G. Frazer, *The Golden Bough,* Vol. III, *Taboo and the Perils of the Soul,* 3rd ed. (London, Macmillan, 1926), pp. 318 ff. In the one-volume abridged edition (1926), Chap. XXII, pp. 244ff.

secret name, but she is not fooled. In the Old Testament, the deity is variously called *elohim,* "god," generically;[2] *shaddai,* "the Almighty";[3] and so on; but his proper name is *Yahweh,* "he who causes to be." The name was treated with great reverence, and we are enjoined in the Ten Commandments not to take it in vain. It later became absolutely sacrosanct and was forbidden to be pronounced. The same taboo was evidently observed with respect to the hidden name of Ra, which as far as we know, was never revealed to mortals at all, but as the text tells us, only to the goddess Isis, and only under dire necessity.

One reason for the origins of this myth may be the fact that Isis was the goddess of magic par excellence. A standard epithet of Isis is *Weret Hekau,* "Great of Magic." In the later story of *The Contendings of Horus and Set,* much of the action results from the magic of Isis, who is one of the principal protagonists. Our present text illustrates her magic and possibly accounts for it in one way by describing how she obtained Ra's secret name of power. She begins by using one widely used technique in sorcery, that of obtaining something emanating from the body of the victim or intimately associated with him by contact, thus embodying his essence, in this case the spittle of Ra. Mixing Ra's spittle with earth, Isis fashions therefrom the serpent that will sting the god. Since she has created the poison and its virulence, only she can recall it. Thus she can blackmail Ra into telling her his secret name. The graphic description of the old age of Ra, of his sufferings, and the dramatic and down-to-earth dialogue all serve to illustrate the vivid and colorful imagery that is a feature of the oriental tale in general.

The text following is in the Turin Papyrus, discovered in the middle of the nineteenth century. This particular papyrus dates

---

[2] The Hebrew form is grammatically in the plural—"gods"—probably intended as the sum total of the divine powers in the early days of monotheism. It was later interpreted as "plural of Majesty."
[3] Possibly originally meaning "he of the mountain."

from the Nineteenth Dynasty (1320–1205 B.C.), but as is the case
with all myths found in ancient writings, the myths are of course
much older than the texts in which they have been put into writing, just as, for instance, the stories in *Grimm's Fairy Tales* are
centuries older than their first published compilation:

The chapter of the divine god who came into being by himself: he
who made the heaven, the earth, and the waters, the breath of life—
and fire and gods and men, cattle and reptiles, flying fowl and fish—
king of men and gods together, to whom aeons are as years. Many
names has he, and even the gods do not know them.

Now, Isis was a woman clever of words. She was more cunning of
heart than a million of mankind. She excelled millions of gods and
was more knowing than millions of the glorious spirits. There was
nothing of which she did not know on heaven or earth like Ra, who
made all the earth. The goddess plotted in her heart to learn the
name of the august god.[4]

Now, Ra entered every day at the head of his boatmen[5] and established himself upon the Throne of the Two Horizons. The Divine
One had become old, his mouth quivered, he spewed forth his spittle
to the ground, and what he spat out fell upon the earth. Isis kneaded
it in her hand together with the earth which was on it, and fashioned
it into a noble serpent, making it in the form of a dart. It did not
move forward alive before her, but she left it lying on the path along
which the great god would go according to his heart's desire through
his Two Lands.

The august god rose and went forth, the gods of the Great Palace
(life, prosperity, and health!) following him, and he strode forth as
was his wont every day. The noble serpent bit him, and the fire of
life went forth from him completely, subduing the Dweller-Among-
the-Cedars.[6] The divine god opened his mouth, and the voice of His

[4] By knowing the secret name of Ra she would be enabled to assume the same
degree of power as the great god himself.
[5] In the divine Solar Bark which sails across the sky.
[6] Rendering Ra sexually impotent? If this surmise is correct, this would be a parallel
motif to that of Gaia's instigation of the castration of Ouranos by Kronos, as related
by Hesiod.

62

Majesty (life, prosperity, and health!) reached up to heaven. The Ennead of the gods cried, "What is it?" And all his gods asked, "What is the matter?" But he did not find the strength to answer. His jaws trembled, and all his limbs quivered as the poison seized his members as the Nile seizes all in its course.

When the great god had made firm his heart, he cried out to those in his following: "Come to me, O ye who came into being from my body, O ye gods who have come forth from me! Be informed of what has happened! A deadly thing has wounded me! My heart knows it, but my eyes have not seen it, nor has my hand made it. It is unknown among all that I have made. I have never tasted pain like unto it, nor is there anything more deadly than this! I am a Ruler and the son of a Ruler, the fluid produced by a god. I am a Great One, the son of a Great One. My father thought out my name.[7] I am many of names and many of forms, and my Being exists in every god. I am proclaimed as Atum and Horus-of-Praise. My father and mother have uttered my name, and it was hidden in my body ere I was born, so that a magician might not be allowed to achieve power over me by his spells. As I was going forth to see that which I had made, and was striding through the Two Lands which I had created, something stung me, I know not what. It is not indeed fire, nor is it indeed water. There is fire in my heart, my limbs are trembling, and my members are full of quiverings. Come, let my children, the gods, be brought to me, those who are glorious over words and who know their magic utterance, whose powerful influences reach unto the heavens!"

And so his children came, and every god there was weeping. And Isis also came, with her glorious power, her mouth endued with the breath of life, and with her plague-destroying spells and her words which cause choked throats to live. And she said: "What is the matter, divine father, what is it? Has a serpent driven sickness into you? Has one of the creatures you have borne lifted its head against you? Then I shall destroy it with effective spells. I shall make it depart at the sight of your rays."

---

[7] His secret name of power. His mother and father are, of course, himself (unless Nun is referred to).

63

The sacred god opened his mouth, saying: "I was passing along the road, striding through my Two Lands and foreign countries, desiring in my heart to see what I had created, when I was bitten by a serpent which I did not see. It is not indeed fire, it is not indeed water. I am colder than water, I am hotter than fire. All my members are drenched with sweat. I am shivering. My eye is unsteady, and I cannot distinguish the heavens. Moisture rises over my face as in the time of summer."

And then Isis said to Ra: "Come, tell me your name, O my divine father, for that one lives over whose name magic power is exerted."

"I am he who made heaven and earth, who fastened together the mountains and created all that exists thereon. I am he who made the waters, causing the Great Flood[8] to come into being. I am he who fashioned The-Bull-of-his-Mother, so that sexual delights came into being.[9] I am he who fashioned the heaven and the hidden recesses of the Two Horizons, within which I placed the souls of the gods. I am he who when he opens his eyes it becomes light, and when he closes his eyes it becomes darkness, at whose command the waters of the Nile rise, and whose name the gods do not know. I am he who creates the hours, and the days come into being. I am the opener of the festivals of the year, the creator of the flowing streams of water."[10] I am he who made living fire, so that the works of houses might be performed. I am Khepri in the morning, Ra at high noon, and Atum in the evening."

But the poison was not repelled from its course, and the great god was not relieved.

Then said Isis to Ra: "Your name is not among those which you have said to me. Come, tell it to me and the poison shall go forth. He shall live whose true name is declared."

And the poison burned with fiery fierceness. It was mightier than flames of fire.

And then the Majesty of Ra said: "I shall allow myself to be

---

[8] The celestial lake, conceived as being in the form of a cow, upon which the sun in his bark sails in his daily course.

[9] In analogy to the cow of the Great Flood? Bull-of-his-Mother is also one of the epithets of the god Amen of Thebes. Shades of Oedipus and Sigmund Freud!

[10] The inundation of the Nile, by which the seasons are measured.

searched out by Isis. My name shall go forth from my body into her body! I, the most divine among the gods, concealed it so that broad might be my seat in the Divine Bark of millions of years.[11] Once it has gone forth from my heart, then tell it to your son Horus, after you have sworn him by the life of the god, and have placed the god in his eyes."[12] The great god then rendered up his name.

Then said Isis, great of enchantments: "Spew forth, poison! Go forth from Ra! O Eye of Horus,[13] go forth from the god who created by his utterances! I, even I, am working this spell! I send forth the powerful poison to fall upon the ground! For behold, the great god has rendered up his name! Ra lives, and the poison dies! The poison dies, and Ra lives!"

So spoke Isis the Great, Mistress of the Gods, who knows Ra in his own name.

Directions: These words are to be recited over an image of Atum together with one of Horus-of-Praise and a figure of Isis and an image of Horus.[14] Write this spell and have the person swallow it. Thus also it may be done on a piece of real linen and placed upon his throat. It may be mixed with beer or wine and drunk by the patient. It is a complete destruction of the poison—successful a million times!

[11] The solar boat in which Ra crosses the sky. His power and authority therein were most secure as long as he had kept his secret name concealed.

[12] Isis may divulge the name to Horus, but only after she has made him take an oath of secrecy while gazing at Ra.

[13] This allusion is rather obscure in this context unless one wishes to connect it with the common mythic motif of the father being rendered impotent by the son, as in the case of Ouranos and Kronos.

[14] These four figures are drawn on the Turin Papyrus, to serve as a model for copying. Atum is shown seated, wearing the Double Crown and the curved beard of divinity. Beside him sits Horus-of-Praise, also with the Double Crown, but falcon-headed. Isis sits beside him, human-headed, and on her coiffure is a miniature throne, her distinctive symbol. Standing beside her is the falcon-headed Horus, wearing the Double Crown and holding the *Was*-scepter of divine lordship and prosperity.

(hieroglyphic text spanning the top of the page)

8   The Goddess Hathor:
Mankind in Peril of Destruction

The text quoted in this chapter introduces us to the great goddess Hathor, who was one of the most ancient deities of Egypt. Like all the very ancient goddesses, Hathor embodies quite ambivalent attributes, being both the "good" and the "bad" mother: All that is beautiful and desirable in woman and the essence of bountiful love and fertility, she is at the same time goddess of bloodshed and destruction, exulting in slaughter. She shares this basic ambivalence with Ishtar of Mesopotamia, Anath of Syria-Canaan and Parvati-Durga (called *Kali*, "the black one") of India. As also in other cultures, in Egypt too we have other goddesses who embody differentiated elements of the ambivalence: Sekhmet, "the powerful one," who is mostly specialized as a war-goddess, and represented as a lioness-headed woman;[1] Neith of the Delta, represented as a woman wearing the crown of Lower Egypt and brandishing a spear and/or a bow and arrows; Isis, the mother and protectress of the younger Horus and adept in magic and spells, who wears the cow's horns originally belonging to Hathor; and Bast, or Bastet, the charming and languorous goddess of the delights of love and pleasure, represented as a cat or a cat-headed woman, the beautiful and domestic feline variant of the wild and savage lioness of Sekhmet.

The name Hathor is, again, the Greek rendering. The Egyptian

---

[1] Throughout the ancient Near East, the formidable mother goddess is associated with the lion and is frequently shown standing on a lion or seated in a chariot drawn by lions, as in representations of Ishtar, Anath, and Atargatis-Cybele.

is *Het-Her,* "the house of Horus," and the hieroglyph of her name is the Horus-falcon within a "house." Horus here is "the Horus of the Double Horizon" or "Horus the elder," who is the same as Ra, and not to be confused with the younger Horus, who is the son of Isis and Osiris. Thus she contains Ra-Horus, that is, she is his mother. Not surprisingly, she is also mentioned in various texts as Ra's consort and also as his daughter.[2]

As fertility-goddess, Hathor is represented as a cow, as a cow-headed woman, or with a woman's face and a cow's ears. In the last form, she is seen heading the magnificent Palette of Narmer of the First Dynasty, and on the handle of her sacred instrument is the sistrum, which consisted of a somewhat oval-shaped frame attached to a handle and crossed by several thick wires loosely inserted in it so that it rattled when shaken. The sacred sistrum of Hathor was sometimes referred to as "the female soul with its two faces." The Hathor head also forms the capital of one type of pillar frequently seen in surviving examples of Egyptian architecture. Her face is usually framed within thick and heavy curls that cling to the cheeks and then curve outward and upward, very much like the "flip" coiffure popular during the 1960's.

This text shows Hathor in her "terrible" aspect, called in by Ra in a fit of pique for the purpose of teaching mankind a bloody lesson. Ra has cause to regret his unleashing Hathor, as, heady with the blood of the many thousands she has already slain, she seems bent on nothing less than the slaughter of all mankind. The great god, however, saves mankind from total destruction by thinking of a clever stratagem, which incidentally reveals the delightful ancient Egyptian sense of humor.

The text is found inscribed on the walls of some of the royal tombs of the Nineteenth Dynasty, but the language points to a much earlier original.

---

[2] In the symbolism of the unconscious, the house often represents the mother and/or the feminine love object in general. The ancient Egyptians knew their Freud!

And it came to pass when Ra, who came into being by himself, had established his kingship over men and gods together. Then mankind planned evil thoughts against Ra. Now as to His Majesty (life, prosperity, and health!), he had become old. His bones were silver, his flesh was of gold, and his hair was real lapis lazuli.

And His Majesty discerned the thoughts that were planned against him by mankind. And His Majesty (life, prosperity, and health!) said to the gods who were among his following:

"Come, fetch for me my Eye,[3] and also Shu, Tefnut, and Geb, together with the Fathers and Mothers[4] who were with me when I was as yet in Nun, the Primeval Waters, together with my god Nun, who shall bring his courtiers with him. Thou shalt bring them cautiously; let not mankind see, let not their hearts be awakened! Thou shalt come with them to the Great Palace, that they may give me their counsel, as they have done since the time when I came forth from Nun to the place wherein I came into being."

And so, when these gods were brought in before him, they placed their heads to the ground before His Majesty, so that he who fashioned mankind, the King of Peoples, might speak his words before the Father of the oldest gods.[5]

Thereupon they said to His Majesty: "Speak to us, that we may hear it."

Then Ra said to Nun:

"O thou Eldest God, in whom I came into being, and ye Primeval Gods! Behold mankind, who came into being from my Eye! They have planned evil thoughts against me. Tell me what you would do about it! Behold I am seeking a solution, and am not slaying them until I hear your opinion."

And then the Majesty of Nun said:

"O my son Ra, who is greater than he who fashioned him and more ancient than he who created him, sitting upon thy throne! Great is the fear of thee when thine Eye is against those who have planned against thee!"

---

[3] See page 50.
[4] Namely, the gods and goddesses.
[5] That is, Nun.

And the Majesty of Ra answered:

"Lo, they are fled to the desert, since their hearts are fearful because of what I may say to them."

And they all said unto His Majesty:

"Let thine Eye go forth to smite for thee those who plan with evil. However, the Eye has not sufficient power within itself to smite them for thee. Let it go forth as Hathor!"

And so, then, this goddess arrived, and she slew mankind upon the desert. And then the Majesty of this god said: "Welcome, O Hathor, for thou hast done that for which I sent thee!"

Then this goddess said: "As thou livest for me, I have prevailed over mankind, and it is delightful in my heart!"

And the Majesty of Ra said: "In diminishing them, I have prevailed over them as king." This was how Sekhmet came into being,[6] the Drunken One[7] of the Night, for to wade in their blood, beginning from Herakleopolis.

Then Ra said: "Come call to me swiftly running messengers who fly like the shadow of a body!" And so these messengers were brought straightway.

And the Majesty of this god said: "Go down to Elephantine and bring me very much red ochre."

And so this quantity of red ochre was brought to him. And the Majesty of this great god caused Him-of-the-Sidelock-Who-Is-in-Heliopolis[8] to grind up this red ochre. And then slave girls bruised barley for beer, and they added this red ochre to the mash, and it became like human blood. Thus seven thousand jars of beer were prepared. And then the Majesty of the King of Upper and Lower Egypt, Ra, came with these gods to see this beer.

And now when the land brightened at dawn, and time came for

[6] Sekhmet was the lion-headed goddess of war and bloodshed. Here she is specifically described as the other, terrible and destructive, aspect of Hathor, who is goddess of love, beauty, and fertility. The ancient great Mother-goddesses always had this dual aspect; for example, Anath in Syria and Parvati-Durga-Kali in India. Eros and Thanatos (or *destrudo*) as ambivalent aspects of the libido!

[7] The Egyptian word means "mixture," "(beer-) mash," hence "drunken"; see further in the text. The orgiastic aspect of the fertility deities was an important feature of their ritual.

[8] One of the titles of the high priest of Ra.

69

the goddess to continue the slaughter of mankind, the Majesty of Ra said: "How fine they are![9] With it I shall protect mankind from her!" Then Ra said: "Come, carry it to the place where she intends to slay mankind!"

And the Majesty of the King of Upper and Lower Egypt, Ra, betook himself very early, while it was still deep night, to have this sleeping-drink poured out. Then were the fields filled three palms deep with the liquor through the power of the Majesty of this god.

And when this goddess went forth at dawn, she found the place flooded with the liquor. Her countenance was beautiful in it. And then she drank, and it was good upon her heart. She came back drunk, without having even perceived mankind. Then the Majesty of Ra said to this goddess: "Twice welcome in peace, O Charming One!" Thus came into being the Beautiful Ones in Iamu.[10]

Then the Majesty of Ra said to this goddess: "Make for them intoxicating drinks on the yearly feasts and entrust it to the slave girls." This is how it came to pass that the making of intoxicating drinks was entrusted to the slave girls by all mankind since that first day.[11]

[9] The jars of red beer.
[10] Literally, "the City of Charm." Ra has called Hathor "Charming One" (iamyt), and one of the epithets of Hathor was "Lady of Iamu." No such site is known, but it may refer to one of the centers of her worship in Lower Egypt. We find punning explanations of place names and personal epithets all through Egyptian literature (as in all myth, for that matter) just as we do in the Old Testament, which is within the same tradition. The "Beautiful Ones in Iamu" are probably the priestesses and/or hierodules of the goddess.
[11] This is an apparent reference to a ritual which was conducted in commemoration of the event, as part of a festival of the goddess.

70

9 The God of
Wisdom and Learning: Thoth

The god Thoth had a most important place in Egyptian thought and religious ideas, being the deity who invented writing, which was called "the words of the god." The written characters were the means by which thought may be transmitted over any distance in space and time, and this is "magic." Thus Thoth was not only the scribe of the gods and frequently their spokesman, but also their "attorney" and keeper of the sacred archives, and the repository of all knowledge and creative intelligence. Indeed, one may have the impression that Thoth was about the only one of the gods who was literate. As source of the magic words, Thoth was the inventor of the arts and sciences and custodian of truth and all that this implies, and as such he supervised and recorded the "justification" of the deceased before Osiris in the Other World. Because of his close association with magic, learning, and the mysteries of the world beyond, the Greeks who became acquainted with Egypt during the mid-first millennium B.C. equated him with their god Hermes, who had several similar attributes. The Alexandrian period saw a profuse development of mystic and alchemical writings in Greek, and this mystic corpus of "Hermetic" texts was naturally attributed to Thoth, whom the Greeks called *Hermes Trismegistos,* "thrice-greatest Hermes."

Thoth was identified totemically with both the ibis-bird and the cynocephalus (dog-headed) ape or baboon, and his most common representation is as a man with the head and long, curved beak of the ibis. He was also closely associated with

71

the moon, and frequently wears the moon-disk resting in a crescent on his head. In most examples, he is shown holding a scribe's palette, into which he is dipping his writing reed.

Thoth describes some aspects of himself in the following selection from Chapter 182 of *The Book of the Dead* in E. A. W. Budge's translation (*The Book of the Dead—The Chapters of Coming Forth by Day,* London, 1898, translation volume, p. 340 ff).

The book of establishing Osiris firmly, of giving breath to the Weary of Heart,[1] while Thoth repulses the foes of Osiris, who comes there in his forms of becoming, and is protected and made holy and guarded in the Other World—that which has done Thoth himself.

I am Thoth, the excellent scribe, whose hands are pure, the lord of the two horns, who makes iniquity to be destroyed, the scribe of right and truth, who abominates wrongdoing. Behold, he is the writing reed of the Lord of All,[2] the lord of laws, who gives forth the speech of wisdom and understanding, whose words have dominion over the Two Lands.

I am Thoth, the lord of right and truth, who judges right and truth for the gods, the judge of words in their essence, whose words triumph over violence.

I have scattered the darkness, I have driven away the whirlwind and the storm,[3] and I have given the pleasant breeze of the north wind unto Osiris, the Beautiful Being,[4] as he came forth from the body of her who gave him birth.

I have made Ra to set as Osiris, and Osiris sets as Ra sets. I have made him to enter the secret habitation to vivify the heart of the Weary of Heart, the Holy Soul who is over the West, and to exult in joy to the Weary of Heart, the Beautiful Being, the son of Nut.[5]

[1] An epithet of Osiris as the "inert one," after he had been done to death by Set.
[2] An epithet of the great primeval god Ra. The rest of the sentence refers to Thoth, not to Ra.
[3] Referring to Set and his turmoil.
[4] *Wen-nefer,* "the Beautiful Being," was one of the most frequently used epithets of Osiris.
[5] Osiris, Isis, Set, and Nephthys were the children of the earth-god Geb and the sky-goddess Nut.

I am Thoth, praised of Ra, the lord of might, who brings to a prosperous end that which he does, the mighty one of enchantments who is in the boat of millions of years,[6] the lord of laws, whose words of power gave strength to her who gave him birth, whose voice subdues opposition and fighting, and who makes the praise of Ra in his shrine.

I am Thoth, who made true the voice[7] of Osiris over his enemies.

I am Thoth, who issues the decree at dawn, and whose sight follows on after his overthrow at his season,[8] the guide of heaven and earth and the Other World, and the creator of the life of all peoples.[9] I gave breath unto him who was in the hidden place[10] by means of the might of the magical words of my utterance, that Osiris might be true of voice over his enemies.

I came unto you, O lord of the Sacred Land, O Osiris, Bull of the West,[11] and you were made flourishing forever. I set eternity as magical protection for your members. I came having magical protection in my hand, and I guarded you with strength during the course of each and every day. Magical protection and life were behind this god, and his Divine Essence[12] was glorified with power.

The king of the Other World, the Ruler of the West, the possessor of the heavens through truth of voice, firmly established upon him

[6] The Solar Bark in which Ra crosses the sky daily, accompanied by several of the major deities. Thoth is always figured among them.

[7] At the famous judgment between Horus and Set, in which Horus contended for the claims of his father Osiris, which he inherited. Thoth acted as "attorney" for Horus and procured the vindication of his and Osiris's claims. The epithet "true of voice," meaning one who is justified before the tribunal, was a standard epithet of Osiris and regularly used after the names of the deceased as being identified with the god.

[8] He orders day to dawn and follows the course of the sun after it sets in its regular time.

[9] Thoth is here considered as ordering not only the visible world but also the world of eternity, and as the creator of life.

[10] Osiris.

[11] Like most of the dying and resurrected fertility gods of the ancient world (for example, Dionysus, with whom Osiris was identified by the Greeks), he was regularly called Bull, the powerful phallic totem par excellence. "The West" was a usual term for the Other World.

[12] *Ka* in Egyptian, the essential element of divinity of both gods and mortals. A mortal's *ka* was created with him and remained in the divine world during his lifetime, guiding and protecting him as a tutelary genius. When a man died, he rejoined his *ka.*

is the *Atef*-crown,[13] he is diademed with the White Crown,[14] and he grasps the Crook and the Flail.[15] Unto him, the great one of souls, the great one of the *Wereret*-crown,[16] every god is gathered together, and love of him who is the Beautiful being, and whose existence is forever unto eternity, goes through their bodies.

Hail to you, O you who are over those in the West, who makes mortals to be born again, renewing your youth and always in your season, and who is more beautiful even than anything in your heart! Your son Horus has avenged you,[17] and the dignities of Atum[18] have been conferred upon you, O Beautiful Being! You are raised up, O Bull of the West, you are made firm, made firm in the body of Nut, who unites herself with you and who comes forth with you. Your heart is raised upon that which supports it, and your breast as it was at its beginning; your nose is made firm with life and prospering; you are living, you are renewed and you are young like Ra each and every day.[19] Great, great is Osiris as one True of Voice and he is firmly established with life!

I am Thoth, and I have made content Horus and have quieted the two Divine Combatants[20] in their season of storm. I have come, and I have washed the Red One, I have quieted the Stormy One,[21] and I have made him swallow all manner of evil things.[22]

---

[13] The *Atef*-crown, which Osiris usually wears, consisted of the tall crown of Upper Egypt in its primitive form, with two ostrich plumes attached on either side and mounted upon a pair of twisted ram's horns.

[14] The tall white crown of Upper Egypt.

[15] The symbols of royal authority, analogous to the scepter of European kings. The flail was usually held in the right hand and the crook in the left, crossed diagonally over the chest.

[16] The tall white crown set into the low red crown of Lower Egypt, and worn by the king as the Double Crown of the Two Lands.

[17] A standard epithet of Horus is "Avenger of His Father."

[18] Ra-Atum-Khepri was the great primal god of Egypt.

[19] All the foregoing refers to the resurrection of Osiris, here represented as being effected by the magic power of Thoth. Note that Isis is not mentioned at all.

[20] Horus and Set.

[21] Set is frequently represented as red in color, and associated with storm and turmoil. The Egyptians identified Set with the great Syro-Canaanite god Baal, who in one of his fertility aspects brings the rainstorm.

[22] One of the various punishments meted out to Set after the great judgment. In the oldest variants of the myth, Set had to carry Horus on his back.

I am Thoth, and I have done the "Things of the Night" in Letopolis.[23] I am Thoth, and I have come daily into the cities of Pe and Depu.[24] I have led along the offerings and oblations. I have given cakes with lavish hand to the Glorious Ones.[25] I have protected the shoulder of Osiris, I have embalmed him, [26] I have made sweet his odor, even as the odor of the beautiful god.[27]

I am Thoth, and I have come each day to the city of Kher-Aha. I have tied the cordage and I have set in good order the *Mekhenet*-boat,[28] and I have brought it from the east to the west. I am more exalted upon my standard than any god, in this my name of "He whose face is exalted." I have opened beautiful things in this my name of *Wep-wawet*, Opener of the Ways.[29] I have ascribed praise and accomplished kissing-of-the-earth to Osiris, the Beautiful Being, whose existence is forever and unto eternity.

---

[23] The city of *Khem*, or *Kherti*, which the Greeks called Letopolis, was situated close to the fork of the Delta. It was the ancient site of the worship of Horus *Mekhenti-irty*, or *Mekhenty-en-irty*, meaning "Horus endued with his two eyes," or "Horus deprived of his two eyes," respectively. This alludes to the episode in the myth of the contendings of Horus and Set in which, in the course of a violent struggle between the two, Set tore out the eyes of Horus and Horus tore out the testicles of Set. When peace was later brought about, these organs were returned to their respective owners. The "Things of the Night" probably refers to the ritual re-enactment of the myth, which constitutes the essential "mysteries" of every cult. Well known in Greece were the mysteries of Dionysus, in which the death and resurrection of the god were re-enacted, and the Eleusinian mysteries, in which were re-enacted the myth of Demeter and Persephone and the latter's "death," that is, her abduction by Hades into his realms below and her later ascent, on the divine plane, and the death and resurrection of Demophoön-Triptolemos on the human level. Compare also the symbolic consuming of the body and blood of Jesus in the Roman Catholic Mass. Most of the ancient mysteries were performed at night, at least in the Graeco-Roman world.

[24] Ancient cities of Egypt.

[25] Beings possessing full attributes of divinity, such as the gods, or endowed with them by magic ceremonial, such as the spirits of the deceased.

[26] Here Thoth is identified with Anubis, the jackal-headed god who superintended the embalming process, which was a sacred rite in itself with a special liturgy. The ritual of embalmment was itself a re-enactment of the primal embalming by Anubis of the body of Osiris, with whom the deceased was identified.

[27] The mummy of the deceased was impregnated with fragrant oils and resins.

[28] Another name of the Solar Bark of Ra.

[29] A dog or jackal-headed deity, probably an aspect of Anubis, who acted as the guide of the deceased on the way to the Other World.

10   The Great Royal Myth
of Egypt: Osiris, Isis, Set, and Horus

A most important god of Egypt and actually visible, literally "in the flesh," was the king himself. He was the god Horus, son of Isis and Osiris; and the first of the five names in the royal titulary was the king's name as "Horus So-and-So." The concept of the reigning king as the living Horus goes back to the most ancient times, and in this sanction of the king as the living, personal deity of Egypt were his absolute power and authority embodied. An appreciation of this fact is essential to an adequate understanding of the literature and art, and indeed the entire cultural complex which prevailed in ancient Egypt.

The position of the king as the living and manifest national god of Egypt found its authority in what might be called the basic myth of Egypt—the story of Osiris, which made a profound impression on all those who came in contact with Egypt from the earliest period through Roman times. As in all primal myths, the motif is a simple one. It will be remembered from The Creation According to Ra, in Chapter 6, that the primordial god Ra-Atum-Khepri produced the gods Shu ("air") and Tefnut ("moisture"), who in turn begot Geb ("earth") and Nut ("sky"). Geb and Nut bore two sons, Osiris and Set, and two daughters, Isis and Nephthys. Geb, as lord of all the earth, bestowed the sovereignty thereof upon his eldest son, Osiris. Osiris ruled over all the earth (Egypt, naturally) in paternal beneficence, teaching mankind agriculture and the other arts of civilization.

His younger brother Set, however, being jealous of his hegemony, conspired against him, slew him, and usurped his throne.
Isis, who was Osiris's loving and devoted sister and consort, observed the ritual period of lamentation and mourning together
with their sister Nephthys and then proceeded upon the search
for her murdered husband's limbs (or drowned body, in another
version). Her main purpose in this was to reconstitute the life of
Osiris so that he might impregnate her and engender an heir who
would avenge his father's murder and take his rightful place upon
the usurped throne.

Eventually Isis found the dead Osiris, and being "great of
magic" (see Chapter 7, Ra, Isis, and the Mystery of the Divine
Name), she brought about his resurrection. After impregnating
Isis, Osiris left the earth forever, to become lord of the Other
World, the World of Eternity where the immortal dead live in
beatitude and glory. In course of time, Isis gave birth to Osiris's
son Horus, who was to avenge his father and assume his rightful
place as king of Egypt. After various struggles with Set, Horus
was victorious and eventually obtained the recognition of the
Council of the Gods as rightful king.

From the earliest times, the royal succession of Egypt was intimately and essentially a repetition of this theme, a re-enactment
of the ongoing myth. The living king upon the throne was always
the god Horus, and regarded as such by all "people," that is,
mortals. The king was not a mortal; he was a god, Horus, the son
of Isis and heir of his father Osiris, the first divine, legitimate heir
to the throne. When the king died, he became, in absolute identification with his father, Osiris; and his heir in turn took his place
upon the throne of Egypt as Horus. Becoming Osiris and Horus,
however, could be effected only by means of ritual magic, and
this was the purpose of the involved ceremonials attending the
burial of the deceased king and the investiture of his successor.

To effect the deceased king's becoming Osiris was the purpose

77

of our earliest body of religious texts from Egypt, the *Pyramid Texts,* so-called because the texts were found inscribed upon the walls of the corridors and chambers of the pyramids of the kings of the Fifth and Sixth dynasties. What these texts are is a series of magic spells which bring this purpose about. It must be remembered that these ritual formulas are not there to tell us the story of Osiris, but to "make" the deceased king Osiris by the magical effectiveness of their words and of the ritual acts which accompanied them. For this reason, we do not find the story in a connected form. As a matter of fact, nowhere in ancient Egyptian literature do we find the entire story in a connected sequence. We find it only in a late text, with many non-Egyptian additions and speculations and written in Greek by a non-Egyptian: the essay *On Isis and Osiris* by Plutarch, who lived during the later first and early second century A.D. Various elements and aspects of the myth, however, are referred to in much of ancient Egyptian literature throughout its history, and one most unusual and amusing text deals anecdotally with *The Contending of Horus and Set.*

Our purpose here is to present the myth from the oldest source at our disposal, namely, the *Pyramid Texts* (see pages 49–57). Since as mentioned, these ritual texts do not tell the story in a connected order, as this was not their reason for being, what we have done is to gather separate spells referring to definite elements of the "story line" and arrange them in as best an ordered sequence as we can. If our compilation seems rather disjointed, it is because the spells, or groups of spells, have been taken out of context and rearranged to "tell" the story. In no way, however, has the meaning of a spell been stretched or changed, except those instances in which the deceased king is addressed or referred to as "Osiris So-and-So" or by his name alone. In these cases we have simply substituted "Osiris," since that was what he was considered to be. The only complete English translation is by the Canadian Egyptologist Samuel A. B. Mercer: *The Pyramid Texts*

(4 volumes, Macmillan, 1952), with commentary and additional essays, of which the translation comprises the first volume.

The texts from the various royal pyramids of the Fifth and Sixth dynasties were collated and published, first partially by Maspéro in 1894, and in a much more complete edition by Kurt Sethe in 1908–1910. Sethe's edition has become the standard one, although from time to time new inscriptions have come to light from Old Kingdom pyramids, with parallel and/or additional texts. Each sentence of the texts (corresponding to a "verse" in the Bible) is referred to as a "spell" by scholars, and each group of spells dealing with a unit of the ritual is called an "utterance." The corpus of texts as published by Sethe is made up of 2,217 spells or fragments of spells, divided into 714 utterances.

[The birth of Osiris]

There come the waters of life which are in the sky; there come the waters of life which are in the earth. The sky burns for you, the earth trembles for you, before the birth of the god.

The two mountains[1] open: the god comes into being, and assumes power over his body.

Behold Osiris! his feet shall be kissed by the pure waters which were in Atum, which the phallus of Shu has made, and which the vulva of Tefnut has caused to be.

Your Mother Nut has given you birth; Geb has wiped your mouth for you!

They have come, they have brought to you the pure waters which are in their father. They purify you and cleanse you as with incense.

A cool libation is poured out at the gate of Osiris. The face of every god is washed.

---

[1] Most likely referring to the vulva of Tefnut, who is mentioned in the next spell.

79

You wash your arms, O Osiris! The renewal of your youthful vigor is
   as a god![2]

[Nut rejoices in the birth of her son, and all the gods rejoice with her]

Nut, the gleaming,[3] the great, says: "This is my son, my first-born,
   Osiris, opener of my womb! This is my beloved, in whom I am
   content." Geb says: "This is my son, Osiris, of my body!"

Nut the great, she who is in the lower mansion,[4] says: "This is my
   son, Osiris, my beloved, my eldest one, who is upon the throne
   of Geb, in whom he is content, to whom he gave his inheritance
   in the presence of the Great Ennead!"

All the gods are in exultation. They say: "How beautiful is Osiris,
   in whom his father Geb is content!"

Nut, this is your son is this one here, Osiris, of whom you have said:
   "One born to your father!" You have wiped for him his mouth.

[Osiris is assigned his place in the genealogy of the gods[5]]

Atum, this your son is this one here, Osiris, whom you have made to
   endure and to live.

Shu, this your son is this one here, Osiris, whom you have made to
   endure and to live.

Tefnut, this your son is this one here, Osiris, whom you have made to
   endure and to live.

Geb, this your son is this one here, Osiris, whom you have made to
   endure and to live.

Nut, this your son is this one here, Osiris, whom you have made to
   endure and to live.

Isis, this your brother is this one here, Osiris, whom you have made to
   endure and to live.

Set, this your brother is this one here, Osiris, who is made to endure
   and to live, so that he may punish you.

---

[2] The king is reborn and his powers are rejuvenated, in and with Osiris.

[3] The word in Egyptian (*akh*) may mean "glorious," "luminous," "beneficial." The
same root is found in the name of the famous Akhenaten (*Akh-en-Aten,* "the glory
of the sun disk.")

[4] Heliopolis.

[5] The genealogy is that of the Heliopolitan theology. See pages 51–52.

Nephthys, this your brother is this one here, Osiris, whom you have
    made to endure and to live.

Thoth, this your brother is this one here, Osiris, who is made to
    endure and to live, so that he may punish you.[6]

Horus, this your father is this one here, Osiris, whom you have made
    to endure and to live!

[Osiris is declared king of Upper and Lower Egypt]

Nut-Nekhbet[7] the great says: "This is my beloved, my son. I have
    given the Two Horizons to him, that he may be powerful over
    them like the Horus of the Two Horizons."[8] All the gods say:
    "It is a true thing that he is your beloved among your children.
    I will exercise divine protection over him eternally!" Nut the
    great, who is within the encircled mansion,[9] says: "This is my
    son, Osiris, of my heart!"

All the gods say [to Nut]: "Your father Shu knows that you love him
    more than your mother Tefnut."

He lives, the King of Upper and Lower Egypt, beloved of Ra, living
    forever!

Heir of Geb, whom he loves, Osiris, beloved of the gods, Osiris, given
    life, endurance, joy, health, all happiness, like Ra!

Osiris, the beloved son of Geb, Osiris, son of Nut, opener of her
    womb, Osiris, endowed with life, endurance, health, like Ra for-
    ever!

[Isis and Nephthys given to Osiris as consorts]

Nut says: "Osiris, I have given to you your sister Isis, that she may
    hold you fast, that she may give you your heart of your body."

Nut says: "Osiris, I have given to you your sister Nephthys, that she

---

[6] One of the few references to Thoth as another brother of Osiris and an accomplice
of Set. In most other texts Thoth is not a "villain" but the scribe and attorney of the
gods and the executor of their decrees.

[7] Nut here is identified with the vulture-goddess Nekhbet, the ancient tutelary deity of
Upper Egypt.

[8] An epithet of Atum, who is also called "the elder Horus," not to be confused with
Horus the son of Isis. The "horizons," of course, are those of the east and the west,
the rising and the setting sun.

[9] The shrine in Heliopolis.

may hold you fast, that she may give you your heart of your
body."

[Thoth aids Set against Osiris[10]]

Behold what Set and Thoth have done, your two brothers, who knew
not how to weep for you!
Set, this your brother is this one here, Osiris, who is made to
endure and to live, that he may punish you!
Thoth, this your brother is this one here, Osiris, who is made to
endure and to live, that he may punish you!

[Set binds Osiris and kills him]

[Horus] beats him who beats you; he binds him who binds you.
Have you [Set] acted against him? Have you said that he would
die? He will not die! Osiris will live a life forever. Osiris is become, in spite of them,[11] as the surviving bull of the wild bulls.
Osiris is at their head; he will live and last forever!

[The search and lamentation for Osiris]

The *hat*-bird[12] comes, the kite[13] comes; they are Isis and Nephthys.
They have come in search of their brother Osiris.
You who are here, weep for your brother! Isis, weep for your brother!
Nephthys, weep for your brother!
Isis sits, her hands upon her head. Nephthys has indeed seized the
tips of her breasts because of her brother Osiris. Anubis is on his
belly, Osiris being wounded.[14]
Isis and Nephthys have seen you; they have found you. Your two
sisters, Isis and Nephthys, come to you. They hasten to the place
in which you are, to the place where you were drowned. Your

---

[10] See note 6.
[11] Set and his followers. "The Followers of Set" are frequently referred to, and are
punished with him. In various texts, reference is made to a series of mythical kings
who reigned before Menes and were called "The Followers of Horus." Possibly "The
Followers of Set" are the opposite numbers of these.
[12] Literally, "the mourning bird," from the verb *hai,* "to mourn."
[13] Isis takes the form of a kite in *The Contendings of Horus and Set* (see Chapter 20).
[14] These are various attitudes of mourning. In many paintings and reliefs, mourning
women are depicted with breasts exposed and lacerated.

sister Isis laid hold of you, when she found you complete and
great, in your name of "Great Black."[15]

The gods in Buto[16] were filled with compassion, when they came to
Osiris, at the voice of weeping of Isis and at the lamentation of
Nephthys, at the wailing of these two spirits.

The souls of Buto dance for you; they smite their flesh for you; they
beat their arms for you; they dishevel their hair for you; they
smite their legs for you!

[The resurrection of Osiris]

It is your great sister who has collected your flesh, who has gathered
your hands, who sought you, who found you on your side on the
shore of Nedyt.[17]

Your two sisters, Isis and Nephthys, come to you. They heal you,
complete and great, in your name of Great Black, fresh and
great, in your name of Great Green![18]

Osiris, your mother Nut has spread herself over you, that she may
hide you from all evil things. Nut has guarded you from all evil;
you are the greatest among her children.

O Osiris, he who comes and comes, you shall not be in need! Your
mother comes; you shall not be in need!

Nut, you shall not be in need; protectress of the great, you shall
not be in need; protectress of the fearful, you shall not be in
need!

She protects you, she prevents your need, she gives back your head
to you; she collects your bones for you; she brings your heart
into your body for you.

Nut has made you to be as a god to your enemy, for you are made
young in your name of Fresh Water.

---

[15] In paintings and vignettes on papyrus, Osiris is colored either black or green, evidently symbolic of his powerful fertility aspects—the fertile black mud of the Nile and
the green of vegetation and water.

[16] Buto was an ancient, semi-mythical center of Lower Egypt. "The Souls of Buto,"
probably the spirits of ancient ancestral kings, are frequently represented performing
their stately ritual dance of mourning for Osiris.

[17] The mythical place on the Nile where the drowned body of Osiris was washed up.

[18] See note 15.

Osiris, who was placed upon his side by his brother Set, he who was
in Nedyt stirs; his head is raised up by Ra. His abomination is
to sleep; he hates to be wearied!
Osiris awakes in peace; he who was in Nedyt awakes in peace. His
head is lifted up by Ra.
He rots not; he stinks not!
"Come, my child!" says Atum. "Come to us!" say they, say the gods
to you, Osiris!
"Our brother is come to us—the eldest, the first-begotten of his father,
the first-born of his mother."
You support the sky on your right side, having life. You live, because
the gods ordained that you live. Osiris supports the sky on his
right side, having life. He lives his life, because the gods have
ordained that you live!
You lean on the earth on your left side, having joy. You live your
life, because the gods have ordained that you live!
Osiris is the blood which came forth from Isis![19] Osiris is the red
blood which came forth from Nephthys!

[Osiris impregnates Isis]

Your sister comes to you, rejoicing for love of you!
Isis comes to you, rejoicing for love of you!
"I have assembled my brother; I have united his limbs. I have come,
I lay hold of you; I have put your heart in your body for you.
I have come, rejoicing for love of you! O Osiris, this source[20] is
within you! I am the water-hole; I am overflowing!"
You have placed her upon your phallus, that your seed may go into
her, pointed like Sothis.[21] Horus the pointed has come forth
from you as Horus who was in Sothis!

---

[19] The menstrual blood of Isis had great life-giving power, and figures significantly in
the spells of *The Book of the Dead.*
[20] That is, of the "water" (semen) of Osiris.
[21] Sothis is the Greek name for the star Sirius, the brightest of the fixed stars. The
Egyptian name for Sirius is *Sepdet,* which means "the pointed one." The phallus of
Osiris, having become "pointed," produced Horus, who in one of his aspects was also
a powerful fertility-god (and equated with the ithyphallic god Min) and therefore
also "pointed."

[The battle of Horus and Set]

It is Horus! He has come to avenge his father Osiris! He has proclaimed a royal decree of death in the places of Anubis.[22]
Everyone hears it and he [Set] shall not live.

Thoth, spare none among those who have wronged the king![23]

[The first company of the "justified" was born] before there was anger,
before there was tumult, before there was strife, before there was
conflict, before the Eye of Horus was plucked out, before the
testicles of Set were torn away.[24]

Horus falls because of his Eye. The Bull[25] Set collapses because of
his testicles.

Horus has moaned because of his Eye. Set has moaned because of
his testicles.

Horus has seized Set; he has placed him under you,[26] that he may
carry you, and that he may quake under you like the quaking of

[22] The jackal-god of the necropolis, who has charge of the ritual embalming of the
deceased, and conducts him before Osiris.

[23] Here, and in many spells of the *Pyramid Texts,* Thoth is the one who executes the
decree of justice upon Set and his followers.

[24] This spell alludes to the physical struggle between Horus and Set. There are many
references to this in Egyptian literature. The combat ends in a draw, namely, Set tears
out the eyes (or Eye) of Horus, and Horus tears out the testicles of Set. It is interesting that in the symbolism of the unconscious as expressed in dreams and myths, the
eyes usually represent the testicles—"displacement from below upwards," as Freud
put it. The classic example of this symbolism is the self-blinding of Oedipus: self-castra-
tion as punishment in "poetic justice" for having copulated with his mother. In the
Egyptian myth, Horus and Set mutually destroy each other's most important divine
attribute, that of fertility. See also note 21. When the strife is over and the dissension
resolved, the vital organs are restored to their respective owners. Also, Horus will
present his Eye to Osiris as a powerful instrument of the latter's reinstauration as
fertility-god. See The Creation, pages 50 and 56, in which the Eye of Ra (who is also
Horus the Elder and Horus of the Two Horizons) figures prominently as a fertility
symbol, and as such is associated with the sun. The race of mankind also proceeded
from the Eye of Ra (see page 56). The Eye of Ra is also Hathor, the ancient fertility-
goddess (see page 69) sometimes represented as the consort of Ra and sometimes as
his daughter.

[25] Every ancient fertility-god is often referred to as "Bull," for obvious reasons. Osiris
is also called "Bull" in many texts.

[26] Osiris is addressed here.

the earth, for you are more exalted than he, in your name of "He of the Exalted Land."

Horus has caused that you seize him with your hand, without his escaping you. O Osiris, Horus has avenged you! He has done it for his *ka* in you, that you may be satisfied in your name of "Satisfied *Ka*."

[The return of the organs of Horus and Set after the battle]

Osiris is the messenger of the gods in search of the Eye of Horus. Osiris searched for it in Buto; he found it at Heliopolis. Osiris snatched it from the head of Set, at the place where they fought.

The messenger of Horus, whom he loves, was Osiris, who has brought back to him his Eye. The messenger of Set, whom he loves,[27] was Osiris, who has brought back to him his testicles.

You, Osiris, shall spit in the face of Horus in order to drive the injury away from him.[28] You shall catch the testicles of Set, in order to drive away his mutilation. That one was born to you; this one was begotten by you.[29]

You have been born, O Horus, as one whose name is "him at whom the earth quakes." You are begotten, O Set, as one whose name is "him at whom the sky trembles." That one [Horus] has not a mutilation; this one [Set] has not an injury. This one has not an injury; that one has not a mutilation.[30]

[Horus gives his Eye to Osiris]

Your son Horus has smitten him; he has snatched back his Eye from him; he has given it to you, that you may become glorious

---

[27] Whether the phrase "whom he loves" serves the purposes of balance is immaterial. After the resolution of the conflict, all the gods live in harmony anyhow. The phrase may also be taken to mean that Set loves Osiris for returning to him his testicles.

[28] Spittle, as one of the body fluids symbolizing semen, has magical, life-giving powers among all ancient and primitive peoples. Ra-Atum-Khepri "spat out" Shu and Tefnut in the process of creating them (page 54). In Greek myth, Polyidus, who had given Glaucus the magic power of divination, made Glaucus spit into his mouth when he desired to recall the magic that he had given him (Apollodorus, *The Library,* III, iii, 2). Magic and divination are strongly connected with the fertility concept.

[29] Horus and Set are often referred to as "brothers."

[30] Chiastic repetition (in which the order is reversed) is frequent in ritual magic.

thereby, that you may become mighty before the Glorious Ones.

O Osiris, arise! Horus comes, he reclaims you from the gods. Horus has loved you; he has equipped you with his Eye.

Horus has given you his Eye, the hard one. He has placed it for you, that you may be strong, and that all your enemies may fear you. Horus has completely filled you with his Eye, in this his name of "fullness of the god."

Horus has opened your eye for you, that you may see with it, in its name of "Opener of the Way."

[In a variant spell, Osiris eats the Eye:] that which you have eaten is an eye.[31] Your body is full of it; your son Horus parts with it for you, that you may live by it.

[Horus as the Avenger of Osiris]

Horus says: Arise for me, father! Stand up for me, O Osiris! It is I; I am your son; I am Horus your avenger. I have smitten for you him who smote you. I have avenged you, O father Osiris, on him who did you evil!

O Osiris, Horus has found you! He rejoices over you. Go forth against your enemy; you are greater than he!

Horus has caused him to carry you; he has delivered you from your enemy. He has avenged you.

Horus has extended your enemy beneath you. You are older than he [Set] for you were born before him.

Horus has caused Thoth to bring your enemy to you. He has placed you upon his back, and he dares not resist you. Sit you down upon him![32]

Mount; sit upon him, so that he dare not resist you!

And the Ennead shall not allow Set to be free from carrying you forever!

---

[31] To eat something is to assimilate its qualities. This is also the basis of cannibalism, which is magical in nature.

[32] The most frequently mentioned token of the submission of Set is that he had to carry Osiris upon his back.

[Set's lying testimony, and his judgment]

Remember, Set, put in your heart this word which Geb spoke, the
   threat which the gods made against you in the house of the
   Prince, in Heliopolis, because you did strike Osiris to the ground!

As you, Set, did say: "I have not done this against him!" that you
   might prevail thereby; that you might be acquitted, and prevail
   in spite of Horus.

As you, Set, did say: "It is he who defied me!" As you, Set, did say:
   "It is he who came too near to me!"

Osiris desires to be justified by that which he has done; since Tefen[33]
   and Tefnut have justified Osiris, since the Two Truths[34] have
   heard him, since Shu has been his advocate, since the Two
   Truths have given verdict, he has encompassed the thrones of
   Geb; he has raised himself to that which he wished.

So that his limbs are united, which were once hidden. He united
   himself with those who are in Nun. He concludes his defense in
   Heliopolis.[35]

[The triumph of Osiris and Horus]

O Osiris, stand up, see that which your son has done for you! Awake,
   hear that which Horus has done for you!

He has caused Thoth to turn back for you the Followers of Set,
   and that he bring them to you all together.

Thoth has seized your enemy for you, so that he is beheaded together
   with his followers;[36] there is not one whom he has spared!

---

[33] Although Shu ("air") is the consort of Tefnut ("moisture"), Tefen, a grammatically
masculine counterpart of Tefnut, is sometimes mentioned.

[34] Goddesses who are personifications of truth and justice, and who also figure in *The
Book of the Dead.* They are double, like many aspects of ancient Egypt.

[35] Before the divine tribunal of the Ennead, which declared Osiris "true of voice,"
that is, justified before the court. This epithet of the deceased king as having become
Osiris and "justified" before the gods was later, in the Middle and New Kingdom
periods, applied to the deceased nobles and commoners who also became Osiris by
virtue of the mortuary spells and rituals.

[36] Differing punishments, including dismemberment, and so on, are assigned to Set
and his followers in various portions of the *Pyramid Texts.* Since they are divine,
however, this does not mean that they are "killed dead." Set was always venerated,
particularly in his city of Tanis-Avaris. The killing and dismemberment of Set and his
followers are to be taken "in a Pickwickian sense."

He has beaten for you him who beats you. He has killed for you him
who kills you, like a wild bull. He had bound for you him who
binds you. He has put him under your great daughter who is in
Kedem.[37]

So that mourning ceased in the Two Palaces of the gods![38]

[The risen Osiris as the ongoing principle of life]

Osiris has come forth this day at the head of the full flood. Osiris is
the crocodile with the flourishing green plume, with head erect,
his breast lifted, the foaming one who has come forth from the
thigh of the Great Tail which is in the gleaming heavens.[39]

Osiris has come to his pools,[40] which are in the land of the flood, in
the great inundation, to the seats of contentment—green of fields,
which are in the horizon.

Osiris makes green and fertile the fields in both lands of the horizon.
Osiris has brought the gleam to the Great Eye in the midst of
the field. Osiris receives his throne which is in the horizon.

Osiris rises as Sebek, son of Neith.[41] Osiris eats with his mouth;

[37] This reference is one of those which are unclear in our present state of information.
All we can say about Kedem is that it probably refers to Syria-Canaan.

[38] Just as the palace of the king is double (for Upper and Lower Egypt), so is the
dwelling of the gods. See also note 34.

[39] The lizard—in Egypt the crocodile, who was also the god Sebek (see below)—the
erect head, "the foaming one," are all of obvious phallic significance, here epithets of
Osiris "at the head of the full flood." He has come forth from the "thigh," that is,
the genital organs (and so frequently metaphorically for euphemism in the Old Testament) of the "Great Tail," who is probably Ra. Elsewhere in the *Pyramid Texts,* Ra
is called "Bull of Bulls," and the deceased king, namely, Osiris, is referred to as
seizing his tail.

[40] As crocodile. Sacred crocodiles were kept in pools in the courtyards of the temples
devoted to them. Many mummified crocodiles have been found, some stuffed with
papyri containing valuable texts that would otherwise have been lost.

[41] Neith was the ancient warrior-goddess of Saïs in the Delta, and is usually represented wearing the clinging, sheathlike single garment worn by women in the Old
Kingdom, and holding a spear. She was sometimes equated with Nut. Her attributes
lend support to the possibility that her name became transposed, by metathesis, into
that of Athena, with whom the Greeks actually equated her. Sebek, as fertility deity,
is identified in Egypt not only with Osiris, but also with Ra and Horus. We find great
powers of fertility attributed to the crocodile by Nilotic peoples even in recent times:
Budge reports that the genitals of male crocodiles were eaten by Sudanese natives as
an aphrodisiac (E. A. W. Budge, *Osiris and the Egyptian Resurrection.* London, P. L.
Warner, 1911, I, p. 128).

Osiris urinates; Osiris copulates with his phallus. Osiris is lord of semen which women seize from their husbands, wherever Osiris wishes, according as his heart conceives.

O you whose life-giving tree becomes green, who is over his field; O opener of flowers, he who is on his sycamore; O you whose riverbanks glisten with verdure, who is over his tree of charm!

O lord of green fields, rejoice this day! Osiris will henceforth be among you; Osiris will go forth in his environs. Osiris will live on that upon which you live.

O Bulls of Atum! Make Osiris green! Refresh Osiris more than the Red Crown which is upon his head, more than the floodwaters which are upon his thighs, more than the dates which are in his fist![42]

---

[42] The reader will now readily recognize the strong phallic symbolism.

11   Amen: An Upstart Who
Rose to Supreme Power and Became Ra

Amen was originally a purely local deity, the god worshiped at the town of Thebes, in Upper Egypt. During the first period of Egyptian history, practically the entire third millennium B.C., when Egyptian civilization was centered in the Delta and Middle Egypt, with the capital at Memphis, both Thebes and her god were practically unknown and completely insignificant. With the rise of the Middle Kingdom at Thebes, however (Chapter 3, The Middle Kingdom), and the re-establishment of Thebes as the capital under the Theban kings of the Eighteenth Dynasty (Chapter 3, The New Kingdom), it was natural that Amen should be elevated to the supreme position in the pantheon. As such, he was accorded the sanction of being completely equated with Ra and was henceforth known as Amen-Ra. This meant, of course, the rise of the Amen priesthood to such great power and wealth as to exert a heavy political influence upon the throne. It was this influence, resented by Amenhotep IV (the later Akhenaten) that resulted in Atenism and the "Amarna Revolution."

Amen was, of course, also equated with Horus (the Elder, of the Double Horizon), and with the ancient phallic fertility god Min, several of whose attributes he assumed. Like Min, he was regularly represented in completely human form and wearing the flat crown surmounted by the two tall plumes, but without Min's ithyphallic attributes.

The text of the following hymn to Amen-Ra, one of the

91

most beautiful in all literature, dates from the Eighteenth Dynasty, although fragments of it have been found in an inscription of the earlier Second Intermediate period. The reader will note the tremendous universalistic concepts as compared with earlier religious texts.

The Great Hymn to Amen

Adoration of Amen-Ra, the Bull of Ionu,[1] the chief of all the gods,
    the good god, the beloved, who gives life to all that is warm,
    and to every good herd:

I

Hail to you, Amen-Ra, Lord of the Thrones of the Two Lands[2] who
    presides in Thebes!
  Bull of his Mother, the first on his field![3]
Wide of stride, first in upper Egypt,
  Lord of the Medjoi, and prince of Punt.[4]
Greatest of heaven, eldest of earth,
  lord of what exists, who endures in all things.
Unique in his nature, like the essence of the gods,
  Bull of the Ennead[5] and chief of the gods.
Lord of Truth, father of the gods,
  who made mankind and created the beasts.

[1] Ionu was the name of the ancient center of the worship of Ra, in the Delta, not far from Memphis. In the Bible it is called On (Genesis 41:45). Since Ra was closely identified with the sun, the Greeks called the city Heliopolis, "city of the sun." The powerfully phallic bull was one of the most widespread fertility totems among the ancients, and was usually a frequent symbol of the great masculine deities. In Egypt, Osiris is frequently called "Bull," and it is also a frequent epithet of both Horus and Amen as "Bull of his Mother," and so forth.

[2] "Thrones of the Two Lands" was a name for the vicinity of Thebes in which the great Amen temple was situated, in modern times called Karnak, the Arabic name of the site.

[3] Probably in reference to the cosmos as the "field" of the god.

[4] The Medjoi were one of the peoples of Nubia. Punt was the name of the fabulous land on the southwestern shores of the Red Sea, from which the Egyptians brought precious incense and spices.

[5] The nine great gods of the Heliopolitan Theology, which see.

Lord of what exists, who created the fruit tree,
  who made the green herb and sustains life in cattle.
Beauteous form which Ptah fashioned,[6]
  the beauteous, beloved youth, he whom the gods praise.
Who made them that are below and them that are above,
  he who illumines the Two Lands.
Who traverses the firmament in peace,
  King of Upper and Lower Egypt, Ra, True of Voice.[7]
The chief of the Two Lands, great of strength,
  lord of reverence, who made all the earth.
More eminent of nature than any god,
  over whose beauty the gods rejoice.
To whom praise is given in the Great House,
  who is crowned in the House of Fire.[8]
Whose sweet savor the gods love when he comes from Punt;
  richly perfumed when he comes down from the land of the Medjoi;
    fair of face, when he comes from the Land of the God.[9]
The gods fawn at his feet, knowing His Majesty to be their lord—
  the fearful, the terrible, great of will, and mighty in appearance,
    who abounds in victuals and creates sustenance.
Jubilation to you who created the gods,
  raised up the sky and spread out the ground!

II

He has awakened, who is in health!
  Min-Amen,[10] the Lord of Eternity, who created Everlasting,
    possessor of praise, who presides over the Ennead.

[6] Ptah, as craftsman-god, has given Amen his form.
[7] It is interesting that the scribe here applies the epithet "True of Voice," usually placed after names of the dead, to Ra, as if he were a deceased king.
[8] The "Great House" and the "House of Fire" were the names of the sanctuaries in the ancient capitals of Upper and Lower Egypt.
[9] A frequent epithet of Punt.
[10] Min was a very ancient god of procreation, always represented with erect phallus and wielding a flail. In all his representations he also wears on his head the two tall plumes which Amen always wears, and like Amen was represented in human form (although Amen in some cases was shown as a ram, Min is always human in form). There was a close connection between Min and Amen, as well as between Min and Horus, and the divine name Min-Horus is often found.

Firm of horns[11] and beautiful of face,
   lord of the Serpent[12] and lofty of plumes,[13]
     with beauteous diadem and tall White Crown.
The *Mehenet*-serpent and the Buto-serpents[14] are above his face,
   the Double Crown, the Headcloth[15] and the Blue Crown.[16]
Fair of face when he takes the *Atef*-crown,[17]
   beloved of the Upper Egyptian Crown and the Lower Egyptian.
Lord of the Double Crown when he takes the *ames*-scepter,[18]
   lord of the *mekes*-scepter[19] who holds the Flail.[20]
Prince crowned beauteously with the White Crown,
   lord of rays, who creates light, to whom the gods give praise.
Who gives his hands to him whom he loves,
   while he assigns his foe[21] to the fire.
It is his Eye[22] which overthrows the enemy;

[11] As "Bull." What follows is a description of the various insignia of royalty borne by the king.

[12] The uraeus-serpent on the king's diadem.

[13] The two tall plumes always worn by Amen.

[14] Buto was the ancient goddess of Lower Egypt and was represented by the cobra.

[15] The striped headcloth which was worn only by the king. In movies, television, and so on, all the Egyptians are usually shown running around in the *nemes*-headdress, an amusing example of the ignorance of the producers of these monstrosities.

[16] A stylized adaptation of the Double Crown, usually covered with small circles or spiral ornaments and colored blue. The king frequently wears the blue crown when riding in his war chariot.

[17] An elaborate headpiece, consisting of two twisted ram's horns spread horizontally, surmounted by one or more Upper Egypt crowns in their primitive form, to which ostrich plumes are attached on either side. The *Atef*-crown is usually shown worn by Osiris.

[18] A scepter in the form of a club or mace.

[19] Another type of scepter, with a flat end.

[20] The Flail and the Crook are the most frequently shown symbols of royal authority, held by the king.

[21] The following lines describe the daily struggle of Ra with his great enemy, the primeval serpent Apep, rendered by the Greeks as Apophis. Apep always attempts to prevent Ra from traversing the heavens in his Solar Bark and is always slain by Ra's spear.

[22] The Eye of Ra, which is, of course, the sun itself, but it includes many more aspects of the god. Basically, it is through his Eye that Ra accomplishes much of what he wills, and it is most usually conceived of as a goddess. In the story of *Hathor and the Destruction of Mankind* (see Chapter 8), Ra sends forth his Eye to accomplish the work of destruction, and it goes forth as the goddess of Hathor. The cobra-goddess is another manifestation of the Eye of Ra.

it thrusts its spear into him who drinks up Nun,[23]
and causes the dragon to vomit forth what he has swallowed.
Praise unto you, O Ra, Lord of Truth,
whose shrine is hidden,[24] lord of gods.
Khepri in his Bark, who commanded and the gods came into being.[25]
Atum,[26] who created mankind, who distinguished their nature and
made their life,
who made the colors different, one from the other.[27]
He who hearkens to the prisoner's prayer,
kindly of heart when one calls to him.
Who rescues the fearful from the oppressor,
who judges between the wretched and the strong.
Lord of Perception, in whose mouth is authority,[28]
for love of him the Nile has come.
The sweet, the greatly beloved,
and when he has come do men live.
He causes all eyes to open that are made in Nun;
his beneficence has created the light.
The gods rejoice in his beauty,
and their hearts live when they behold him.

III

O Ra adored in Karnak,
appearing great in the House of the Benben,[29] he of Ionu!

[23] Nun is the Primeval Waters out of which Ra appeared, and is here conceived as the celestial ocean across which Ra sails his Solar Bark, and which the Apep-dragon would swallow in order to frustrate Ra's course.

[24] The word for "hidden" is *amen*. The Egyptians ascribed a great deal of significance to puns and other plays upon words. We all do the same in our dreams and other unconscious associations of ideas and their resultant feelings.

[25] *Khepri* means "he who comes into being," or "he who brings into being."

[26] *Atum* means "he who completes," or "he who perfects," and is one of Ra's aspects as creator. See The Theology of Heliopolis in Chapter 6.

[27] All races and peoples are the children of (Amen-) Ra.

[28] *Sia* ("perception"), and *Hu* ("authoritative utterance"), as attributes of Ra were also personified as individual deities and were sometimes represented in the Solar Bark.

[29] The benben was the Primeval Hillock which Ra caused to rise out of the waters of Nun at creation, so that he might have upon which to stand. See The Theology of Heliopolis. The benben was also symbolized by the pyramidion, the miniature pyramidal capstone of the pyramids of the Old Kingdom.

Lord of the ninth day of the month,
  in whose honor men keep the sixth and the seventh day.[30]
Sovereign and Lord of all the gods;
  Falcon[31] in the midst of the horizon;
lord of the Silent Ones[32] among men,
  whose name is hidden from his children, in his name of Amen.[33]
Praise unto you, O Fortunate One,
  lord of joy and mighty in his appearing!
Lord of the Serpent and lofty of feathers,
  with beauteous diadem and tall White Crown,
the gods love to look upon you,
  when the Double Crown rests on your brow.
Love of you is spread throughout the Two Lands,
  when your rays shine in the eyes.
The well-being of mankind are you when arising,
  and the beasts are languid[34] when you shine.
You are beloved in the southern sky
  and are pleasant in the northern sky;
Your beauty captivates the hearts,
  and the love of you makes languid the arms.
Your beauteous form makes feeble the hands,[35]
  and the hearts are forgetful[36] when looking upon you.
You are the Only One, who made all that is;
  The One and Only, who made what exists.
From whose two eyes mankind issued,[37]

[30] Festivals connected with Ra and/or Amen. They may have been moon festivals, and as such connected with *Khonsu,* the son of Amen of Thebes and associated with the moon.
[31] The falcon is a frequent symbol of Ra and/or Horus.
[32] The blessed dead in the necropolis.
[33] See note 24. Note also the association of "silent" and "hidden."
[34] That is, relaxed and content.
[35] See previous note.
[36] Of care.
[37] Alluding to the myth of the creation of mankind from the tears of Ra. Another play upon words, the Egyptian *remyt* meaning "tears" and *remet,* meaning "mankind." See The Theology of Heliopolis.

and from whose mouth the gods came into being.[38]
He who made herbage for the cattle
   and the fruit tree for men,
who made that whereon live the fish in the river,
   and the birds who inhabit the sky;
who gives breath to that which is in the egg,
   and causes to live the son of the worm.
He who made that whereon gnats live,
   the worms, and flies likewise.
He who made that which the mice in their holes need,
   and nourishes the birds on every tree.
Praise unto you, who did make all this,
   Unique One and Only, with the many hands![39]
Who passes the night wakeful, when all men sleep,
   seeking the best for his creatures.
Amen, who endures in all things!
   Atum, and Horus of the Double Horizon![40]
Jubilation unto you because you weary yourself with us;
   reverence unto you, because you did create us!
"Praise unto you!" says every beast,
   "Jubilation unto you!" says every wilderness,
as high as is the heaven,
   as broad as is the earth,
     as deep as is the Great Green![41]
The gods make obeisance unto Your Majesty,
   and extol the might of their creator.
They rejoice when he who begot them draws nigh,
   and they say unto you: "Welcome, in peace!
Father of the fathers of all gods,

---

[38] Again in reference to the Heliopolitan Theology. Ra "spat out what is Shu, and emitted what is Tefnut." This may also indicate Amen-Ra's assimilation of the attributes of Ptah, who created "what the heart conceived, and the tongue uttered." See The Theology of Memphis.

[39] As having accomplished all this creation.

[40] "Horus of the Double Horizon" or "Horus the Elder" was another aspect of Ra-Atum-Khepri.

[41] This colorful metaphor was the regular Egyptian name for the (Mediterranean) Sea.

who raised up the sky and set down the ground,
who made that which is,
   and created what exists!
O Sovereign, chief of the gods!
We revere your might, because you created us,
   we shout for joy to you, because you have fashioned us,
      we offer you praise, because you wearied yourself with us!
Praise unto you, who made all that is,
   Lord of Truth and father of the gods.
Who made mankind and created beasts,
   lord of grain, who made the sustenance of the beasts of the desert.
O Amen, Bull of the beautiful countenance, beloved in Karnak,
   great of appearings in the House of the Benben,
      crowned again in Ionu!
You who judged between the Two[42] in the Great Hall,
   chief of the Great Ennead.
Unique One and Only, without peer,
   he of Ionu, who presides in Thebes,
      the head of his Ennead, living daily on Truth.
Dweller in the Horizon, Horus of the East!
The wilderness creates for him silver and gold,
   and real lapis lazuli for love of him,
myrrh and incense mixed from the land of the Medjoi,
   and fresh myrrh for your nostrils.
Fair of face when he comes from the land of the Medjoi,
   Amen-Ra, Lord of the Thrones of the Two Lands, presiding in
      Thebes,
      He of Ionu, presiding in his harem![43]

IV

The sole king, unique among the gods,
   with multitudinous names, whose number is not known,[44]

---

[42] Horus and Set.
[43] There was a grade of priestesses of Amen who were considered "the women of the god," and who dwelt in his "harem."
[44] The ancient gods had many names, some of them absolutely secret. See Chapter 7.

98

Who arises on the eastern horizon,
  and sets on the western horizon,
Who is born early every day,
  and every day overthrows his enemies![45]
Thoth lifts up his eyes, and delights in his excellence,
  the gods rejoice in his beauty, and the *hetet*-apes[46] exalt him.
Lord of the ship of evening and the ship of morning;
  they traverse Nun for you in peace.
Your crew[47] rejoices in seeing the enemy overthrown,
  and how his limbs are consumed by the knife.
The fire has devoured him,
  and his soul is consumed yet more than his body.
The dragon, an end is made of his going;
  the gods shout for joy
    and the crew of Ra is in contentment.
Ionu is in joy: the foe of Atum is overthrown;
  Thebes is content, and Ionu exults.
The gods of Babylon are in jubilation,
  and they of Letopolis[48] kiss the earth when they see him.
The Mistress of Life[49] is glad:
  the foe of her lord is overthrown.
Strong is his might,
  the most mighty of the gods,
Righteous One, Lord of Thebes,
  in this your name of Creator of Right![50]
Lord of victuals, Bull of provisions,
  in this your name of Bull of his Mother![51]

---

[45] Apophis and his fellow malevolent monsters.
[46] A group of divine apes, frequently represented as jubilating over the sun-god at his arising.
[47] The entourage of Ra in his Bark, consisting of the great divinities.
[48] Babylon (not to be confused with the great city of the same name in Mesopotamia) and Letopolis were cities not far from modern Cairo.
[49] The goddess of the Eye of Ra.
[50] In Egyptian, *Maat,* "right, truth, justice" and so forth, and also personified as a goddess.
[51] See note 1.

Who made all men that are and created all that is,
  in this your name of Atum-Khepri!
Great Falcon, who makes festive the body,
  fair of face who makes festive the breast!
With pleasing form and the tall plumes,
  the Two Serpents rearing on his brow.
He to whom men's hearts come nestling,
    who suffers mankind to come out to him,
      who gladdens the Two Lands with his going forth!
Praise unto you, Amen-Ra,
    Lord of the Thrones of the Two Lands,
      whose arising his city loves!

12 Atenism and the "Amarna Revolution"

Toward the middle of the fourteenth century B.C., there occurred a remarkable phenomenon in the history of Egypt and of human civilization. This was the political, religious, and cultural revolution promoted, as far as we know, by a most unusual and talented king, encouraged and aided by his unusual and beautiful queen. The king has come down in history not by his original name, which was *Amen-hotep,* "Amen is content," or "pleasing unto Amen," but as *Akh-en-Aten,* "the glory of the Aten." He assumed this new name himself, an outward token of a profound change in inner attitudes that was a radical revolt against fifteen hundred years of the most strongly ingrained, conservative religious and cultural traditions of Egypt. With good reason has Akhenaten been called "the first individual in history" by James H. Breasted.

Akhenaten, who came to the throne as Amenhotep IV, was the son of Amenhotep III, the "Louis XIV" of ancient Egypt, under whose reign the empire reached the zenith of its prosperity and of its highly sophisticated, cosmopolitan culture. Riding the wave of this wealth and prosperity was the priesthood of Amen at Thebes, enormously enriched during the previous generations of the Eighteenth Dynasty by the tribute pouring into Egypt with the expansion of the empire. In gratitude to Amen for according them their great victories and imperial hegemony, the Pharaohs donated a large proportion of the booty

and tribute to the god, which meant, of course, to the temples
and the priesthood—the Amen "establishment." With wealth
came power, and the Amen priesthood became, evidently, the
real power behind the throne. It is tempting to compare this
all-powerful influence with that of Richelieu, Mazarin, and
Dubois (all cardinals of the Roman Church) under Louis XIII
and his successors in France during the seventeenth and eighteenth centuries.

It seems that the young Amenhotep IV continued to worship
Amen down to the fifth year of his reign (his regnal dates are
1367–1350). We do not have many details of the particular
events of Akhenaten's reign, since with his disappearance from
the scene the Amen priesthood attempted to obliterate his
memory from Egypt and from history, and a great many of his
inscriptions were destroyed. In fact, we do not know exactly
what happened to him, whether he was assassinated or whether
he died a natural death, and we are likewise ignorant of the
fate of Nefertiti his queen. We do know, however, that after
about five years he renounced all allegiance to Amen, unseated
the god from his royal supremacy, and elevated instead as head
of the pantheon an ancient personified aspect of Ra, namely,
the *Aten,* which is the disk of the sun itself. Henceforth it is
the Aten, always represented by the sun-disk, protected by the
uraeus-serpent, and sending forth rays ending in hands which
bless the king and his family and which hold the *ankh,* the sign
of eternal life. To avoid the (understandably) malevolent
presence of the Amen priesthood, he, together with his family
and a large retinue of his Aten-priests, officers, administrators,
and courtiers, removed from Thebes altogether and built a
completely new capital, with an elaborate palace and temple to
the Aten, at a site about halfway down the Nile between Thebes
and Memphis, and called the new city Akhet-Aten, "the horizon
of the Aten."

Akhenaten, with his queen, *Nefert-Iti* ("the Beautiful One

has come"), both of whom were evidently totally uninterested in the affairs of the empire, seem to have immersed themselves completely in the worship of their god and the beautification of the new palace at Akhet-Aten. There an entirely new form of art appears, a style startlingly "modern," showing, in delineation of human beings from the king down, a radical departure from the rigid conventions of Egyptian art. We see both in sculpture and relief, a stark, exaggerated realism, in its development pushed almost to the point of caricature that is strongly suggestive of the post-Impressionists of the early twentieth century. In the rendering of plant and animal life we are struck with a new and bold love of free-flowing natural forms replete with movement and grace. The many fascinating examples of the art produced at Akhet-Aten came from the busy royal studio-workshop staffed by a corps of excellent artists who were taken along by the king with his entourage, and headed by a master named Thothmes. Even the many trial pieces we have found in the ruins of the workshop, practice carvings on scraps and flakes of stone, are treasured as masterpieces today by museums the world over. The many representations of the king and his queen seated under the beneficent rays of the Aten and dandling their little daughters on their knees, or graciously throwing down gold collar-necklaces from their balcony to the courtiers below (in these scenes the king and queen are frequently depicted in the nude) are but one of the many charming aspects of the art.

But these idyllic glories were not to last. After about fifteen years, Akhenaten and Nefertiti disappear from history. The last, and completely ineffectual, scion of the family, the boy originally named *Tut-Ankh-Aten,* "the living image of the Aten," went back (was most likely taken back) to Thebes, and significantly enough, we find his name changed to *Tut-Ankh-Amen,* "the living image of Amen." Akhet-Aten was allowed to sink buried beneath the sands blowing in from the desert, to remain undiscovered for almost thirty-five hundred years. Toward the end of the nineteenth century the first discoveries began to be made at the site, now known by its Arabic name of *Tell-el-Amarna.* The term Amarna is hence applied to Akhenaten's period and its various aspects.

The seeds of the "Amarna Revolution," which in its full flowering was due to the efforts of Akhenaten and Nefertiti, are to be found, however, in the latter part of the previous reign, that of Amenhotep III. We have several inscriptions from Amenhotep's time indicating reverence for the Aten, and some evidence of a special cult of the Aten at Thebes. In the art, one interesting relief represents Amenhotep as a man of advancing years, slumped languidly on his throne with one arm thrown listlessly over its back; the expression on the king's face is tired and blasé —a radical departure from the usual rigidly majestic and idealized representation of the kings of Egypt, and foreshadowing the free movement and realism of the Amarna art which was to come. An excellent example of the beginnings of Atenism, in which both Amen and the Aten are hailed as aspects of Ra, is the poetic hymn to Amen and the Aten, quoted later in this chapter. This "joint hymn" is declared to be a joint composition of the twin brothers Suti and Hor (Set and Horus), and it is quite possible that the Egyptians, who attached much importance to puns and other similarities, made much of the implied (and expressed) duality here, and it is possible that although the hymn was obviously composed at a time when Amen was quite the supreme deity, the Aten had already assumed such an importance that the two could be regarded as "twins."

Hymn to Amen and the Aten by Suti and Hor

We have a rather interesting text containing a double hymn, to Amen and to the Aten, composed, appropriately enough, by twin brothers. As the reader can see from the colophons of the text, they were "Overseers of the Works of Amen" (something like engineers in charge of construction) and also "Directors" or superintendents of the huge temple-complex of Amen at Thebes, the vast ruins of which are at the Arab village of Karnak. And like many kings, administrators, and others of high position in ancient Egypt, they were not only skilled in their particular office, but were highly cultured persons and men of parts, who composed poetry.

The names of the brothers provide an interesting insight into Egyptian ways of thinking. The fact that they were twins gave them a certain aura, since twins always were regarded by ancient peoples, and by peoples today who think mythopoeically, as something uncanny, and hence connected with the mythic. Jacob and Esau, Castor and Pollux, and to take a contemporary example, the Marassa, the Divine Twins in the Voodoo religion, are but a few cases in point.

Duality was basic to ancient Egypt since earliest times, conditioned first by the originally distinct areas of the Delta and Upper Egypt and their consequent union. This duality was recognized throughout its history: the country was called the Two Lands, the king was the Lord of the Two Lands, the national tutelary deities were the Two Goddesses (the vulture-goddess Nekhbet of Upper Egypt and the cobra-goddess Buto of Lower Egypt) with whom the king was also identified, the royal treasury and granaries were "Double," and so on. On the mythic level— and it is to be remembered that the ancients did not distinguish between the mythic and the "real"—Ra was "the Horus of the Double Horizon," *Ra-Her-Akhety,* and there was also Horus, son of Isis, with whom he was frequently identified or confused.

Likewise, in the basic myth of Egypt, there are the two contending gods, Horus and Set. Although according to strict genealogy Set is the brother of Osiris, and as such, the uncle of Horus, this made no difference to the Egyptians, since Horus is another aspect and the inheritor of Osiris anyway; and they are regularly

105

referred to as "the divine pair" and "the brothers." Set may be the villain of the piece, but he is a god and hence to be venerated, as he is very powerful. Besides, the contendings took place on the divine plane. As a matter of fact, as far back as the Second Dynasty we have a record of a king with both a Horus and a Set name, and we have a representation of a king and/or a divine figure with a human body and both the falcon head of Horus and the head of the Set animal. It was thus a "natural," so to speak, for twins to be named Horus and Set. To differentiate between the actual deities and the men named for them, we are using here the Egyptian names of the twin brothers. *Hor, Her,* is the original name of the god rendered by the Greeks as *Horus.* The name of Set has variant versions in Egyptian: *Setekh, Setesh,* and *Suti,* and in this text it is the latter variant that is found.

It has long been recognized by scholars that the worship of the Aten was not introduced by Akhenaten, although he elevated the Aten to supremacy in the pantheon in order to eliminate Amen, and that this was certainly not monotheism. We see from this text that the Aten was accorded equal honors with Amen in the time of Akhenaten's father, Amenhotep III (about 1405–1367 B.C.). Of course, in this text the Aten is another aspect or manifestation of Ra, with whom Amen was identified after Thebes had risen to supremacy in the Eighteenth Dynasty.

This double or "twin" hymn, composed by the twin brothers (who had "twin" jobs, as will be seen) is inscribed upon a stele now in the British Museum.

Hymn to Amen
and the Aten by Suti and Hor

Praise of Amen when he rises as Horus of the Double Horizon, by the Overseer of the Works of Amen, Suti, and the Overseer of the Works of Amen, Hor. They say:

106

Hail unto you, O Ra, beautiful one of each day,
  who rises at dawn and never makes cessation,
    Khepri wearying in his works!
Your rays are in one's face without their being known;
  even fine gold is not like your brilliance.
The Ptah of yourself,[1] you did fashion your limbs:
  one who gives birth, but was not born.[2]
Unique in his qualities, traversing eternity over the ways;
  millions are under his guidance.
Your radiance is like the radiance of the heavens,
  and your color gleams more than the covering thereof.
When you sail[3] across the sky all faces behold you,
  but your going is hidden from their sight.[4]
You present yourself at dawn every day,
  and vigorous is your sailing under Your Majesty.
In but a short day you run a course of millions of hundred thou-
      sands of measures;
  a moment is every day under you, and when it passes you set.
You complete the hours of the night likewise;
  you measure it without a pause in your labors.
All eyes see through you,
  and they do not finish when Your Majesty sets.
You rouse yourself early to shine in the morning;
  your brilliance opens the eyes of the wakeful.
And when you set in Manu,[5]
  then they sleep in the manner of death.
Hail unto you, O Sun-disk [Aten][6] of the day,
  creator of all things and making their life!
Great Falcon,[7] many-colored of plumage,

[1] Ptah was the great creator god of Memphis, who had absorbed all the creative
aspects of the primordial Ra (see The Theology of Memphis in Chapter 6).
[2] Ra-Atum-Khepri, according to the Theology of Heliopolis, (see Chapter 6), rose
self-created out of the Primeval Waters of Nun.
[3] Ra, as the sun, was considered to sail across the sky in his Solar Bark.
[4] The actual movement of the sun is not discerned, as it seems to stand still in the sky.
[5] The mythical land in the west, into which the sun sets.
[6] Amen-Ra as the actual sun-disk.
[7] Ra as Horus the Elder, or Horus of the Double Horizon, was depicted as a falcon,
or falcon-headed.

who came into being, and then raised himself up.[8]
Who brought himself into being, and who was not born;
  O Horus, the first from the midst of Nut![9]
For whom is made jubilation in rising,
  and in his setting likewise.
He who fashions what the ground produces:
  the Khnum and the Amen of mankind,[10]
    who holds the Two Lands, from the great to the little.
Glorious Mother[11] of gods and men,
  craftsman patient and laborious, as their maker without number.
Herdsman valiant and strong, driving his cattle:
  their refuge, and the maker of their life.
Racer, runner, and courser! Khepri who determines his birth,
  causing his beauty to rise in the body of Nut,[12]
    and the Two Lands to shine with his Disk.
Primordial One of the Two Lands, who made himself
  and beholds what he has made.
Unique Lord, possessing the lands every day,
  and beholding those who tread thereon.
Rising in the sky, his form is the sun;

---

[8] Ra brought the Primeval Hillock up out of Nun and stood himself thereon.

[9] A beautiful example here of the fusion of the deities. The goddess Nut was the sky, the consort of the earth-god Geb, and the mother of Osiris, Isis, Set, and Nephthys. Horus was begotten of Isis by Osiris, first-born of Nut. Naturally, Horus the son of Isis is fused with the Elder Horus (Horus of the Double Horizon), who is Ra, who is Amen, and who is the Aten.

[10] *Khnum* (meaning "the joiner-together") was another creator god, who fashioned mankind on his potter's wheel. Since Amen means "hidden," the Egyptian phrase could also be taken in the sense of "the hidden fashioner of mankind." The Egyptians attached great significance to these plays upon words.

[11] An allusion to the bisexuality of the primeval creator god, a concept common in primitive cosmogonies. Whether this is conscious or not here cannot, of course, be known. The Egyptian word for "mother" is *mut,* and is written ideographically as a vulture. The vulture-goddess mother, the goddess Mut, was the consort of Amen of Thebes.

[12] The association of Nun and Nut, the Primeval Waters with the heavens.

he makes the seasons according to months.
Warmth when he wishes, and coolness when he wishes;
  he makes lax the limbs when he enfolds them.
Every land is in chattering at his shining forth,[13]
  every day in order to praise him!

The Overseer of the Works, Suti, and the Overseer of the Works,
  Hor; each says:
I was the Director in your Southern Harem,[14] the loyal Overseer
of the Works in your sanctuary, which was made for you by your
son, your beloved, the Lord of the Two Lands, Neb-Maat-Ra,[15] given
life.

My Lord made me Director of your Monuments. I was vigilant, I
served as a vigorous Director of your Monuments, performing the
true things of your heart. I was one knowing that you are content
over justice, and I exalted you, doing it upon earth. I performed it,
and you exalted me. You set my favors over the land in the Chosen
of Places,[16] and I was among your followers when you shone forth.

I am one of truth, who despises wrongdoing. I do not take pleasure
in any words which say falsehood. Besides me, my brother is like myself. I take pleasure in his counsels. He came forth from the womb
together with me on the same day, the Overseers of the Works of
Amen in the Southern Harem, Suti, and Hor.

I was Director over the western side, and he was over the eastern
side. We were Directors of the great monuments of the Chosen of
Places before Thebes, the City of Amen.

May I be joined with the favored ones,[17] going forth[18] in contentment! May you give to me sweet breath when the bandlets are made

[13] An allusion to the divine apes who are represented as greeting Ra-Atum-Khepri
on his rising with their chattering.
[14] A name of the temple-complex of Amen at Karnak. The priestesses of the god
were considered to be his concubines. Suti and Hor are still addressing the god.
[15] The "son of Ra" name of Amenhotep III, and meaning "Lord of the Truth of Ra."
[16] A frequently used name for the Temple of Amen at Karnak.
[17] The blessed dead.
[18] One of the euphemisms for dying.

firm and donned on the day of the Festival of the Rising of the Sun![19]

Akhenaten's Hymn to the Aten

The following hymn to the Aten, composed, in all probability, by Akhenaten himself, reveals the poetic and sensitive soul of this "first individual." Here is the universalism usually ascribed to monotheism (although we see much of this even in the Amen hymn)—in fact, Akhenaten's "monotheism" was Breasted's particular hobbyhorse, which that scholar continued to ride to the end, and which has been glibly repeated by pot-boiling popularizers who had never even read a translation of the hymn. We know today, however, that Akhenaten was much influenced by the ancient cult of Ra at Heliopolis, and that he revered other deities, notably Thoth. This is not monotheism, and the theory of Akhenaten's monotheism is not held by any serious scholar today. See, for example, the statements of John A. Wilson, Breasted's successor at the Oriental Institute of the University of Chicago, in *The Culture of Ancient Egypt.*[20]

Several parallels have been indicated between parts of Akhenaten's hymn and Psalm 104. They are no doubt an example of the strong cultural influences of Egypt upon Israel lasting through several centuries. It is important, however, to call attention to at least two basic differences between the Atenism of Akhenaten and ethical monotheism as developed in Israel by the later prophets. Akhenaten's Atenism was essentially the cult and faith belonging to the king and royal family. The king was both high priest and prophet of the Aten, and in his hymn he declares: "There is no one who knows

---

[19] An obscure allusion. It may possibly have something to do with the mortuary rituals.
[20] (Chicago, University of Chicago Press, 1956), Chapter IX.

110

you [the Aten] save your son, Nefer-Khepru-Ra Wa-en-Ra,"
the "King of Upper and Lower Egypt" name of Akhenaten;
literally, "beautiful are the becomings (or forms) of Ra, the
Unique One of Ra"; Akh-en-Aten was his "Son of Ra" name.

Atenism was not a religion for all the people. Indeed, at
Tell-el-Amarna were found many images of Bes, the bandy-
legged, phallic, dwarf god of fertility and good luck, and other
popular deities. Another important difference is the absence of
ethical considerations or precepts in the Aten texts, considerations that are essential in Israelite monotheism.

The text of the hymn was found inscribed in the tomb of
Ay, who reigned briefly after Tut-Ankh-Amen and who may
have been the latter's uncle. The tomb is at Tell-el-Amarna
and was obviously prepared while the court was at Akhet-
Aten, during Akhenaten's reign.

The Great Hymn to the Aten

Praise of *the Living Ra,*[21] *Horus of the Double Horizon, Rejoicing
on the Horizon, in His Name of Shu*[22] *Who is in the Aten,* living
forever unto eternity; Aten living and great, he who is in the Jubilee

---

[21] The appellations of Ra italicized here are within two cartouches in the original, like
royal names. This is unusual, as the names of deities are rarely found within cartouches.
Usually, only the last two of the five names in the titulary of the king are in cartouches.
[22] The god Shu ("air") and the goddess Tefnut ("moisture") were produced by Ra
from his own body by masturbation, when first he stood alone on the Primeval Hillock
(see The Theology of Heliopolis in Chapter 6). Shu and Tefnut, in turn, begot the
earth-god Geb and the sky-goddess Nut in the usual manner. In many representations,
Shu is shown holding up the body of Nut, who is bowed like an arc over the earth,
her toes and the tips of her fingers touching the ground and her body covered with
stars. Interpretation of "Shu who is in the Aten" is difficult: Shu as the sun-disk
holding up the sky? We do have a hymn to Shu translated by E. A. Wallis Budge in
his *From Fetish to God in Ancient Egypt* (London, Oxford University Press, 1934),
p. 418, in which the god is addressed as "Leader of the Eye of thy father Ra." The
sun was one of the aspects of the Eye of Ra. Sir Alan H. Gardiner has interpreted
Shu here as "sunlight" (*Egypt of the Pharaohs,* New York, Oxford University Press,
1961, p. 218).

Festival, Lord of all that the Aten encircles, Lord of the Heavens and Lord of the Earth, Lord of the House of Aten in Akhet-Aten. The King of Upper and Lower Egypt, Living in Truth, the Lord of the Two Lands, Nefer-Kheperu-Ra Wa-en-Ra, Son of Ra, Living in Truth, Lord of Diadems, Akh-en-Aten, Great in his Duration, and the Great Wife of the King, his Beloved, the Lady of the Two Lands, Nefer-Neferu-Aten Nefert-Iti, living, healthy, and youthful forever unto eternity. He says:

Beautiful is your shining forth on the horizon,
    O living Aten, beginning of life!
When you arise on the eastern horizon,
    you fill every land with your beauty.
You are bright and great and gleaming,
    and are high above every land.
Your rays envelop the lands,
    as far as all you have created.
You are Ra, and you reach unto their end,
    and subdue them all for your beloved son.[23]
You are afar, yet are your rays upon earth;
    you are before their face, yet one knows not their going![24]
When you go down in the western horizon,
    the earth is in darkness, as if it were dead.
They sleep in their chamber, their heads enwrapped,[25]
    and no eye sees the other.
Though all their things were taken while under their heads,
    yet would they not perceive it.[26]
Every lion comes forth from his den,
    and all serpents that bite.
Darkness is without and the earth is silent.
    for he who created it rests in his horizon.

[23] Akhenaten.
[24] The actual movement of the sun is not discerned. The same idea is expressed in the Hymn to Amen and the Aten by Suti and Hor, which see.
[25] To protect their heads from the night chill.
[26] Their most precious possessions were kept under their heads while sleeping, in order to prevent them from being stolen.

When the earth brightens[27] and you rise on the horizon,
  and shine as the Aten in the day,
When you scatter the darkness and offer your beams,
  the Two Lands are in festival,
They[28] are awake and they stand on their feet,
  for you have raised them up.
They wash their bodies, and they take their garments,
  and their hands praise your arising.
    The whole land, it performs its work!

All beasts are content upon their pasture,
  and the trees and herbs are verdant.
The birds fly out of their nests,
  and their wings praise your Divine Essence.[29]
All wild beasts prance upon their feet,
  and all that fly and alight.
    They live when you shine forth for them!

The ships voyage downstream and upstream likewise,
  and every way is open, since you have arisen.
The fish in the river leap up before your face,
  and your rays are in the midst of the Great Green.[30]

You who bring children into being in women,
  and make fluid into mankind,
Who nourishes the son in the womb of his mother,
  who soothes him so that he weeps not,[31]
    O nurse in the womb!
Who gives breath in order to keep alive
  all that he has made;
When he comes forth from the womb on the day of his birth,
  you open his mouth in speech, and give all that he needs.

---

[27] The usual idiomatic expression for "dawn" in Egyptian.
[28] That is, the people.
[29] Literally "your *ka*."
[30] The usual Egyptian expression for the Mediterranean Sea.
[31] In its mother's womb.

The chick in the egg chirps in the shell,
  for you give it breath therein to sustain its life.
You make its completion for it in the egg in order to break it;
It comes forth from the egg at its completion,
  and walks on its feet when it comes forth therefrom.

How manifold are the things which you have made,
  and they are hidden from before man![32]
    O unique god, who has no second to him!
You have created the earth according to your desire,
  while you were alone,[33]
With men, cattle, and wild beasts,
  all that is upon earth and goes upon feet,
    and all that soars above and flies with its wings.

The lands of Syria and Kush,[34]
  and the land of Egypt,
You put every man in his place,
  and supply their needs.
Each one has provision
  and his lifetime is reckoned.
Their tongues are diverse in speech,
  and their form likewise;
Their skins are distinguished,
  for you distinguish the peoples of foreign lands.

You make the Nile in the Other World,[35]
  and bring it whither you wish,
In order to sustain the people,
  even as you have made them.
For you are lord of them all,
  who weary yourself on their behalf,
The lord of every land, who arises for them,
  O Aten of the day, great of majesty!

---

[32] Their number is too great to be conceived of.
[33] Another allusion to the Heliopolitan Theology.
[34] Nubia and/or Ethiopia.
[35] It was believed that the Nile and/or the inundation rose in the Other World.

All strange foreign lands,
   you make that whereon they live.
You have put a Nile in the sky,[36]
   that it may come down for them,
And make waves on the hills like the sea,
   to water their fields in their townships.
How excellently made are your designs, O Lord of Eternity!
   the Nile in heaven, you appoint it for foreign peoples,
     and all beasts of the wilderness which walk upon feet;
The Nile upon earth,
   it proceeds from the Other World for the Beloved Land.

Your rays suckle every field,
   and when you shine forth
     they live and flourish for you.
You make the seasons
   to cause to continue all you have created:
The winter to cool them,
   and the warmth that they may taste of you.
You have made the sky afar off to shine therein,
   in order to behold all you have made.
You are alone, shining in your forms as living Aten,
   appearing, shining, withdrawing, returning,
     you make millions of forms of yourself alone!
Cities, townships, fields, road, and river,
   all eyes behold you against them,
     O Aten of the day above the earth!

You are in my heart,
   and there is no one who knows you save your son,
Nefer-Khepru-Ra Wa-en-Ra,
   whom you made understanding of your designs and your might.
The earth came into being by your hand,
   even as you have created them.
When you arise they live,

---

[36] The waters above the earth, which descend in the form of rain.

and when you set they die.
But you have eternity in your members,
   and all creatures live in you.
The eyes look on your beauty until you set;
   all work is laid aside when you set in the west.
When you rise you make all to flourish for the King,
   you who made the foundations of the earth.
You raise them up for your son,
   he who came forth from your body,[37]
the King of Upper and Lower Egypt, Living in Truth, the Lord of
the Two Lands, Nefer-Kheperu-Ra Wa-en-Ra, Son of Ra, Living in
Truth, Lord of Diadems, Akh-en-Aten, Great in His Duration, and
for the Great Wife of the King, his Beloved, the Lady of the Two
Lands, Nefer-Neferu-Aten Nefert-Iti, living and youthful forever unto
eternity.

[37] As son of Ra.

13 The Divine Conception of the King-Queen Hatshepsut and of King Thothmes III

The divinity of the king was one of the oldest concepts forming the foundation of the Egyptian state, and we already find this assumption fully developed in the *Pyramid Texts,* in which the deceased king becomes Osiris and his living son upon the throne is the god Horus incarnate, son of Osiris and Isis. This *mystique* served as sufficient sanction for the divine aura surrounding the king until the occurrence of something hitherto unique in Egyptian history—a woman made herself king and had herself represented as a man. It was true that in ancient Egypt all inheritance descended in the female line, and no man could become king unless he were married to a princess of the blood royal, whether it be his sister, half sister, or another woman of the royal line. However, a woman could not be the actual sovereign.

The Divine Conception of Queen Hatshepsut

This woman who made herself king and ruled as a "man" was the famous *Hat-shepsut* ("foremost in nobility"), who ruled from 1490 to 1468 and whose tomb-temple at Deir-el-Bahri is one of the most majestically beautiful sights of Egypt. The precise genealogy of Hatshepsut and her successor, Thothmes III, who was her nephew, or stepson, or both, is still not absolutely clear. Most of the evidence indicates that (a) Hatshepsut was the daughter of Thothmes I (1528–1510) and of his queen,

Aahmes, and that she was married to Thothmes II (1510–1490), who was the son of Thothmes I by a concubine; and (b) the boy who later became Thothmes III was a son of Thothmes II by one of *his* concubines. This can get rather complicated. Be that as it may, at the death of Thothmes II, Hatshepsut, although ostensibly regent for her nephew-stepson, declared herself the actual sovereign. She was aided in this achievement by a man of remarkable abilities whose origin seems to have been an undistinguished one—Senmut, who became her vizier.

Thothmes III was kept in complete subjection for some twenty years. After the disappearance of Hatshepsut and Senmut from the scene—that they were "eliminated" would not surprise anyone, although we just have no evidence—he at last ruled in his own right (1468), and he went on to become one of the greatest conquerors Egypt had ever known. Of course, he dated his reign from the death of his father, not only officially ignoring the reign of Hatshepsut but also having the inscriptions and statues of Hatshepsut and Senmut hacked to pieces.

Hatshepsut, during the twenty odd years that she reigned with Senmut at her right hand, proved to be an efficient ruler, and her reign was distinguished as an era of peace, fruitful commerce, and building activity. As "king," she had herself frequently represented in the statuary with masculine build and wearing the artificial square chin-beard worn by the king on state occasions. She shows, however, a definite consciousness of her femininity in many other statues of her, which show her with the typically Egyptian feminine contours and frankly as a woman, and quite a charming woman at that.

In order to establish her sanction to reign as king, however, she produced a "legal fiction" in the form of a statement by Amen himself, to the effect that it was actually he, the god Amen, who was her true father. Inscribed on the walls of the Deir-el-Bahri complex is a detailed description of how Amen entered the palace by night and embraced Queen Aahmes in love and decreed that she would bear a daughter, and that it was his very desire that this daughter should reign as king. As the reader will note, the "love scene" is quite lyrical.

The Divine Conception
of Queen Hatshepsut

Amen declares the following to these gods [the Great Ennead] concerning the heir of the Lord of the Two Lands:

Lo, I have loved the mate whom he [Thothmes] has loved, the Mother of King Ka-Maat-Ra [Hatshepsut], endued with life, the Queen Aahmes. I was the protector of her body when she was exalted. I have endowed her with all lands and foreign countries, that she may lead all the living.

I have joined the Two Lands unto her in contentment. She builds your temples and makes them holy; she keeps fresh your sacrifices and offering tables. Cause the dew in the heavens to come down for her at its proper time, and make a Great Nile[1] for her at its proper time. Extend about her your protection of life and good fortune!

He who shall praise her shall live, but he who shall speak evil of the name of Her Majesty, to him will I give the gift of death forthwith!

The Great Ennead answers:

We have come to extend our protection of life and good fortune about her. She shall build her beautiful monuments in these Two Lands.

[Amen announces his intention to Thoth, who will escort him into the presence of Queen Aahmes. Thoth replies:]

This princess of whom you have spoken, Queen Aahmes is her name. She is more beautiful than all the women in this entire land. She is the wife of the Sovereign, King Aa-Kheper-Ka-Ra ["great is

[1] A good inundation.

the becoming of the *ka* of Ra," that is, Thothmes I], given eternal life. His Majesty is a child of royalty, and thou mayest then go!"[2]

And then he came, this august god Amen, Lord of the Two Lands, and he assumed the form of the Majesty of her husband, King Thothmes. They [the god and the form of the king] found her as she was reclining in the beauty of her palace.

She awakened at the fragrant odor of the god,[3] and laughed in joy before His Majesty. And then he came to her straightway. He was passionate for her. He gave his heart unto her. He let her see him in his divine form after he came to her. She rejoiced when she beheld his beauty; his love went through her limbs. The Palace was flooded with the divine fragrance, and all his odors were those of Punt. The dearest and loveliest one—the Majesty of this god did everything that he desired with her. She let him rejoice over her. She kissed him.

Then spoke the Wife and Mother of the God, Queen Aahmes, to the Majesty of this god, Amen, Lord of the Thrones of the Two Lands:

My Lord, how great is thy splendor! Magnificent it is to see thy presence! Thou hast filled my Majesty with thy glory! Thy sweet savor pervades all my members!

Thus she spoke after the Majesty of this god did everything that he desired with her.

Then spoke Amen, Lord of the Thrones of the Two Lands, unto her:

Hat-Shepsut ["foremost in nobility"] shall be the name of this daughter whom I have implanted in thy body. She shall exercise beneficent kingship in this entire land. My spirit shall be hers. My power shall be hers. My exaltation shall be hers. My crown shall be hers. She shall rule the Two Lands in kingship, and shall lead all the

---

[2] Thothmes' mother was of non-royal blood, and his sole legal claim to the throne was his marriage to the princess Aahmes, who was evidently a scion of the royal line. Hence a specific declaration by Thoth, the scribe and archivist of the gods, is needed to sanction the royal rank of Hatshepsut's father as a man befitting for Amen to impersonate.

[3] The deities of the classical world were also distinguished by their divine fragrance, for example, Aeschylus, *Prometheus Bound,* 1.115.

living over all that the heavens embrace and all over which I shine. I have joined unto her the Two Lands in all her names, and upon the throne of Horus of the Living. She shall be under my divine protection every day, together with the god thereof. She is my beloved daughter, out of my own seed.

The Designation and Divine Conception of Thothmes III

As already mentioned, Thothmes III considered Hatshepsut to have been an absolute usurper. Although he officially dated his reign from the death of his father Thothmes II, he evidently felt that he, too, needed a divine sanction. Accordingly, he caused to be inscribed upon the walls of the great temple of Amen at Karnak (to which he contributed magnificent enlargements in gratitude to the god) a story of how, when he was still a child and serving as a priest in the temple, the image of Amen recognized him as it was borne in solemn procession, and how the god then spoke to him and declared that he, Amen, was his father. Amen then proceeded to invest the young Thothmes with the royal titulary and the other prerogatives of sovereignty.

It is interesting that Thothmes was impelled to interpolate: "... this is not a lie; there is no untruth in it... These things really happened, and it is not an untruth," going on to disarm any possible further skepticism by stating that this miracle was not to be discerned by mere men but only by himself, Thothmes.

The Designation and

Divine Conception of Thothmes III

Amen—he is my father, and I am his son. He commanded me to be upon his throne when I was still one who is a bird in his nest. He begot me within his inmost being, and he designated me for the kingship (this is not a lie; there is no untruth in it) when My Majesty was but a child, when I was still a suckling in his temple,[4] and before my induction as priest had taken place.

I was in the vestments and role of a "Pillar-of-his-Mother" priest,[5] like Horus in his youth at Khemmis. I was standing in the north papyrus-pillared hall,[6] and Amen was going forth from the "Holiness of His Horizon."[7] He made heaven and earth festive with his beauty, and he began a great wonder with his rays in the eyes of mankind, like Horus of the Double Horizon.[8] All people gave him praise in his temple. Then His Majesty[9] offered him incense upon the flame and brought a great sacrifice of oxen, cattle, and wild beasts of the desert.

The god proceeded around the papyrus-pillared hall on both its sides, and it was not in the mind of those who were present at his doing that he was searching for My Majesty in every place.[10] And then he recognized me, and he halted. Then I threw myself upon my belly before him; I lifted me up from the ground and bowed again before him, and he placed me before His Majesty. I was set upon the Place of the Lord,[11] and then he marveled over me. These things really happened, and it is not an untruth. They were not manifest in the faces of men, but kept secret in the hearts of the gods who knew it. There was no one who knew these things, no one who understood them.

[4] The child Thothmes, like other royal princes, received the regular education of a scribe in the temple school. In the regular course of events, he would be inducted into the various grades of the priesthood.

[5] In reference to the childhood of Horus, who was born at Khemmis, in the Delta marshes, and there nurtured by his mother Isis. Because of the identification with Horus, this priestly office could be assumed, evidently, only by a scion of royalty.

[6] In the temple of Amen at Karnak, built by Thothmes I. The two most frequent types of column capitals in Egyptian temples are stylized forms of the open papyrus flower and the closed papyrus bud.

[7] The image of Amen (in which the god himself was believed to reside) was being solemnly borne forth from its shrine. Since Amen was completely identified with Ra, his shrine would be called his "horizon."

[8] Another name of Ra was "Horus of the Double Horizon" or "Horus the Elder," not to be confused with Horus, son of Isis.

[9] Thothmes I or II, whoever reigned at the time.

[10] Those assembled there did not realize that the god, by forcing his bearers to make the circuit of the hall, was looking for Thothmes.

[11] The particular spot in the temple where only the king stood.

He[12] opened for me the gates of the heavens; he threw open for me the portals of his Horizon. I flew up to the sky as a divine Falcon,[13] in order to see his Divine Mystery in the heavens and adore His Majesty. I saw the glorious forms of the God of the Double Horizon on his mysterious paths in the sky.

Ra himself established me; I was adorned with the diadems upon his head, and his Only One[14] was fixed upon my brow. I was endued with all his glories; I was made full with the excellencies of the gods, like Horus when he made estimation of himself[15] at the house of his father Amen-Ra; I was endued with the dignities of a god.

He established my diadems, and affirmed my Titulary himself:[16]

He set my Falcon upon the Facade;[17] he made me powerful as a powerful bull, he made me to shine forth in Thebes in this my name of Horus, the Powerful Bull, Shining Forth in Thebes.

He made me to put on the Two Ladies;[18] he caused to endure my kingdom like that of Ra in the heavens, in this my name of The Two Ladies, Enduring of Kingship like Ra in the Heavens.

He fashioned me as a falcon of gold. He gave to me his power and his strength, and I was august with these his splendors, in this my name of The Horus of Gold, Powerful in Strength, August in Splendors.

---

[12] All of what follows describes the transfiguration of Thothmes, his acceptance and designation by Amen-Ra. The "Heaven" and the "Horizon" also denoted the inner sanctums of the temple, the dwelling of the god, into which Thothmes evidently entered and experienced his ecstatic theophany.

[13] The falcon was the bird and emblem of Horus (both the Elder and the Son of Isis), and so of the king, who is the living Horus upon earth.

[14] The uraeus-serpent.

[15] When he assessed his dignities at the assumption of the kingdom after his victory over Set.

[16] Here follows the fivefold titulary of the king in New Kingdom times: (1) as Horus, (2) as the Two Ladies, the tutelary goddesses of Egypt (Nekhbet, the vulture-goddess of Upper Egypt, and Buto, the cobra-goddess of Lower Egypt), (3) as the Horus of Gold, (4) as king of Upper and Lower Egypt, and (5) as Son of Ra. The king had an individual name in each of these five aspects. Here these names are being given to Thothmes by Amen-Ra himself.

[17] The first, or Horus, name was inscribed within an ornamental upright rectangle stylized to represent the ancient palace facade, and surmounted by the Horus-falcon.

[18] See note 16.

He caused me to shine forth as King of Upper and Lower Egypt.[19] He made firm my forms of becoming like Ra, in this my name of Firm Are the Becomings of Ra.

I am his son, who came forth from within him, perfect of births like Thoth. He united all my becomings, in this my name of Son of Ra, Born of Thoth,[20] United of Becomings, Living Forever unto Eternity.

He caused all foreign lands to come and bow to the power of My Majesty. The terror of me is in the hearts of the Nine Bows,[21] and all lands are under my sandals. He has placed victory in the power of my hands, in order to broaden the boundaries of Egypt.

My father Amen has done these things through the greatness of his love for me. He rejoices over me more than any other king who was in the land since it was created. I am his son, beloved of His Majesty. That which his Divine Essence desires, that is what shall be done.

[19] The fourth and fifth names are the ones written in cartouches.
[20] The Egyptian name of the god is *Djehwty,* rendered by the Greeks as "Thoth." Unfortunately, it has become conventional to use the Greek renderings (usually slaughterings) of Egyptian royal and divine names. In the original, the name is *Djehwty-mes,* "born of Thoth." Likewise, *Ra-messes,* "Born of Ra," and so on. The name "Moses" is the Egyptian *mes,* "born (of)" with its preceding god-name deleted by the original compilers of the Bible.
[21] The traditional enemies-in-general of Egypt since ancient times. During the course of its history, the various people with whom the Egyptians fought were filled into the "Nine Bows" to suit the times.

124

III
Man and
the Supernatural
World

14 The Book of the Dead

To the average person, *The Book of the Dead* is probably the best-known text, at least by title, from ancient Egypt. This title, however, like many popular notions about ancient Egyptian civilization, is a complete misnomer, and these texts were never called by that name. The title of this collection of magic religious texts, as given at the head of the so-called *Book of the Dead* itself, is *The Chapters of Coming Forth by Day*. This is quite a different matter, and indicates a completely different complex of associations to these texts in the minds of the Egyptians themselves. During the nineteenth century, when Europeans began coming to Egypt in droves to search for antiquities, and proved quite willing to pay for them, tomb-pillaging became a profitable venture for the Arab peasants and "antica" dealers. In breaking open the mummy cases and stripping the jewels and other ornaments from the mummies (which they then broke to pieces, together with the mummy cases since they could get much more by selling the parts and ornaments separately than they could for the whole package) the robbers frequently found with the dead a rolled-up papyrus manuscript written in hieroglyphic characters and often illustrated with little vignettes. These scrolls were, of course, "books," and since they were found with the dead, the Arabs called them *kitab-el-mayyitun,* "the book of the dead." Like many erroneous popular appellations, the name stuck, and it is used today by everyone, Egyptologists included.

The usual impression fostered by most popular media such as the press, the movies, commercial television, and cheap fiction is that the ancient Egyptians were a gloomy and humorless people, constantly preoccupied with thoughts of death and the tomb, and somehow most adept at working out weird spells, usually for the purpose of revivifying mummies, who turn out to be rather unpleasant and malevolent characters who know all "the mysterious wisdom of ancient Egypt," and are hence especially dangerous. Far from this ridiculous nonsense, the ancient Egyptians were a warm, gay, and vibrantly wide-awake people with a high degree of intelligence and sensitivity and a highly sophisticated sense of humor, as even a cursory reading of some of the texts in this book will show. In fact, so much did they love life and all the good things which sheer living brings that they wanted to secure a continual life, with all its good things, for all eternity. They believed that "you *can* take it with you!"

It was for this reason that the tomb and its furnishings was all-important, and to their "House of Eternity" they took along as many as they could of the possessions that they enjoyed upon earth. That is why we find so many objects of beauty in the tombs —exquisite ornaments, furnishings, vessels, games, and toilet articles, models of their boats in which they enjoyed yachting on the Nile, dancing girls and concubines and "every good thing." On the walls of the tomb are reliefs and murals depicting the deceased enjoying all the happy aspects of his life—overseeing his estates, fishing and fowling in the marshes with his wife and children, enjoying together with his family and guests elaborate banquets graced with musicians and delightful nude dancing girls, and enjoying other such activities as would make a good time, or as he would put it, "a good place." We must keep in

128

mind that models and paintings serve just as well as the real thing, since all this is taking place upon another plane entirely (see page 35 for further exposition of this concept), and that the deceased is taken to this other plane by the magic of the mortuary rituals and the texts of the spells inscribed on the walls and/or in his copy of *The Chapters of Coming Forth by Day.*

The Book of the Dead is thus essentially a series of magic spells which ensure the safe journey of the deceased to the Other World and his acceptance and beatification there by Osiris, its Lord and Ruler. The deceased must, however, justify himself before Osiris by proving that he has been a man just and true. Hence the crucial scene of The Weighing of the Heart in *The Book of the Dead,* in which the heart of the deceased is weighed in the balance against the Feather of Truth, and in the declarations uttered by the deceased. Here and in The Negative Confession the reader will get an idea of the high ethical concepts which thoroughly permeated the faith of the Egyptians.

In order to understand much of the sense of these texts, we must know the main lines of their development. Basically, the "chapters" are descended in a direct line from the *Pyramid Texts.* It will be remembered that in the Old Kingdom the king (and only the king) became Osiris after his death, and that the *Pyramid Texts* were the spells which brought this about. During the First Intermediate period (see Chapter 3), the nobles had enjoyed several generations of personal rule, which evidently included the privilege of also becoming Osiris after death. Although the nobles had to surrender their political autonomy to the strong Pharaohs of the Middle Kingdom, they retained their prerogatives in the Other World. Inscribed upon all the outer and inner surfaces of the rectangular wooden coffins in which the mummies of the nobles were placed during the Middle Kingdom, we find hundreds of spells which were to enable them to become Osiris after their demise. These spells were adapted from the *Pyramid Texts* of the Old Kingdom, with certain additions and omissions to fit them to the situation. We call these magic formulas the *Coffin Texts*.

With the establishment of the New Kingdom and the expansion of Egypt to imperial power, the tremendous increase in wealth and in international commerce resulted in a broadening of the base of prosperity among the lower orders of administrators, priests, merchants, artisans, and independent farmers, who constituted the "commons." One result of this was that now not only the king and nobles but also "commoners" could become Osiris after death. Quite possibly this movement saw its beginnings during the social upheavals that accompanied the decay of the Middle Kingdom and the Hyksos rule. At any rate, this again necessitated further revisions and additions to the ritual spells of entering the Other World and becoming Osiris. It is this "much revised and greatly enlarged" recension of the previous spells of the *Coffin Texts,* which make up the 190 *Chapters of Coming Forth by Day,* which we call *The Book of the Dead.*

None of our many papyrus scrolls of *The Book of the Dead* actually contain all the 190 chapters. That number was gathered together by Egyptologists of the nineteenth century, who studied the various papyri, culminating in the inclusive publication of a collation of the best available texts by E. A. W. Budge of the British Museum. Budge's "standard edition" of all the chapters appeared in 1898 (no other complete publication has appeared since, although there have been several editions of individual papyri), and as a basis for this he used the *Papyrus of Ani,* which contains more chapters than any other, and filled in from other papyri, notably those of *Nebseni* and *Nu.* This is why, in our selections, the reader will meet "the Osiris Ani," "the Osiris Nu," "Inhay," and so on.

Selections from
The Chapters of Coming Forth by Day

The Opening Chapter

In this first, opening chapter, the deceased, speaking sometimes in the first person and sometimes in the third,[1] pro-
claims his identification with Osiris and requests that the
regularly ordained mortuary offerings be given him, and
that he be safely guided to the Other World.

The beginning of the Chapters of Coming Forth by Day, of lifting
up and glorifying, of coming forth and entering into the Domains-
under-the God,[2] which are beneficial in the beautiful Land of the
West.[3] They are to be recited on the day of entombment, the day of
entering-in after coming forth.

Recited by the Osiris Ani:

The Osiris, the Scribe Ani: Hail to thee, O Bull[4] of the Land of the
West! Thoth, King of Eternity, is with me! I am the Great God
aboard the Divine Ship.[5] I have fought for thee. I am one of those
gods, the Divine Magistrates, who justified the voice of Osiris before
his enemies on the day of the weighing of the words![6]

I am thy kinsman, Osiris! I am one of those gods, the children of
Nut, who cut in pieces the enemies of Osiris and who chained the
rebels for him!

---

[1] These spells were in all probability recited by the priests during the long and
intricate funerary ceremonies. The various "parts," the speeches of the various
deities and of the deceased, would have been assigned to different priests. All ancient
religious rites (and many modern ones) are actually forms of drama, and we know
that the drama actually did originate in religious ritual.

[2] That is, under Osiris, one of the many names for the Other World.

[3] The Other World was believed to be situated in the west, and one of the several
euphemisms for dying was "to go west." In the earliest, prehistoric burials found in
Egypt, the deceased is found curled up in the "embryonic" position and facing west.

[4] Like all powerful fertility gods, Osiris is frequently called "Bull."

[5] In the various vignettes accompanying the spells in the papyri, both Osiris and the
deceased are represented in the divine bark of Ra as he sails through the heavens.

[6] Here and further, the deceased is identified with the deities in the "justification" of
Osiris, already discussed in our selections from the Pyramid Texts.

131

I am thy Kinsman, Horus! I have fought for thee. I have come for thy name's sake!

I am Thoth, who justified the voice of Osiris before his enemies on the day of the weighing of the words in the Palace of the Great and Ancient One who is in Heliopolis![7] Ra said: "Thoth, justify the voice of Osiris before his enemies!" Let his command be done for me by Thoth!

I am together with Horus as the avenger of the left shoulder of Osiris, which is in Sekhem.[8] I enter and come forth among the gods who are therein, on the day of the destruction of the rebels in Sekhem. I am together with Horus on the day of the festivals of Osiris, when offerings are made on the sixth day of the Denit Festival in Heliopolis.

O ye who cause perfect souls to approach the House of Osiris, cause the excellent soul of the Osiris, the Scribe Ani, justified of voice,[9] to approach with you the House of Osiris! Let him hear you, let him have sight even as ye have sight, let him rise up even as ye rise up, and let him take seat even as ye take your seats![10]

O ye who give the bread and beer offerings to the perfect souls in the House of Osiris, give bread and beer offerings twice each day to the soul of the Osiris, the nobleman Ani, justified of voice before the gods, Lords of Abydos,[11] whose voice is justified with you!

O ye who open the way, who guide perfect souls on the way to the House of Osiris, open indeed the way for him, and guide the soul of the Osiris, the Scribe and Registrar of the offerings of all the gods,[12] the nobleman Ani, whose voice is justified with you!

---

[7] That is, Ra.

[8] A town in the Delta, where the left shoulder of Osiris was preserved as a sacred relic. At Sekhem, too, the great battle between the followers of Horus and Set was believed to have taken place. Several localities figured in the Osiris-Set myth and were the scenes of the regular re-enactment of the story at the Osiris festivals.

[9] The regular epithet applied to the deceased as identified with Osiris and justified before the gods in his contendings with Set.

[10] Giving the deceased sight, hearing, movement, and speech in the Other World was all accomplished during the funerary ceremonies by the magic spells, recitations, and rituals performed by the mortuary priests. Many of the chapters in *The Book of the Dead* are the texts of these spells.

[11] Abydos, in Upper Egypt, was the birthplace of Osiris, and there his head was preserved. Abydos was naturally the great center for the worship of Osiris.

[12] Evidently the priestly office held by Ani during his life on earth.

May he enter in boldness, and may he come forth in peace from the House of Osiris! May he not be opposed, and may he not be sent back! May he enter in praise and come forth beloved, in that his voice is justified!

May his commands be done in the House of Osiris! May his words proceed forth with you, and may he be glorious with you! May he not be found to be wanting in the Balance,[13] which is free of fault!

The Opening of the Mouth

This chapter was considered one of the most important spells, as it gave the deceased speech in the Other World, enabling him to speak for his "justification" before Osiris and his magistrates. Many vignettes in the papyri and paintings and reliefs on the walls of the tomb represent the priest performing this rite before the standing mummy, using a peculiar ritual instrument, a sort of chisel, with which he literally "opens the mouth" of the deceased.

The Chapter of Giving a Mouth to the Osiris, the Scribe and Registrar of the offerings of all the Gods, Ani, justified of voice, for his benefit in the Domains-under-the-God.

Recitation:
I have risen forth from the Egg which is in the Secret Land! May my mouth be given to me that I may speak therewith before the Great God, the Lord of the Other World! Let not my arm be repulsed by the Magistrates of any God. I am Osiris, Lord of the Necropolis. May the Osiris Ani, justified of voice, share portion with him who is at the top of the Steps![14] I have come, at the desire of my heart, from the Island of Flame[15]; I have extinguished the flame.

Hail to thee, Lord of Brightness, he who is head of the Temple above, Lord of Twilight![16] I have come unto thee. I am glorious, I

[13] The balance in which the heart of the deceased was weighed against the Feather of Truth.
[14] Osiris, in the judgment scene, is frequently represented enthroned in state on a dais raised above several steps.
[15] One of the several perilous obstacles encountered by the deceased on his journey to the Other World.
[16] That is, Osiris.

am pure! My arms are about thee, thy divine ancestors hold thee.
Give unto me my mouth, that I may speak therewith! I guide my
heart at its season of flame and of night.

The Weighing of the Heart

This is the central, culminating scene in the deceased's
journey to the Other World. He has come before the
presence of Osiris, where his heart is weighed in the
balance of Maat, goddess of truth and justice. In one pan
of the scales stands the heart of the deceased, and in the
other the Feather of Truth. Both must balance, as evidence
that the deceased has been upright and just and deserving
of eternal beatitude. Thoth is always present to preside
over the weighing and to record and announce the results.
In the event that the heart proves lighter, there crouches
at the foot of the balance a hideous she-monster, Amemet,
"the devourer," ready to devour the wanting heart. Fortunately for the deceased, the heart balances in every case,
as he has been provided with the necessary magic rites
and spells, and poor Amemet is eternally deprived of
nourishment.

The Speech of the Osiris, the Scribe Ani. He says:

O my heart of my mother! O my heart of my mother! O my heart
of my various forms! Rise not up against me as a witness! Do not
oppose me among the Magistrates! Do not incline against me before
the Keeper of the Scales! Thou art my Divine Essence[17] which is
within my body, the god Khnum[18] who makes prosper my limbs!
Come forth to the beautiful place whither we go. May no falsehood
be said against me at the side of the beautiful gods, and mayest
thou hear good things!

[17] The *ka*, the divine aspect or essence of a man, created with him and remaining
in the divine realm as his tutelary genius. When a man departs this mortal life, he
"rejoins his *ka*."
[18] Khnum was a ram-headed god, represented as fashioning men on his potter's
wheel. The reference is metaphorical here.

134

Words spoken by Thoth, Judge of Truth of the Great Ennead of the Gods, before Osiris:

Hear ye these words! In very truth has the heart of Osiris been weighed, and his animating spirit[19] has borne witness for him. His conduct has been justified on the Great Balance. There hath not been found any wickedness in him. He has not appropriated any offerings due to the temples. He has not injured [anyone] by his deeds, nor has his mouth gone forth in evil counsel during his existence upon earth!

Words spoken by Anubis, he who is in the Embalming-chamber:[20]

Pay good heed, O true and righteous judge, to the Balance in setting it aright! Pay good heed also in judging the heart, in the Balance, of the Osiris, the Chorister of Amen, Inhay,[21] justified of voice, and place her heart in the seat of truth before the Great God!

Words spoken by the Great Ennead[22] to Thoth, who is in Hermopolis:

That which comes forth from thy mouth is accurate and true. The Osiris, the Scribe Ani, has not committed any sin or done evil against us. Amemet shall not be allowed to prevail over him! There shall be given to him offerings, and coming forth into the presence of Osiris, and a permanent grant of land in the Field of Offerings,[23] like unto the Followers of Horus!

At this point in the papyrus there follows a description[24] of the monster Amemet, who devours those whose hearts are found wanting in the balance:

---

[19] Another aspect of a man, his *ba*, which was evidently the spirit animating him while he dwelt upon earth. The *ba* accompanies the deceased to the Other World and is represented as a bird with a man's head, hovering about the scales at the judgment scene.

[20] Anubis is the jackal-headed god who presides over the entire sacred rite of the embalming of the deceased and sees him on his way.

[21] This section is from the Papyrus of Inhay, who was a singing priestess of Amen. Women, too, become Osiris in the Other World.

[22] The great council of the gods.

[23] The fields of the beatified.

[24] This description is the actual "caption" written next to the representation of Amemet in the illustration of the weighing scene.

Amemet—her forepart is a crocodile, the middle of her body is a lion, and her hindquarters are those of a hippopotamus.

The Presentation Before Osiris

After the heart of the deceased has been proven true in the Balance, the justified is presented to Osiris by Horus, son of Osiris and Isis:

Words spoken by Horus, son of Isis:

I have come to thee, O Beautiful Being,[25] and I have brought to thee the Osiris Ani. His heart is righteous; it has come forth from the Balance. It has not committed wrong before any god or any goddess. Thoth has weighed it according to the decree pronounced unto him by the Ennead. It is most exact and true! Grant that there be given unto him bread and beer, and that he come forth before Osiris! Let him be like the Followers of Horus[26] forever!

Words spoken by the Osiris Ani; he says:

Behold, I am before thee, O Lord of the West! There is no evil-doing in my body. I have not spoken untruth knowingly, never, never! Grant that I may be like the favored ones who are among thy following, and an Osiris greatly favored by the Good God, and beloved of the Lord of the Two Lands—I who am a true scribe of the King, whom he loves, Ani, justified of voice before Osiris!

THE CHAPTER OF NOT LETTING THE BODY PERISH
Words spoken by the Osiris Nu:

Hail to thee, O my Divine Father Osiris! I came to heal thee! Do thou heal me, that I may be complete, and that I may be, indeed, like unto my divine father Khepri, the divine type of him who never corrupted. Come, then, make powerful my breath, O Lord of Breath, who exalts those divine beings who are like him! Come, make me endure, and fashion me, O thou Lord of the Sarcophagus!

Grant that I may descend into the Land of Eternity, according

[25] *Wen-Nefer,* one of the regular epithets of Osiris.
[26] The early legendary kings of Egypt, considered to be of the entourage of the primal Horus, and the first of the beatified dead.

136

as that which was done to thee together with thy father Atum, whose body did not see corruption, nor did he himself see decay.

I have never done that which thou hatest, but have acclaimed thee among those who love thy Divine Essence. Let me not putrefy, as you do unto every god and every goddess, every animal and every reptile, when they perish, when their animating spirits go forth after their death.

Hail to thee, O my father Osiris! Thou livest with thy members. Thou didst not decay, thou didst not become worms, thou didst not wither, thou didst not putrefy. I am Khepri, and my limbs shall have eternity! I shall not decay, I shall not rot, I shall not putrefy, I shall not become worms, I shall not see corruption before the eye of Shu! I shall exist! I shall exist! I shall live! I shall live! I shall flourish! I shall flourish!

I shall wake up in contentment; I shall not putrefy; my intestines shall not perish; I shall not suffer injury. My eye shall not decay; the form of my face shall not disappear; my ear shall not become deaf. My head shall not be separated from my neck. My tongue shall not be removed, my hair shall not be cut off. My eyebrows shall not be shaved away, and no evil defect shall befall me.

My body shall be enduring, it shall not perish. It shall not be destroyed, nor shall it be turned back whence it entered into this Land of Eternity!

The Purging of Guilt: The "Negative Confession"

The following selections are interesting because of the strong ethical criteria connected with the beatification of the deceased. In the Papyrus of Nu, the deceased identifies himself with the ancient creator, Ra-Atum-Khepri.

Chapter 125 of *The Book of the Dead* is probably the most famous and is usually referred to as "The Negative Confession." Assisting in the judgment are the forty-two "assessors," or magistrates, of Osiris. In the Papyrus of Nu, the deceased addresses them collectively, enumerating various offenses against the gods and against men which he has *not* committed. Ani, in his papyrus, addresses each of the assessors in turn, declaring before each his innocence of one specific offense. We acquire an understanding here of the high standards of ethics entertained by the ancient Egyptians, many of whose values we find incorporated in the later ethical codes of the Old Testament.

Recited by Steward of the Keeper of the Seal Nu, justified of voice, when he shall reach the Hall of the Two Truths,[27] so that he may be purged of all wrongdoings which he has done, and that he may behold the faces of the Gods.

Words spoken by the Steward of the Keeper of the Seal, Nu:

Hail to thee, great God, Lord of the Two Truths! I have come before thee, O my Divine Lord, I have been brought so that I may behold thy beauties. I know thee, and I know thy name! I know the names of the forty-two Gods who are with thee in the Hall of the Two Truths, who live by guarding over evildoers, and who feed upon their blood on the day when the characters of men are reckoned up before the Beautiful Being.

Lo, "The Two Daughters, the Two Beloved Ones, the Two Eyes, the Two Goddesses, the Two Truths" is thy name![28]

Behold, I have come before thee, I have brought the Two Truths unto thee! I have crushed evil for thee!

I have not done evil against people.

I have not caused misery to my associates.

I have not committed wrong in the judgment hall, the Seat of Truth.

I have not known evil and worthless men.

I have not done evil things.

I have not caused the first work of the day to be done for me.

I have not brought forward my name for dignities.

I have not deprived a humble man of his property.

I have not done what is hateful to the Gods.

I have not vilified a slave to his master.

[27] Another name for the Hall of Judgment, because of the presence of the goddess Maat, here conceived of as double, like many aspects of ancient Egypt.
[28] The concept of Maat as identified with Osiris.

I have not inflicted pain.

I have not made anyone hungry.

I have not made anyone weep.

I have not committed murder.

I have not commanded to murder.

I have not caused anyone to suffer.

I have not stolen the offerings in the temples.

I have not fornicated[29] or masturbated in the sanctuaries of the God of my city.

I have not added to the weight of the scale, nor have I depressed the pointer of the balance.

I have not taken away milk from the mouths of children.

I have not driven cattle from their pastures.

I have not caught fish with [bait of] their bodies.[30]

I have not held back water in its season of flowing, nor have I dammed up flowing water.[31]

I have not extinguished a fire in its season of burning.

I have not driven off the cattle of the estates of the gods.

I have not turned back a god on his appearances.

I am pure! I am pure! I am pure! I am pure!

In the following text, from the papyrus of Ani, the deceased addresses each of the forty-two magistrates of the Other World in turn, making a declaration of guiltlessness to each. He hails each of them by name and epithet, adding his negative declaration beginning with:

O Wesekh-Nemtet ["wide of stride"], who comes forth from Ionu [Heliopolis], I have not done evil.

[29] In the papyrus, the scribe has written the word twice (dittography), as if he had become a little excited here.

[30] This is reminiscent of the Old Testament injunction against seething a kid in its mother's milk, although here the etiological background is different (boiling a kid in milk, not necessarily its mother's, was part of an important Canaanite ritual connected with the birth of the gods).

[31] In order to keep the water of the irrigation canals in his own fields, thus depriving his neighbor.

Without troubling the reader with the names and epithets of all the magistrates, these are the ensuing declarations:

I have not stolen.
I have not plundered.
I have not slain people.
I have not stolen grain.
I have not committed a crime.
I have not stolen the property of a god.
I have not said lies.
I have not taken away food.
I have not cursed.
I have not copulated with men.
I have not caused anyone to weep.
I have not eaten my heart [indulged in useless misery?].
I have not led anyone astray.
I have not been deceitful.
I have not stolen cultivated land.
I have not gossiped.
I have not slandered.
I have not been contentious in affairs.
I have not copulated with the wife of [another] man.
I have not copulated with the wife of [another] man. [Repeated, after hailing the next magistrate.]
I have not fornicated.
I have not caused terror.
I have not gone astray.
I have not become heatedly angry.
I have not turned my countenance from words of truth.
I have not blasphemed.
I have not sent forth my hand [in violence].
I have not stirred up strife.
I did not think hastily.
I have not eavesdropped.
I have not multiplied my words in speech.

140

I have not wronged, I have not done evil.

I have not reviled the king.

I have not waded upon water.

I have not raised my voice.

I have not reviled a god.

I have not been arrogant.

I have not stolen the offerings of the gods.

I have not carried away the cakes of the glorified spirits [of the deceased].

I have not taken away the bread of a child, to blaspheme my local god.

I have not slain the cattle of a god.

These are the words to be spoken by the true of heart, in whom there is no evil, when he comes forth as one justified in the broad hall of the Two Truths; they shall be said when he arrives before the gods who are in the Other World:

Hail to you, O ye gods who are in your broad hall of the Two Truths! I know you; I know your names! I shall not fall before your knives. You shall not bring up any wickedness of mine to this god in whose following you are.

No evil deed of mine has come before you. You shall speak truth about me before the Lord of All, inasmuch as I have done justice in the Beloved Land. I have not reviled a deity, nor has any evil deed of mine come before a king who is in his day!

Hail to you, who are in your broad hall of the Two Truths, in whose bodies there is no falsehood, who live in Truth and who feed upon Truth before Horus who is in his sun disk!

May you deliver me from Babi, who lives on the entrails of the dead on that day of the Great Judgment!

Behold me who have come before you! I am without sin, without guilt, without evil. I have no accusers, and there is no one against whom I have done anything.

I have lived in Truth; I have fed upon Truth. I have performed the decrees of mankind, and that which pleases the gods.

I have gratified the god with that which he desires: I have given bread to the hungry, and water to the thirsty, and clothing to the naked, and a boat to the stranded one. I have given the gods their sacred gifts, and offerings of invocation to the Glorified Spirits.

Deliver ye me, then, protect ye me, then, and do not make report against me before the Great God! I am pure of mouth and pure of hands. I am one to whom those who see him say: "Come in peace! Come in peace!"

The Ushabti Figurine

Every collection of Egyptian antiquities contains these little figurines, found in the tombs, in the form of a standing mummy and inscribed with lines of hieroglyphs. These figurines are variously called *ushabtis* or *shawabtis.* The Egyptian word is *weshebti,* meaning "answerer," and they served quite a useful purpose to the deceased. When you had justified yourself before Osiris and were received into his domains, you could not just sit back and enjoy yourself in beatific complacency. You had to earn your keep by plowing in the fields of Osiris every day, or performing any other necessary labors there. Every morning the roll was called, and you had to answer "Here!" and go to work. But being a clever Egyptian, you availed yourself of an excellent stratagem. If you took along one or more figures of yourself inscribed with the appropriate magic text, the figure would answer to your name and do the work, while you yourself did whatever you enjoyed doing. These little "answerers" hold a little hand plow in each fist, ready to perform their labors. Some of the ushabtis are beautifully carved and decorated, but many of them were mass-produced from molds and cheaply done. In some tombs there were found chests containing 365 ushabtis, one for each day in the year.

The Chapter of making the ushabti to do work for a man in the Other World.

Words said by the scribe Neb-Seny, the draughtsman in the Temples of the North and South, highly venerated in the Temple of Ptah. He says:

O this ushabti of the scribe Neb-Seny, the son of the scribe Tchena, True of Voice, and of the lady of the house Mut-Resti, True of Voice; if I be called, or if I be assigned to do any work whatsoever of the labors which are to be done in the Other World— for indeed an obstacle is presented therein[32]—by a man in his turn,[33] let the assignment fall upon you instead of upon me always, in the matter of sowing the fields, of filling the water courses with water, and of bringing the sands of this east to the west. "Here I am!" shall you say!

---

[32] That is, all is not smooth sailing; one has to do work in one's turn.
[33] Literally, "as a man toward those-things-he-is-under." The phrase has also been justifiably translated "as a man in his duties." This is one example of the difficulties with which one must sometimes contend in attempting to convey the meaning of the Egyptian idiom.

143

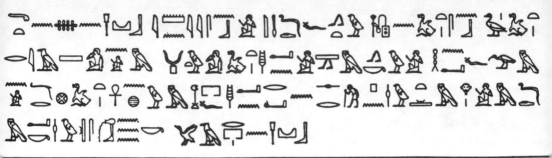

15 Incantations of Healing Magic

Like all ancient peoples (and many primitive and not so primitive peoples today), the Egyptians believed that illnesses, and the swellings, fever, and other malfunctions caused by the bite of insects and reptiles could be driven out by magic spells. In Egypt, the incantation consists of the recital of a myth in which one deity expels the poison from the body of another. By sympathetic magic, just as the goddess or god (usually the former) expelled the poison from the god so-and-so in the myth, so will she drive out the poison from the body of this particular person (see Chapter 7).

I

The following is one of a number of incantations for driving out the poison of a scorpion bite. This text is interesting, not only because it is a fairly long and connected one but also because of the unconscious symbolism which it manifests. Written, according to Gardiner, sometime during the reign of Ramesses II (1290–1224 B.C.) the text is also an excellent example of cultural syncretism during New Kingdom times. The protagonist is the great Syrian goddess Anath, goddess of fertility and also of war and destruction, and thus quite similar to Hathor of Egypt. During the New Kingdom the Syrian goddesses Anath and Astarte were introduced into the Egyptian pantheon, and in *The Contendings of Horus and Set* they are represented as

daughters of Ra, and given to Set in compensation for the loss
of the throne of Osiris, which had been awarded to Horus.

First, a rather obscure myth is told, involving Anath, Set,
and Ra. Set, true to his wildly lecherous character, commits a
sexual assault upon Anath. Ra, who happens to be passing
by, witnesses the scene. Some of Set's poisonous semen flies
up and hits the Great God between the eyes. Ra becomes ill
as a result. While he lies bedridden in his palace, Anath visits
him. Ra greets her, but ends his greeting with some quite inco-
herent statements. It is difficult to decide whether the text is
corrupt or whether the obscurity is intended to indicate that
Ra is delirious. At any rate, Isis suddenly appears and pro-
nounces her magic spell of healing.

The spell itself proceeds quite methodically. The various
bodily parts of the patient are enumerated, beginning with the
forehead and working down to the toenails. The illness is ad-
jured not to "take its stand" in any of them, and for each part
a protective deity is named, who repels the invading poison.

AN INCANTATION FOR A MAN
WHO HAS BEEN BITTEN BY A SCORPION

The goddess Anath was disporting herself in the stream of Khap,
and bathing in the stream of Hemkat. Now the Great God[1] had gone
forth to walk, and he saw Set as he mounted on her back, leaping
her even as a ram and covering her.

Then some of the semen poison[2] flew to his forehead, to the parts
of the brows of his eyes. Thereupon he lay down upon his bed in
his Residence, being ill.

Then came Anath, the Divine Goddess, she the victorious, the
woman who is a warrior, clad as a man and begirt like a woman,
to Ra her father. And he said to her:

---

[1] Ra.
[2] In Egyptian, the very same word (*mtwt*) means both "semen" and "poison."

145

Lo, what is it, Anath the Divine, the victorious, woman who is a warrior, clad as a man and begirt like a woman? I reached home in the evening, and I know that you will say "I have come to beg Set from the semen poison." Is it not a child's punishment to cause to chew the semen poison given to the wife of the God above, that he copulate with her with fire and open her with a chisel?

Then said Isis the Divine:

I am a Nubian woman, and have come down from the heavens. I have come to lay bare the semen poison which is in the limbs of So-and-so, born of the woman So-and-so,[3] to cause him to depart in health to his mother, even as Horus departed in health to his mother Isis. So-and-so, born of the woman So-and-so, shall exist! As Horus lives, so shall live So-and-so, born of the woman So-and-so!

Thou shalt not take thy stand in his forehead;
   Hekayit is against thee—Lady of the Forehead!
Thou shalt not take thy stand in his eyes;
   Horus Mekhenty-irty is against thee—Lord of the Eyes!
Thou shalt not take thy stand in his ears;
   Geb is against thee—Lord of the Ear!
Thou shalt not take thy stand in his nose;
   Khenem-tchau[4] of Hesret is against thee—Lady of the Nose!
   Beware lest she subdue the North-wind from before the Great
     Gods!
Thou shalt not take thy stand in his lips;
   Anubis is against thee—Lord of the Lips!
Thou shalt not take thy stand in his tongue;
   Sefekh-aahui is against thee—Lady of the Tongue!
Thou shalt not take thy stand in his neck;
   Wadjety[5] is against thee—Lady of the Neck!
Thou shalt not take thy stand in his throat;
   Meret is against thee—Lady of the Throat!
   Beware lest her voice be stilled before Ra!
Thou shalt not take thy stand in his nipple;

---

[3] In the actual incantation, the name of the sufferer was to be pronounced here.
[4] Literally, "breeze-sniffer."
[5] The serpent-goddess Buto, mistress of Lower Egypt.

Nut is against thee—Lady of the Nipple!
She who bore the gods, and gives suck to them!
Thou shalt not take thy stand in his arms;
  Montu[6] is against thee—Lord of the Arms!
Thou shalt not take thy stand in his back;
  Ra is against thee—Lord of the Vertebrae!
Thou shalt not take thy stand in his side;
  Set is against thee—Lord of the Side!
Thou shalt not take thy stand in his liver, in his lung, in his spleen,
    in his intestines, in his ribs, or in any flesh of his body;
  Mesti, Hapi, Dewa-mutef, and Kebekh-senuef,[7] the gods who are
    in his body, are against thee!
Thou shalt not take thy stand in his buttocks;
  Hathor is against thee—Lady of the Buttocks!
Thou shalt not take thy stand in his phallus;
  Horus is against thee—Lord of the Phallus!
Thou shalt not take thy stand in his perineum;
  Reshpu[8] is against thee—Lord of the Perineum!
Thou shalt not take thy stand in his thighs;
  Horus is against thee—Lord of the Thighs,
  Walking on the desert alone!
Thou shalt not take thy stand in his knee;
  Sia is against thee—Lord of the Knee!
Thou shalt not take thy stand in his shin;
  Nefer-tem is against thee—Lord of the Shins!
Thou shalt not take thy stand in his soles;

[6] Montu was a war god. There is also a pun here: *khepesh,* the word used for "arm," actually the hind leg of an animal, was also, because of its shape, the name for the curved "sickle-sword," which came into use during New Kingdom times. Hence the punning association of Montu with the *khepesh.*
[7] The four gods called "The Sons of Horus." They are usually depicted as four small mummies standing before Osiris in the judgment scene of *The Book of the Dead.* They have the heads, respectively, of a man, a baboon, a jackal, and a falcon. The covers of the "Canopic Jars," containing the embalmed internal organs of the deceased, are usually in the form of these four heads.
[8] Reshpu, or Reshef, was an important Syro-Canaanite fertility deity who, along with Anath and Astarte, assumed a position in the Egyptian pantheon during the cosmopolitan New Kingdom period. The prominent fertility deities (Hathor, Horus, Reshef) protected the genital and adjacent regions of the body.

Nebet-debut is against thee—Lady of the Soles!
Thou shalt not take thy stand in his toenails;
   Anket is against thee—Lady of the Toenails!
Thou shalt not take thy stand in a bite;
   Selket[9] is against thee—Lady of the Bite!

Thou shalt not take thy stand! Thou shalt not find refreshment there! There is no place for you to settle there! Go down to the ground! I have incanted against thee, I have spat upon thee, I have drunk thee! As to his mother is Horus, thus So-and-so, born of the woman So-and-so, is to his mother. As Horus lives, so does he. Go down to the ground! I know thee, I know thy name! Come from the right hand, come from the left hand! Come in saliva, come in vomit, come in urine!

Come hither at my utterance according as I say! Behold, Ra is before thee! Grant a path to So-and-so, born of the woman So-and-so! As the sun shall rise, as the Nile shall flow, as the services shall be performed in Heliopolis, so shall So-and-so, born of the woman So-and-so, be better than he was!

So saith [here follows a list of the names of nine goddesses and a god, each name preceded by "so saith"]. Cause to go forth the semen poison that is in the limbs of So-and-so, born of the woman So-and-so, so as to permit him to depart in health to his mother Isis! The protection of Horus is a protection!
THIS SPELL IS TO BE RECITED FOUR TIMES. Open and examine the wound inflicted by the scorpion. If thou open and examine the wound inflicted by the scorpion, and painful is thy finding . . . [The text breaks off here.]

II

ANOTHER SPELL:
Flow forth, scorpion, thou of long back and many joints!
Come hither at my utterance, according as I say! I am the god who
   came into being of himself![10]

[9] The scorpion-goddess.
[10] Namely, Atum-Ra-Khepri.

Come, issue forth at the command of the wives of Horus!
  I am Horus, the physician soothing the god. Flow forth from the
    limbs!
Come, issue forth at the command of Sefdet, wife of Horus!
  Behold, I am Horus, the physician soothing the god. Flow forth from
    the limbs!
Come, issue forth at the command of Wepet-sepu, wife of Horus!
  Behold, I am Horus, the physician soothing the god. Flow forth
    from the limbs!
Come, issue forth at the command of Sefet-sepu, wife of Horus!
  Behold, I am Horus, the physician soothing the god. Flow forth
    from the limbs!
Come, issue forth at the command of Metemut-nefret-iyes, wife of
    Horus!
  Behold, I am Horus, the physician soothing the god. Flow forth
    from the limbs!

III

[An unidentified goddess is addressed:]
  Hail to thee, O She upon whose head are seven serpents, She to
whom the seventy-seven hearts are entrusted in the evening and in
the night! If So-and-so, born of the woman So-and-so, be not cured,
Ra will not manifest himself, Thoth will not manifest himself, Horus
will not manifest himself!
  As the sun shall rise, as the disk shall shine, as the services shall
be performed in every temple, so shall he be better than he was,
for his mother, even So-and-so, born of the woman So-and-so!
TO BE RECITED FOUR TIMES.

IV

The next spell is interesting for its description of the
actual manipulations performed by the magician-priest
and for the symbolism. The significance of all this remains,
naturally, quite enigmatic.

149

ANOTHER SPELL:

I have enclosed in my right hand; I have enclosed in my left hand. I have embraced Set and Horus. I have enclosed within it seven knots. Horus looked behind him and found Set following him, and so did that other in turn. That Bennu-bird[11] which sat, two ends of a sinew were drawn forth from its brow and made into seven knots. It was reported to Ra, the chest which came forth from Heliopolis, and what was in it was known. A seal was in it, of black stone. Come forth, poison, come forth!

So saith Sepertu-erset Sepenes-ta,[12] the first body of Ra! She tells her name to Horus every three years, the hidden blood being on her thighs, since Horus opened her. Come to me and draw forth these painful fluids[13] which are in the limbs of So-and-so, born of the woman So-and-so, even as Horus went away to his mother Isis on the night when he was bitten!

V

The following is a spell against a severe headache. The complaint was termed *ges-maa,* "half-temple," or *ges-tep,* *"half-head."* Incidentally, we still use the term, originated in Egypt, today. "Half-head" was literally translated by the Greeks into *hemikrania,* which eventually became migraine and megrim.

A SPELL FOR EXORCISING HEADACHE:

O Ra, O Atum, O Shu, O Geb, O Nut, O Anubis who is before the Divine Shrine, O Horus, O Set, O Isis, O Nephthys, O Great Ennead, O Little Ennead, come ye and see your father who enters

[11] A heronlike bird, often translated as "phoenix," which was associated with both Ra and Osiris.

[12] A goddess name since it has the cobra determinative usual after names of goddesses. *Sepertu-erset* can be literally translated "one approaches her," and *Sepenes-ta* something like "the earth is her portion." The first name, with slightly different spelling, is given in another papyrus as one of the wives of Horus. These names are probably epithets of Isis.

[13] Note the association of the vital fluids—the vaginal and/or menstrual blood of Isis and the semen poison, and their magical interaction.

clothed in radiance to see the horn of Sekhmet! Come ye to remove
that enemy, dead man or dead woman, male adversary or female
adversary who is in the face of So-and-so, born of woman So-and-so!
TO BE RECITED OVER A CROCODILE OF CLAY WITH GRAIN IN ITS
MOUTH, AND HAVING AN EYE OF FAÏENCE SET IN ITS HEAD. LET ONE
TIE IT TOGETHER WITH A DRAWING OF THE GODS INSCRIBED UPON
FINE LINEN AND PLACE IT UPON HIS HEAD. TO BE RECITED OVER
AN IMAGE OF RA, ATUM, SHU, MEHYT, GEB, NUT, ANUBIS, HORUS,
SET, ISIS, NEPHTHYS, AND AN ORYX WITH A FIGURE STANDING ON ITS
BACK AND CARRYING A SPEAR.

VI

In the next spell, the malevolent spirit causing the affliction is blasted according to usual procedure. However, if by
any chance this does not work, the magician threatens to
desecrate and even destroy the gods themselves, and to
overturn the very heavens. Such threats against the deities,
if they do not accede to human wishes, are quite in the
tradition of ancient religion. Although not explicit, such a
threat (possibly in milder form) is implied in some of
the patriarchal narratives in Genesis (for example, Genesis
28:20, 21) where the protagonist says in effect, to God: "If
what I desire will come to pass, then Yahweh will be to
me as a god." And if it will not come to pass?

ANOTHER CHARM FOR DRIVING AWAY HEADACHE
AS FOR THE HEAD OF So-and-so, born of the woman So-and-
so, it is the head of Osiris Wen-Nefer,[14] on whose head were placed
the three hundred and seventy-seven Divine Uraei, and they spew
forth flame to make thee quit the head of So-and-so, born of the
woman So-and-so, like that of Osiris. If thou dost not quit the
temple of So-and-so, born of the woman So-and-so, I will burn thy
soul, I will consume thy corpse! I will be deaf to any desire of thine

[14] Literally, "The Beautiful Being," one of the many epithets of Osiris.

151

concerning thee. If some other god is with thee, I will overturn thy dwelling place; I will shadow thy tomb, so that thou wilt not be allowed to receive incense, so that thou wilt not be allowed to receive water with the beneficent spirits, and so that thou wilt not be allowed to associate with the Followers of Horus.

If thou wilt not hear my words, I will cause the sky to be overturned, and I will cast fire among the Lords of Heliopolis! I will cut off the head of a cow taken from the Forecourt of Hathor! I will cut off the head of a hippopotamus in the Forecourt of Set! I will cause Sebek to sit enshrouded in the skin of a crocodile, and I will cause Anubis to sit enshrouded in the skin of a dog![15] I will cause the sky to split open down its middle! I will cause the Seven Hathors[16] to fly up to the sky in smoke! I will cut off the testicles of Horus, and I will blind the Eye of Set![17]

Then indeed shalt thou come forth from the temple of So-and-so, born of the woman So-and-so! I will make for thee the magic amulet of the Gods, their names being pronounced ON THIS DAY. TO BE RECITED OVER THESE GODS INSCRIBED UPON FINE LINEN AND PLACED UPON THE TEMPLE OF A MAN.

On the papyrus there follows a drawing of "these Gods," as a model to be copied on the strip of linen: two jackals, four seated human-headed gods, four Eyes of Horus, and four uraeus-serpents.

[15] Sebek is represented with the body and/or head of a crocodile, and Anubis with that of a jackal.

[16] Aspects of the great fertility goddess who presided over the birth of children and governed their destiny.

[17] During the monumental struggle between Horus and Set, Set tore out the Eye of Horus, and Horus tore out the testicles of Set. The threat is to overturn the very order of the cosmos and the divine *mythos* of Primal Time.

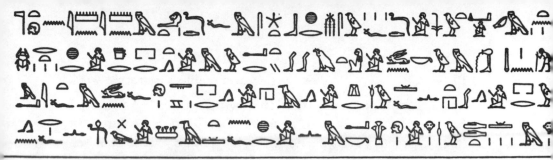

16 The Interpretation of Dreams

The ancient Egyptians placed much importance on dream interpretation. The extent to which it permeated popular culture can
be discerned in the Joseph narrative of the Bible; the entire
episode has a completely authentic Egyptian background, and
is shot through with Egyptianisms—literal translations into
Hebrew. Likewise, Joseph is the interpreter of dreams *par excellence,* and dreams and their interpretation are responsible
for the two decisive moments in his life: his own dreams as a
youth (Genesis 37:5–11), which his brothers and his father
were quite quick to analyze, and which were responsible for
his being brought down to Egypt; and his interpretations of the
dreams of the Pharaoh's chief butler and chief baker and of
those of the Pharaoh himself (Genesis 40:8–23; 41:1–40), as a
result of which Joseph was made vizier.

We are fortunate in having an Egyptian dream book, published by Sir Alan H. Gardiner in 1935.[1] The manuscript is
presumed to come from Thebes, and is dated during the Nineteenth Dynasty (about 1300 B.C.). The language is, to a large
extent, classic Egyptian, and Gardiner cites internal evidence
indicating the derivation of material from Twelfth Dynasty times
(2000–1800 B.C.).

The text is arranged in double columns reading across from
right to left. The dream is in the first column and opposite
it in the second column is the interpretation, preceded by the

[1] The hieratic papyrus Chester Beatty III: *Hieratic Papyri in the British Museum,
Third Series, Chester Beatty Gift,* Alan H. Gardiner, ed. (London, The British
Museum, 1935), I, 9–23; II, Plates 5–8.

153

word "good" or "bad" (the latter written in red; however, I have used capital letters). In front of each double column, in large characters reading down, is the phrase; "If a man see himself in a dream—" to be understood before each dream-picture described, much as today one might write the phrase and then put a large bracket before the dream column.

Many of the interpretations are in terms of contraries, for example, to see oneself dead means that one has a long life in prospect. Others are based upon symbolism (which in turn is founded upon the association of ideas) such as the dreams of Joseph in the Bible. Many others, again, are founded on puns, most of which, naturally, cannot be carried over from one language into another. A good deal of modern psychoanalytic dream interpretation is also based upon the natural tendency of the unconscious mind to suit the sound or appearance of the word to the concept and vice versa. As a matter of fact, it is quite interesting to note the sometimes uncanny (and unconscious, of course) interpretations in what today we would call purely psychoanalytic terms. Indeed, the reader familiar with the principles of psychoanalysis will find all through Egyptian mythic thought and expression a beautiful working out of the methods of expression of the symbols of the unconscious as discovered by Freud.

IF A MAN SEE HIMSELF IN A DREAM:

with his mouth opened,	*good:* something which is a fear in his heart will be opened by the god.[2]
munching lotus leaves,	*good:* there are things with which he will gladden his heart.
shooting at a mark,	*good:* good things will happen to him.

[2] Literally, "with his mouth broken, or split open . . . the god will break it open." In other words, the god will free him of the anxiety which depresses him by causing it to go out through his mouth. Here and subsequently, "the god" or "his god" refers to his local city-god.

reminding a man of his wife,	*good:* his evils will retreat from him.
his penis becoming large,	*good:* this means that his possessions will multiply.
with a bow in his hand,	*good:* a great office will be given to him.
dying violently,	*good:* this means that he will live after his father dies.[3]
seeing a serpent,	*good:* this means food.
his mouth full of earth,	*good:* he will devour his townsfolk.
eating the flesh of a crocodile,	*good:* this means that he will eat the possessions of an official.[4]
looking out of a window,	*good:* his cry will be heard by his god.
white bread being given to him,	*good:* this means things at which his face will light up.[5]
copulating with his mother,	*good:* men of his province will cleave unto him.[6]
copulating with his sister,	*good:* this means that possessions will be decreed unto him.

---

[3] An excellent bit of intuitive psychoanalysis, over three thousand years before Freud. The dreamer, as a result of his unconscious and repressed wish for his father's death, fulfills in his dream the consequent wish for his own violent death as expiation for his overwhelming guilt.

[4] A satiric dig, comparing officials to the greedy and rapacious crocodile, and the wish-fulfillment implied.

[5] An example of the operation of the "dream-work" by puns. In Egyptian, the word for "white" and "bright," "brighten," "light up," and so on is the same. Unfortunately not many of these can be carried over into English.

[6] JOCASTA (*to Oedipus*) . . . But fear not regarding marriage with your mother. Many men ere now in dreams have lain with their mothers.—Sophocles, *Oedipus the King,* lines 980–982.

This is the *locus classicus,* of course, cited by Freud in *The Interpretation of Dreams.* In our Egyptian text we see the Oedipal wish fulfilled in dreams a thousand years before Sophocles. This text was published in 1935, while Freud was still alive. He would have been quite happy to be aware of it, and would no doubt have made some interesting comments on this and many other dreams in the collection. Unfortunately, the majority of scholars working in the area of ancient civilizations have no knowledge of, or interest in, the principles of applied psychoanalysis. Such a knowledge would be most valuable in leading to deeper insights and understandings not only of ancient cultures but of the human psyche in general.

upon a palm tree,	*good:* his heart will be gladdened at what his Genïus has done.[7]
seeing his face as that of a leopard,	*good:* he will perform the office of a head man.
sitting upon a sycamore tree,	*good:* the subjugation of all his evils.
sight-seeing in the city of Osiris,	*good:* he will have a great old age.
binding fast injurious people by night,	*good:* he will take away the utterances of his enemies.
destroying his clothes,	*good:* his release from all evils.
seeing himself dead,	*good:* a hale and hearty life is before him.
drinking his own urine,	*good:* it means consuming his son's possessions.[8]
eating excrement,	*good:* it means consuming his possessions in his house.[9]
mating with a cow,	*good:* it means passing a happy day in his house.[10]
plunging into the river,	*good:* this means that he will be cleansed of all evils.
breaking into a boat that has foundered,	*good:* it means the giving to him of his woman.[11]
seeing himself weak,	*good:* this means that a man will find his enemies dead.[12]
seeing himself together with one greater than he,	*good:* this means that he will be made great by his *ka*.[13]

[7] His *ka*, the Divine Essence of a man which is created with him, and which remains in the Other World during his life on earth, and which acts as his presiding Genius, prompting him in his inclinations and deeds.

[8] Note the unconscious symbolism: urine = semen = offspring, and also the unconscious desire of the father to subjugate (= castrate) the son.

[9] Another symbol of the unconscious: excrement = gold, money, possessions.

[10] The cow is the symbol *par excellence* of the mother-goddess. This is, of course, a typical Oedipal wish-fulfillment.

[11] The classic dream symbolism of hollow receptacles (cups, vases, boats, and so on) as women.

[12] The phenomenon of *displacement:* He wishes his enemies dead; therefore he feels guilt; in self-punishment he displaces his wish onto himself, but in the milder form of weakness. In the earlier dream, whose interpretation involves the death of his father, his punishment must be a violent death, as his crime is much more serious.

[13] See note 7.

156

copulating with a jerboa,	BAD: it means a judgment against him.
drinking warm beer,	BAD: this means that suffering will come upon him.
seeing his face in a mirror,	BAD: it means another wife.[14]
eating hot meat,	BAD: this means that he will not be found justified.[15]
copulating with a woman,	BAD: this means mourning.
being bitten by a serpent,	BAD: this means magic spells will be made against him.[16]
writing on a papyrus,	BAD: it means the tallying of his misdeeds by his god.
fire spreading over his bed,	BAD: this means driving out his wife.
folding wings about himself,	BAD: he will not be justified with his god.
seeing a dwarf,	BAD: it means taking away of half of his life.
shaving his lower parts,	BAD: this means mourning.
putting incense upon a fire to a god,	BAD: the power of a god is against him.
putting a bench in his boat,	BAD: this means putting away his wife.
seeing people far off,	BAD: his death is near.
smearing himself with fat,	BAD: his people will be taken away from him.
seeing a woman's vulva,	BAD: it means the extremity of misery upon him.[17]

---

[14] Gardiner comments on this passage: "To see one's face in a mirror is to discover a second self, which second self must have another wife: hence the interpretation 'it means another wife.'" A possibly more closely analytic interpretation might be the "second self" as another wife with whom one identifies, or as *doppelgänger*.

[15] Literally, "true of voice"; this is a technical term applied to the victorious litigant in a court decision. In the primeval struggle between Horus and Set, Horus and his father Osiris were declared "true of voice" by the Divine Ennead, and in the judgment of the deceased before Osiris in the Other World, the deceased is declared "true of voice" or "justified" also.

[16] Note the connection of the serpent with magic.

[17] And the desire to return to the womb?

copulating with his wife in the open by day,	BAD: his misdeeds will be seen by his god.
looking after monkeys,	BAD: a change is before him.
making a bridal chamber,	BAD: his misdeeds will be brought to light.

Despite the manifold possibility of bad dreams, all is not lost by any means. There is always a way out. After the enumeration of dreams comes what to the ancient Egyptian was indispensable: the magic spell for the protection of the dreamer and the exorcism of bad dreams. The spell is in the form of a dialogue between the dreamer, as Horus, and his mother Isis, who in addition to her other attributes is the great mistress of magic words of power. In addition, a ritual act must as usual accompany the incantation, in the form of a "prescription" to be applied locally.

TO BE RECITED BY A MAN WHEN HE WAKES UPON HIS PLACE:
Come to me, come to me, O my mother Isis! Behold, I am seeing things which are far from my dwelling place!

Here I am, my son Horus; let there come out what you have seen, so that the afflictions pervading your dreams may go out, and fire spring forth against him who frightens you. Behold, I am come to see you, and to drive forth your evils, and root out all that is horrible!

Hail to thee, O good dream which is seen by night or by day! Driven forth are all horrible things which Set, son of Nut, has made! Even as Ra is justified against his enemies, so am I justified against my enemies!

THIS SPELL IS TO BE SPOKEN by a man when he wakes upon his place, there being given to him *pesen*-bread together with a few fresh herbs moistened with beer and myrrh. Let a man's face be smeared with it, and all evil dreams which he has seen will be driven away.

IV
Between Man and Man and Between Man and Himself: Wisdom Literature in Ancient Egypt

In the Bible we have three interesting books that constitute what scholars have called "wisdom literature." These are Proverbs, Ecclesiastes, and the Book of Job. All three of these works are reflections on the various problems encountered by the individual in his relation both to the human society in which he must live and to the very existential problems inherent in the human condition. How shall man so conduct himself as to give some sort of meaning to his life, and what is very important, how can he attain earthly success and well-being? What ought to be the relation of man to his fellow man? What is man's place, if any, in the divine scheme? And for that matter, how to account for the presence of evil in the world? Perplexing questions these, and these three Biblical works are attempts to deal with them from essentially varying points of view, each an exemplar of a basic philosophy of life.

When we examine the extra-Biblical literature of the world of the ancient Near East, we find that we have also quite a body of texts from both Mesopotamia and Egypt that deal with the very same problems and that were composed for the purpose of handing on to a younger generation an accumulated fund of experience. We find that this body of teachings and reflections on life constituted an important literary genre of didactic tradition, of which the "wisdom books" of the Old Testament are but part.

17 Instructions and Maxims

We have several ancient Egyptian texts which are quite similar in both content and outlook to the Book of Proverbs—in fact, a portion of the Biblical book is obviously closely paraphrased from one of the largest and most important "wisdom" books, the *Proverbs of Amen-em-Ope*. It is obvious from a reading of both the Biblical book and the Egyptian texts that they are observations on life and human nature made by men of sagacity and keen insight, who had acquired a great deal of experience of the world and the conduct of men. Obviously familiar with the etiquette of the court and the ways of kings, they were evidently highly placed and "men of distinction" whose positions gave them excellent opportunities for studying the complexities of human affairs: we are told that Rekh-mi-Ra, Ptah-Hotep, and Ka-Gemni are viziers, Amen-em-Ope boasts of his high offices, and Amen-em-Hat is actually a king. The manner and formal style of these texts, however, is that of the schools. From remotest antiquity, the teacher was considered *in loco parentis,* addressing his pupil as "my son"—the form, again, which we find throughout the Biblical Book of Proverbs.

To maintain their positions of power and emolument amid the subtle intrigues surrounding royalty, these men would have had to develop faculties of intelligent and practical judgment. For the edification and benefit of younger aspirants to high station and worldly success, they embodied the results of their accumulated experience in a corpus of didactic literature that constituted a school of practical wisdom. As in the Biblical work, the secret of practical wisdom is justice. The reader will note the important stress that these royal and noble writers place upon ethical concepts. Righteous and just behavior toward one's fellow man is the correct and proper way to estimation, well-being, and success. It pays off: certainly a pragmatic and essentially humanistic viewpoint!

Instructions to the Vizier Rekh-mi-Ra

The tomb of Rekh-mi-Ra at Thebes is generally more noted for its most beautiful mural paintings than for these texts inscribed on its walls. This great nobleman of ancient Egypt was vizier of Upper Egypt during the reign of Thothmes III (1468–1436 B.C.).

Regulation laid upon the vizier Rekh-mi-Ra. The council was conducted into the audience hall of Pharaoh, Life! Prosperity! Health![1] One[2] caused that there be brought in the vizier Rekh-mi-Ra, newly appointed.

Said His Majesty to him: "Look to the office of the vizier; be watchful over all that is done therein. Behold, it is the established support of the whole land.

"Behold, as for the vizierate, it is not sweet; behold, it is bitter, as he is named.[3] Behold, he is copper enclosing the gold of his lord's

---

[1] A standard formula after mention of the king or his name, after reference to the royal palace, its gates, chambers, etc. It was written or inscribed with three hieroglyphic signs which are abbreviations of these three words, and meaning, "May he (or it) live, prosper (or flourish), and be healthy."

[2] The king. This type of oblique reference was often used with honorific intent.

[3] He cannot hide behind the fact of being just a cog in the bureaucratic machine; everyone knows his office and his name, and so he must bear public responsibility for each of his actions.

house.[4] Behold, the vizierate is not to show respect of persons to princes and councilors; it is not to make for himself slaves of any people.

"Behold, as for a man in the house of his lord, his conduct is good for his lord. But lo, he does not the same for another.[5]

"Behold, when a petitioner comes from Upper or Lower Egypt, even the whole land, see to it that everything is done in accordance with law, that everything is done according to the custom thereof, giving to every man his right. Behold, a prince is in a conspicuous place, water and wind report concerning all that he does. For behold, that which is done by him never remains unknown.

"When he takes up a matter for a petitioner according to his case, he shall not proceed by the statement of a department officer.[6] But the matter shall be known by the statement of one designated by him, the vizier,[7] saying it himself in the presence of a department officer with the words: 'It is not that I raise my voice;[8] but I send the petitioner according to his case to another court or prince.' Then that which has been done by him has not been misunderstood.

"Behold, the refuge of a prince is to act according to the regulation, by doing what is said to him. A petitioner who had been adjudged shall not say: 'My right has not been given to me!'

"Behold, it is a saying which was in the vizieral installation of Memphis[9] in the utterance of the king in urging the vizier to moderation: 'Beware of that which is said of the vizier Kheti. It is said that he discriminated against some of the people of his own kin in favor

---

[4] As "First Man," he is the buffer and intermediary between the divine king and the people.

[5] The vizier must always be loyal to his lord, the king, and even "cover up" for him if necessary, as in the previous paragraph. But as to anyone else, he must have no loyalties or preferences. This is the main point.

[6] Who probably knows it at second hand.

[7] He must refer cases to the proper courts of appeal only on the statement of a trusted personal representative.

[8] "I am not adjudicating the case myself."

[9] Referring to the case of Kheti, a vizier way back in Old Kingdom times, who "leaned over backward" and discriminated against his own kin so as not to be suspected of favoritism. This is not justice either!

163

of strangers, for fear lest it should be said of him that he favored his kin dishonestly. When one of them appealed against the judgment which he thought to make him, he persisted in his discrimination. Now that is more than justice.'[10]

"Forget not to judge justice. It is an abomination of the god to show partiality. This is the teaching. Therefore, do you accordingly. Look upon him who is known to you like him who is unknown to you; and him who is near the king like him who is far from his house. Behold, a prince who does this, he shall endure here in this place.

"Pass not over a petitioner without regarding his speech. If there is a petitioner who shall appeal to you, being one whose speech is not what is said,[11] dismiss him after having let him hear that on account of which you dismiss him. Behold, it is said: 'A petitioner desires that his saying be regarded rather than the hearing of that on account of which he has come.'

"Be not wroth against a man wrongfully; but be you wroth at that at which one should be wroth.

"Cause yourself to be feared. Let men be afraid of you. A prince is a prince of whom one is afraid. Behold, the dread of a prince is that he does justice. But indeed, if a man cause himself to be feared a multitude of times,[12] there is something wrong in him in the opinion of the people. They do not say of him: 'He is a man indeed.' Behold, the fear of a prince deters the liar, when the prince proceeds according to the dread one has of him. Behold, this shall you attain by administering this office, doing justice.

"Behold, men expect the doing of justice in the procedure of the vizier. Behold, that is its customary law since the god.[13] Behold, it

[10] Justice implies the observation of the golden mean of strict impartiality, leaning neither to one side nor the other.
[11] That is, who has spoken improperly or not to the purpose. It may also refer to one whose statements do not agree with the testimony of witnesses.
[12] But he must not overdo it, with the obvious purpose of instilling fear in order to establish his own security, or the people will see through this device and lose regard for him.
[13] The phrase "since the god" or "since the time of the god" was frequently used referring to the beginnings of time, when Ra established the cosmos and its laws. The true administration of justice is a sacred custom, established at the beginning

is said concerning the scribe of the vizier: 'A just scribe' is said of
him. Now, as for the hall in which you hear, there is an audience
hall for the announcement of judgments. Now, as for 'him who shall
do justice before all the people,' it is the vizier.[14]

"Behold, when a man is in his office, he acts according to what
is commanded him.[15] Behold, the success of a man is that he act
according to what is said to him. Make no delay at all in justice,
the law of which you know. Behold, it becomes the arrogant that
the king should love the timid more than the arrogant!

"Now may you do according to this command that is given you—
behold, it is the manner of success—besides giving your attention to
the crown lands, and making the establishment thereof. If you happen
to inspect, then shall you send to inspect the overseer of the land-
measuring and the patrol of the overseer of land-measuring. If there
shall be one who shall inspect before you, then shall you question
him.[16]

"Behold the regulation that is laid upon you."

The Instruction of Ptah-Hotep

The text has come down to us in several papyri of both
Middle and New Kingdoms, an indication of the great
popularity of the work. Ptah-Hotep tells us that he was
vizier of King Isesi, who reigned during the Fifth Dynasty
of the Old Kingdom (about 2540 B.C.).

of time by Ra-Atum-Khepri. Note the ethical concepts connected with the cosmogony, a theme which runs through all ancient texts from the ancient Near Eastern
and Mediterranean worlds dealing with the beginnings.

[14] Just as the audience hall is known as the place where judgments are rendered,
just so is the vizier proverbially known as "he who does justice to all the people."
Live up to it!

[15] Therefore, do your job well, according to these precepts.

[16] One of the most important duties of the vizier was the management of the huge
royal estates. The vizier is here enjoined, when he inspects the operations, to inspect
also the overseers and their underlings. In view of the context, this implies that his
responsibility is to see that the right thing is done by all the echelons of the super-
visory personnel, and that they do not abuse the peasantry working on the crown
lands.

The instruction of the superintendent of the capital, the vizier, Ptah-Hotep,[17] under the majesty of King Isesi, who lives forever and ever.

So spoke he unto the majesty of King Isesi: Old age has come and dotage has descended. The limbs are painful, and the state of being old appears as something new. Strength has perished for weariness. The mouth is silent and speaks not. The eyes are shrunken and the ears deaf. The heart is forgetful and remembers not yesterday. The bone, it suffers in old age, and the nose is stopped up and breathes not. To stand up and to sit down are alike ill. Good is become evil. Every taste has perished. What old age does to a man is that it fares ill with him in all things.

Let therefore the servant there[18] be bidden to make him a staff of old age; let my son be set in my place, that I may instruct him in the discourse of those who hearken, and in the thoughts of those who have gone before, those who have served the ancestors in times past. May they do the like for you, that strife may be banished from among the people, and the Two Riverbanks may serve you.

Said His Majesty: "Instruct you him in discourse first. May he set an example to the children of the great; may obedience enter into him, and every right conception of him who speaks unto him. There is no child that [of itself] has understanding."

The beautiful expressed utterances, spoken by the prince and count, the Father of the God[19] and Beloved of the God, the bodily son of the king, the superintendent of the capital and vizier, Ptah-Hotep, while instructing the ignorant in knowledge and in the rules of elegant discourse, the weal of him who will hearken thereto and the woe of him who shall transgress them.

Be not arrogant because of your knowledge, and have no confidence in that you are a learned man. Take counsel with the ignorant as with the wise, for the limits of art cannot be reached,

[17] "Ptah is content."
[18] "The servant there" was a frequent expression of humility denoting the speaker.
[19] "Father of the God" and "Beloved of the God" were priestly titles, probably connected with the worship of the king. In the Bible, Joseph is appointed "Father to Pharaoh" (Genesis 45:8); this Biblical phrase can be explained only in the light of our Egyptological knowledge.

166

and no artist fully possesses his skill. Good words are more hidden than the precious green stone, and yet it may be found with slave girls over the milestones.

If you find an orator at his time,[20] with sound sense and better than you, bend your arm and bow back.[21] But if he speaks ill, then fail not to withstand him, in order that men may call out to him: "Ignorant one!"

But if it is an equal of yours, show yourself by silence to be better than he, when he speaks ill. Then will he be praised by the listeners, but your name will be accounted good among the great.[22]

If he is a humble person, who is not your equal, be not wrathful against him, for you know that he is of no account. Disregard him, and so he punishes himself. It is bad if one injures one that is despicable. You smite him with the punishment of the great.[23]

If you are a leader and give command to the multitude, strive after every excellence, until there be no fault in your nature. Truth is good and its worth is lasting, and it has not been disturbed since the day of its creator,[24] whereas he who transgresses its ordinances is punished. It lies as a right path in front of him who knows nothing.[25] Wrongdoing has never yet brought its venture to port. Evil may indeed win wealth, but the strength of truth is that it endures, and the upright man says: "It[26] is the property of my father."

If you are one who sits where stands the table of one who is greater than you, take when he gives that which is set before you.

---

[20] In the full exercise of his art.

[21] In submission.

[22] That is, this man will probably be praised by the rabble, but you will be esteemed by those on your own level.

[23] By just ignoring him.

[24] Maat, meaning "truth, justice, that which should be," was considered to have been established by the gods. The king was supposed to govern by the concept of Maat, which we would call the natural, unwritten principles of human justice. Maat was also personified as a goddess, her symbol being the Feather of Truth which she wears on her head. In the well-known scene of the weighing of the heart of the deceased before Osiris in the Other World, the heart is balanced against the Feather of Truth.

[25] That is, the ingenuous person, who allows his actions to be prompted by natural human ethics.

[26] Maat, which my father has bequeathed me.

Look not at that which lies before him, but look at that which lies before you. Shoot not many glances at him, for it is an abhorrence to the *ka*[27] if one offends it.

Cast down your countenance until he greets you, and speak only when he has greeted you. Laugh when he laughs. That will be well pleasing in his heart, and what you do will be acceptable; one knows not what is in the heart.

A great man, when he sits behind the food, his resolves depend upon the command of his *ka*. A great man gives to the man that is within reach of him, but the *ka* stretches out the hands for him further.[28] Bread is eaten by the decree of the god.

If you are one of the trusted ones, whom one great man sends to another, act rightly in the matter when he sends you. You shall deliver the message as he says it. Be not secretive concerning what may be said to you, and beware of any forgetfulness. Hold fast to the truth and overstep it not, even if you recount nothing that is gratifying. Beware [also] of worsening words, such as might make one great man contemptible to the other through the manner of speech of all men. "A great man, an insignificant one"—that is what the *ka* abhors.[29]

If you plow, and there is growth in the field and the god gives it to you liberally, satisfy not your mouth beside your kindred.

If you are a humble person and are in the train of a man of repute, one who stands well with the god, know you nothing of his former insignificance. Raise not up your heart against him on account of what you know about him aforetime. Reverence him in accordance with what has happened unto him, for wealth comes not of itself. It is the god who creates repute.

Follow your *ka* so long as you live,[30] and do not more than is

---

[27] The *ka* was that part of a man's being which was created at his birth, and which remains as a supernatural tutelary genius, guiding and counseling the individual during his life upon earth. When one dies, one rejoins his *ka*. In this volume, we have translated the word as "divine essence." In the present context, one could translate it as "personality," meaning here that looking at him and his food would "get on his nerves."

[28] If he is in a good mood, he will stretch out his hand further and give to you also.

[29] That is, a nincompoop in important office.

[30] Let yourself be guided according to right conscience.

said. Diminish not the time in which you follow the heart, for it is an abhorrence to the *ka* if its time is diminished.

If you are held in esteem, and have a household, and beget a son who pleases the god—if he does right, and inclines to your nature, and hearkens to your instruction, and his designs do good in your house, and he has regard for your substance as it befits, search out for him everything that is good.

He is your son, whom your *ka* has begotten for you; separate not your heart from him.

But if he does wrong and trespasses against your designs, and acts not after your instructions, and his designs are worthless in your house, and he defies all that you say, then drive him away, for he is not your son, he is not born to you.

If you stand or sit in the vestibule,[31] wait quietly until your turn comes. Give heed to the servant who announces; he who is called has a broad place. The vestibule has its rule, and every arrangement therein is in accordance with the measuring cord. It is the god who assigns the foremost place—but one attains nothing with the elbow.

Proclaim your business without concealment. Give out your thoughts in the council of your lord. One ought to say plainly what one knows and what one knows not. He is then silent and says: "I have spoken."

If you are one to whom petition is made, be kindly when you hearken to the speech of a petitioner. Deal not roughly with him, until he has swept out his body,[32] and until he has said that on account of which he has come. A petitioner likes it well if one nods to his addresses, until he has made an end of that about which he came. A favorable audience gladdens the heart.

But whoso acts churlishly toward petitioners, then men say: "Why, pray, does he do so?"

If you would prolong friendship in a house to which you have admittance, as master, or as brother, or as friend, into whatsoever place you enter, beware of approaching the women. It is not good in the place where this is done. Men are made fools by their gleam-

---

[31] Of the audience chamber.
[32] Meaning, until he has unburdened himself.

ing limbs of carnelian.[33] A trifle, a little, the likeness of a dream, and death comes as the end of knowing her.

If you desire your conduct to be good, to set yourself free from all that is evil, then beware of covetousness, which is a malady, diseaseful, incurable. Intimacy with it is impossible; it makes the sweet friend bitter, it alienates the trusted one from the master, it makes bad both father and mother, together with the brothers of the mother, and it divorces a man's wife. It is a bundle of every kind of evil, and a bag of everything that is blameworthy. Long-lived is the man whose rule of conduct is right, and who goes in accordance with his [right] course. He wins wealth thereby, but the covetous has no tomb.[34]

Be not covetous regarding division, and be not exacting, except with regard to what is due to you. Be not covetous toward your kindred; the request of the meek avails more than strength. Just the little of which he has been defrauded, creates enmity even in one of a cool disposition.

If you are a man of note, found for yourself a household, and love your wife at home, as it beseems. Fill her belly, clothe her back; unguent is the remedy for her limbs. Gladden her heart, so long as she lives; she is a goodly field for her lord.[35] But hold her back from getting the mastery. [Remember that] her eye is her stormwind, and her vulva and her mouth are her strength.[36]

Satisfy your intimates with that which has accrued to you, as one favored of the god. To do this is prudent, for there is none who

[33] Reading according to John A. Wilson [*Ancient Near Eastern Texts*, John B. Pritchard, ed. (Princeton, N. J., Princeton University Press, 1950, 1955)]. The smooth red carnelian stone (believed to be what is meant by the Egyptian word *herset*) is a nice simile here. On the other hand, the Erman-Blackman translation [in *The Ancient Egyptians, A Sourcebook of Their Writings*, William Kelly Simpson, ed. (New York, Harper Torchbooks, 1966)] reads, "Men are made fools by their gleaming limbs and lo! they are [already] become herset-stones," with the footnote: "The shining limbs attract you, but after brief enjoyment they appear discoloured to you as the herset-stone, which is accounted elsewhere as the sign of affliction." In this case the meaning might also be that in a short time these limbs will be decayed and wrinkled, as is usual among the rapidly aging women of Mediterranean countries.
[34] The sign of extreme poverty.
[35] She produces children, something most desired (especially males) among oriental peoples, then as now.
[36] Literally, "her two hands."

knows his condition, if he thinks of the morrow. If, therefore, a misfortune befalls the favored one, it is the intimates that still say "Welcome!" to him.

If you are a man of note, who sits in the council of his lord, fix
your heart upon what is good. Be silent—this is better than *teftef-*
flowers. Speak only if you know that you can unravel the difficulty.
It is an artist who can speak in council, and to speak is harder
than any other work.

Approach not a great one in his hour,[37] and anger not the heart
of him that is laden. This is a dangerous thing, which detaches the
ka from him who loves him, who supplies food together with the god.

Instruct a great one in that which is profitable to him; that will
also be of advantage to you, for your sustenance depends upon his
ka, and your back will be clothed thereby.

If you be grown great, after you were of small account, and have
gotten you substance, after you were aforetime needy in the city
which you know, forget not how it fared with you in time past.
Trust not in your riches, that have accrued to you as a gift of the
god. You are not better than another who is your equal, to whom
the same has happened.

Bend your back to him who is over you, your superior of the
king's administration. So will your house endure with its substance,
and your pay be duly awarded. To resist him who is set in authority
is evil. One lives so long as he is indulgent.

If you look for a state of friendship, ask no question, but draw
near him and be with him alone. Prove his heart by a conversation.
If he betrays anything that he has seen, or does anything with which
you are vexed, then take heed, even in your answers.

Have a cheerful countenance when you celebrate a feast and
distribute bread there.

If you take to wife one who is well nurtured, one who is cheerful,
one whom the people of her city know, put her not away, but give
her [food] to eat.

If you hear[38] this that I have spoken to you, your whole state will
be as good as that of them who have gone before. What remains

---

[37] Of wrath.

[38] In the sense of "obey" or "take to heart," just as we say: "If you listen to me . . ."

over of their truth is noble, and the remembrance of them perishes not in the mouth of men, because their maxims are so goodly. Every word of theirs will be used always as a thing imperishable in this land, and will beautify the utterances with which the princes speak.

It is that which teaches a man to speak to posterity that it may hear it, and to be an artist, one who has heard what is good, and that now on his part speaks to posterity that it may hear it.[39]

If a good nature is formed in him who is the one set in authority, he will be excellent forever and all his wisdom will endure eternally; the wise man's soul is glad when he causes his beauty to endure on earth.

Then men see how admirable he is: His heart is evenly balanced to his tongue, and his lips are exact when he speaks; his eyes see, and his ears together hear what is profitable for his son who does right and is free from lying.

To hear[40] is excellent for a son who has heard; the hearer enters as one who has heard,[41] and he who has heard becomes a hearer[42] who hears well and speaks well. Everyone who has heard is something excellent, and it is excellent for one who has heard to hear. To hear is better than all that is, and fair favor accrues thereby. How good is it for a son to receive it, when his father speaks; thereby old age becomes his portion.

He whom the god loves, hears, but he whom the god hates hears not. It is the heart[43] that makes its owner into one who hears or one who hears not. His heart is a man's fortune.

How good is it when a son hearkens to his father, and how happy is he to whom this is said! A son who is good as a master of hearing, namely one who has heard, he is honored of his father. The memory of him remains in the mouth of the living, of those who are now upon earth and those who shall be.

If a son accepts it, when his father says it, not one of his plans miscarries. He will be esteemed among the magistrates, whereas evil

[39] You will in turn hand on the wise precepts of the past, which you have heard.
[40] The next section is built on a series of plays upon the word "hear."
[41] As one who has acquired wisdom.
[42] A judge, who we also say "hears cases."
[43] By "heart" all the ancients meant a man's intellectual faculties and feelings.

comes on him who hears not. A wise man rises early in order to establish himself, but the ignorant does not so.

As for the fool who hears not, he can do nothing at all. He regards knowledge as ignorance, and good as bad. He will do everything that is blameworthy, so that complaint is laid against him every day. He lives on that wherefrom others die, and it is his food to speak ill. This his nature is known to the magistrates; daily does death threaten him, and men shun him because of the multitude of misfortunes that are daily upon him.

A son who has heard is a worshiper of Horus.[44] He prospers after he has heard. When he has grown old and has attained honor, he talks in like manner to his children and renews the instruction of his father. And everyone who is so instructed should talk to his children, and they again to theirs. May the people who shall see them say: "He is as that one was,"[45] and also the people who shall hear of them shall say: "He is as that one was."

Take no word away, and add nothing thereto, and put not one thing in the place of another.

Your lord also shall say: "This is the son of that one," and they who hear it shall say: "Praised be he to whom he was born." May the magistrates that will hear it say: "How goodly are the utterances of his mouth."

So act that your lord may say concerning you: "How goodly was the instruction of his father. He issued from him, from his body, and he has told it unto him, and it is all in his body, and what he has done is yet greater than what was told to him. Behold, this is a good son, one whom the god gives, one who did more than what was told him by his lord. He does right and his heart does according to its right course."

May you reach me[46] being sound in body, and so that the king is satisfied with all that has been done, and may you pass many years in life. It is not little that I have wrought upon earth. I have spent a hundred and ten years in life,[47] which the king has given

[44] The living king.
[45] Like the great and wise men of old.
[46] That is, join me in the Other World.
[47] A good and ripe old age was considered by the Egyptians to be the age of 110. Joseph, in Egypt, lived to this age (Genesis 50:26).

me,[48] and with rewards beyond those of them who have gone before, because I did right for the king up to the place of reverence.[49]

It has come from its beginning to its end, like that which was found in the writing.[50]

The Instruction of Ka-Gemni

Ka-Gemni's instruction is in the same Middle Kingdom papyrus as Ptah-Hotep. King Huni, mentioned at the end of the text, was the last king of the Third Dynasty, since we know that Seneferu, who, Ka-Gemni tells us, succeeded Huni, was the first king of the Fourth Dynasty (beginning about 2600 B.C.).

The humble man flourishes, and he who deals uprightly is praised. The innermost chamber is opened to the man of silence. Wide is the seat of the man cautious of speech, but the knife is sharp against [the one] who forces a path, that he advance not, save in due season.

If you sit with a company of people, desire not the food, even if you want it;[51] it takes only a brief moment to restrain the heart, and it is disgraceful to be greedy. A handful of water quenches the thirst, and a mouthful of melon supports the heart. A good thing takes the place of what is good,[52] and just a little takes the place of much.

If you sit with a glutton, eat when he is finished;[53] if you sit with a drunkard accept a drink, and his heart will be satisfied.[54] Rage not

[48] Everything, even years of life, is given by the king (who is, of course, the god Horus).
[49] The dead were called "the revered ones."
[50] The usual formula found at the end of texts copied by the scribes.
[51] Do this out of politeness; it makes a good impression.
[52] Possibly, "A small but good dish can satisfy you as much as a large portion of something else."
[53] So that he will not fear that you won't leave enough for him.
[54] The drinker likes everyone to drink with him. Human nature has not changed.

against the meat in the presence of a glutton;[55] take what he gives you and refuse it not, thinking it will be a courteous thing.

If a man be lacking in good fellowship, no speech has any influence upon him. He is sour of face to the glad-hearted who are kindly to him. He is a grief to his mother and his friends. All men say: "Let your name be known! You are silent in your mouth when you are addressed!"

Be not boastful of your strength in the midst of young soldiers.[56] Beware of making strife; one knows not what may chance, what the god will do when he punishes.

The vizier had his sons and daughters called, when he completed his writings on the ways of mankind and on their character as encountered by him. And he said to them:

"All that is in this book, hearken unto it as if I said it."[57] Then they placed themselves upon their bellies.

They read it as it stood in writing, and it was better in their heart than anything that was in this entire land. They stood and they sat in accordance therewith.[58]

The majesty of the king of Upper and Lower Egypt, Huni, came to the landing place,[59] and the majesty of the king of Upper and Lower Egypt, Seneferu, was raised up as beneficent king in this entire land. Then was Ka-Gemni made governor of the capital and vizier.

The Instruction of King Amen-em-Hat

The story behind these instructions is the familiar one of palace intrigue and skulduggery. Amen-em-Hat I was the

---

[55] The glutton eats only for the sake of eating regardless of whether the food may be inferior. If he offers it, take it and let him think you like it; don't try to be polite in this case.

[56] Don't try to show off your strength to them as it is their business to fight, and they are trained for it. You will be good and sorry.

[57] That is, follow these precepts even when I am not here, as if I were saying them to you in person.

[58] They regulated their entire conduct in accordance with it.

[59] "To come to the landing place" or "to come to port" was one of the several euphemisms for dying.

first king of the Twelfth Dynasty, and died about 1960 B.C.
We know that he had associated his son Senusret on the
throne with himself, as coregent during his lifetime—a
practice followed by most of his successors. This was done,
no doubt, in order to forestall just such assassination attempts as are described in our text. This event is also
quite likely the one referred to at the beginning of *The
Story of Sinuhe.*

The text was evidently popular as a school exercise, as
it is found in several papyri, tablets, and ostraca dating
from the Eighteenth to the Twentieth dynasties. *Sinuhe*
was also a popular school text. Both have the elements of
adventure and excitement, and their use as school texts is
an indication of the excellent pedagogic insight of the
ancient Egyptian educators.

Beginning of the instruction which the majesty of the king of
Upper and Lower Egypt, Sehetep-ib-Ra,[60] Son of Ra, Amen-em-
Hat,[61] True of Voice,[62] made, speaking in a message of truth to his
son, the Lord of All. He said:

"You who have appeared as a god,[63] hearken to what I say to
you, that you may be king over the land, and ruler over all the
riverbanks, and that you may do good even in excess of what is
expected.

"Be on your guard against subordinates, lest unforseen terrors
happen. Approach them not, for you are alone! Trust not a brother,
know not a friend, and make not for yourself intimates; in these
things is no satisfaction.

"When you lie down, guard your heart your very self, for on the
day of adversity a man has no adherents. I gave to the poor and

---

[60] Literally, "He who makes content the heart of Ra."
[61] Literally, "Amen to the fore."
[62] This formula, always applied to the deceased, was no doubt inserted by the later
copyist.
[63] That is, you have become king.

nourished the orphan; I caused him who was nothing to reach the goal, even as him who was of account.

"It was he who ate my food who raised arms against me; it was he to whom I gave my hand who aroused fear therewith. They who clothed themselves in my fine linen looked at me as at a shadow,[64] and they who anointed themselves with my myrrh poured out water . . .[65]

"My images are among the living, and my shares in the offerings of men,[66] and yet they contrived a conspiracy against me without it being heard, and a great contest without it being seen. Men fought on the place of combat and forgot yesterday.[67] Good fortune does not attend one who knows not when he should know!

"It was after the evening meal, when night had come. I had taken an hour of repose and laid me down upon my bed. I was weary, and my heart began to follow after slumber. Then it was as if weapons were brandished, and as if there was inquiring after me, and I became like a snake of the desert.[68]

"I roused me to fight, and I was alone. I found that it was a hand-to-hand fighting of the bodyguard. Had I quickly taken weapons into my hand, I had driven back the dastards by smiting around. But there is no bravery by night, and one cannot fight alone, and success could not come without you, who protect me.

"Behold, the vile thing came to pass when I was without you, when the courtiers had not yet heard that I passed on my sovereign power to you, when I did not yet sit together with you.[69] Let me, then, make your counsels. I was not fearful of them;[70] my heart did not bring to mind the slackness of servants.

"Had women ever set the battle in array?[71] Had assailants ever been fostered within the house? No misfortunes had come behind

[64] That is, wishing for my death.
[65] In some ritual of sorcery? The rest of the line is corrupt in the text.
[66] So honored am I.
[67] They forgot, or took no account of, all my good deeds.
[68] Remaining quiet but watchful.
[69] Amen-em-Het had not yet officially announced the coregency of Senusret.
[70] I had no suspicions concerning the members of my own household.
[71] One does not ordinarily imagine women as marshaling the fighting forces. Could I imagine members of my harem instigating this armed conspiracy?

me since my birth, nor had there existed the equal of me as a doer of valiance.[72]

"I trod Elephantine and I marched into the Delta.[73] I stood upon the boundaries of the land and beheld its circuit. I carried forward the boundaries of my power by my might and by my prowess.

"I was one who produced barley, and was beloved of the grain-god.[74] The Nile greeted me on all its reaches. None hungered in my years, none thirsted in them. Men dwelt in peace through that which I wrought, and talked of me. All that I commanded was what it should be.

"I overcame lions, and I captured crocodiles. I cast the Nubians under my feet, and carried off the peoples of the south. I caused the Asiatics to go as dogs.[75]

"I made for myself a house adorned with gold; its ceilings are of lapis lazuli; its doors are of copper and their bolts are of bronze. They are made for everlasting, and eternity is in awe of them. I know every dimension thereof, being Lord of All!

"O my son, King Senusret, by your feet do I walk! You are my own heart, and my eyes look upon you! The children have an hour of happiness beside the people, when they give you praise!

"Behold, that which I have done at the beginning, let me set it in order for you at the end. I will come to the landing place for him who is in my heart.[76] All men together set the White Crown on the Off-spring of the God,[77] fixing it in its due place for what I have begun for you. There is exultation in the Boat of Ra![78] Your kingdom has been from primeval time. Raise up monuments and make beautiful your tomb. I have fought against him whom you know,[79] for I desire not that he should be beside Your Majesty—Life, Prosperity, and Health!"

---

[72] And so there was no reason to suspect that anyone would want to get rid of me.
[73] I set in order the southern and northern frontiers of the realm.
[74] Since he gave me prosperous harvests.
[75] So docile did I make them.
[76] See note [59]. When the king dies, his beloved son will assume full rule.
[77] That is, Senusret.
[78] The deceased was believed to take his place with the other deities in the Solar Bark of Ra that daily crossed the heavens, and to help guide it.
[79] A half brother of Senusret? Was he the candidate of the harem conspirators?

The Proverbs of Amen-em-Ope

The most important of the "wisdom books," and the longest, is Amen-em-Ope. It has often been compared to the Biblical Proverbs, with which it has many points of contact both in thought and in actual phraseology: In reading Amen-em-Ope, even the reader who has but a nodding acquaintance with Proverbs will note the remarkable similarity in phrasing to Proverbs 22:17–24:22. Another important point of similarity is the religious tone and attitude which permeates Amen-em-Ope.

The particular copy of the papyrus which has come down to us has been variously dated from the Twenty-second Dynasty (about 900 B.C.) to the Twenty-sixth (about 650 B.C.), with some authorities holding that the original text goes back to the Eighteenth Dynasty (1580–1320 B.C.). There has naturally been quite some discussion as to whether Amen-em-Ope influenced Proverbs or vice versa. The general consensus of scholars today is that such polemics are gratuitous: both books reflect the ethical and pragmatic teachings of previous generations and are intimately part of the common cultural tradition of the ancient Near East.

The beginning of instruction for living
   and precepts for well-being;
of everything for entering into the councils of the elders,
   and of precepts for courtiers;
of knowing how to return answer to him who speaks,
   and how to bring back report to one who sent him;
to set one right on the ways of life,
   and to cause him to prosper in the world;
   so that his heart will descend into its shrine;
to guide him away from evil,
   and to rescue him from the mouths of the vulgar,

179

that he might be estimated in the mouths of people.
Done by the Overseer of the Fields,
 one skilled in his office
 and the seed of a scribe of the Beloved Land,[80] etc., etc.
[Here follow the various titles and offices of the author]
the owner of a tomb in Abydos,
AMEN-EM-OPE, THE SON OF KA-NAKHT,
 declared Justified in Abydos.
For his son, the youngest of his children,
 the smallest of his fold:
He-who-is-over-the-secrets-of-Min, Bull of his Mother,
 and Pourer of Water for Osiris,[81] etc., etc.
[Here follow the other titles of Amen-em-Ope's son and those of his
mother]
HE SAYS:
Give your ears and hear what is said;
 apply your heart,[82] in order to understand!
It is beneficial to put these things in your heart,
 but hurtful to him who rejects them!
Let them rest within the coffer of your belly,[83]
 and turn them over and over in your heart;
that if a hurricane of words arrive
 they may act as a peg upon your tongue.
If you spend your time-of-life with these things in your heart

---

[80] Egypt.

[81] Min was a very ancient, ithyphallic fertility god. The epithet *Ka-Mutef*, "Bull of
his Mother," was originally applied to Ra, and then extended to other powerfully
procreative deities, such as Min and Amen. The unconscious (?) Oedipal implications
of this epithet are evident. Osiris, as chthonic fertility deity, was closely connected
with water, and the symbolic water pouring was one of his rites. It was common
for both men and women of the nobility and royalty to hold several priestly offices
simultaneously.

[82] Throughout the ancient Near East, the heart was regarded as the seat of the intellect
and the understanding. As a matter of fact, in Egypt the heart was carefully embalmed and placed in a "canopic jar" with the other embalmed internal organs, and
a special heart-scarab was inserted in its place in the body of the mummy. The brain
was discarded.

[83] The "belly" is the interior of the body in general and is frequently used metaphorically, as we would say "within you."

you will find it will bring good fortune;
you will find my words a treasure house of life,
    and your body will prosper upon earth!

I

Be wary lest you rob the afflicted,
    lest you oppress the weak.
Do not put forth your hand against the approach of an old man,
    just as you would not take speech to the great.[84]
Do not cry out against him whom you have injured,
    nor give him answer to justify yourself.
He who does evil, the riverbanks cast him forth,
    and his own flood waters carry him away.
The north-wind descends, and ends his hour;
    it unites with the tempest.
The storm cloud thunders, and evil are the crocodiles!
    O man of heat,[85] how are you now?
He cries out, and his voice reaches heaven above;
    O Moon-god,[86] raise up his crime against him!

II

Do not attempt to harness the quarrelsome one with a hot mouth,[87]
    nor spur him with words.
Rather be sluggard before an enemy,
    and bend back before an attacker.
Sleep on it[88] before you say anything,
    for the storm breaking loose like a fire through straw
    is the heated man in his hour!

---

[84] That is, show as much respect to the aged as you would to the great.
[85] The hotheaded, rash man at the mercy of his emotions. In the text, the phrase "man of heat" is followed by the determinative of a kneeling captive with his hands tied behind his back, as if to indicate that one who has let his temper get the best of him is captive to his own passions.
[86] Thoth, as the scribe and attorney general of the gods.
[87] This expression is followed by the "serpent" and "bound captive" determinatives. See note 85. The serpent might denote "burning."
[88] Literally, "sleep before talking."

Recoil from before him, let it rebound to his own face;
  the god will know how to answer him.
If you spend your time-of-life with these things in your heart,
  then your children shall see [how well off you have been].
As for the heated man of a temple,
  he is like a tree growing in a preserve:
at the end of a moment it loses its branches,
  and it is brought to its end in the shipyards;
it is floated from its place,
  and the flame is its burial.
But the true man of quietude keeps himself in his own place;
  he is like a tree which grows in a garden;
it flourishes in greenery and redoubles in its fruit;
  it stands before its master.
Its fruit is sweet and its shade is pleasant,
  and it comes to its end in the garden.

III

Do not say, "Today is like tomorrow,"
  for how could these things end?
When tomorrow comes, and today is gone,
  the flood may have become a sandbank,
  the crocodiles uncovered of water,
  the hippopotamuses on dry land,
  the fish gasping for breath,
  the wolves sated and the birds in festival![89]
But the quiet man will say in the temple,
  "Great are the favors of Ra!"
Come, be a man of quietude, and you shall find life;
  your body shall flourish on earth!

---

[89] That is, for all we know, catastrophic upheavals, such as a disastrous sinking of
the river, may occur overnight, leaving the river creatures stranded on dry sand to
become victims of wolves and birds of prey. The composed man, however, will not
complain of the seeming monotony of existence, but will thank the gods for their
daily gifts.

IV

Remove not the boundary stone from the limits of a field;
  do not change the position of the measuring cord.
Covet not even a cubit of land,
  and violate not the boundary of a widow.
He who wrongfully seizes a furrow in a field,
  even though he claim it with false oaths,
  he will be seized captive by the power of the Moon-god!
Plow in your own fields and you shall find what you need;
  get your bread from your own threshing floor.
Better a bushel which the god gives you
  than five thousand taken wrongly.
Better is poverty in the hand of the god
  than wealth in a storehouse.
Better is bread with a happy heart
  than riches with sorrow!
Do not cast your heart after riches;
  no one ignores the Fortune-goddess![90]
Let not your heart long for externals;
  every man has his appointed hour!
Toil not after riches, to seek excess
  when your needs are assured;
if you obtain wealth through thievery,
  it will not remain overnight with you.
At daybreak it is no more in your house—
  the earth has opened its mouth and swallowed it;
  it has sunk in the underworld.
It has grown wings like geese,
  and has flown away to the sky!
Rather praise the Sun when he shines forth,
  and say, "Give me well-being and health!"
And he will give you needs for this life,
  and you will be free from fear.

---

[90] Everyone does frantic obeisance to the fortune-goddess; be a nonconformist and keep out of the rat race.

V

Try to be respected by people;
  then will every man greet you!
Keep your tongue free from evil words,
  and you will be liked by men.
Do not call a man a sinner
  when his circumstances are hidden from you.
Whether you hear good or evil,
  leave it outside, as if you had not heard it,
or else place the good on your tongue,
  while the evil lies hidden within you!

VI

Do not associate with the hotheaded man,
  nor be close with him in conversation.
Guard your tongue in answering your superior,
  and be careful not to insult him;
    for he can throw his words to lasso you!
Do not talk falsely with a man;
  it is an outrage to the god!
Do not divide your heart from your tongue,
  and all your plans will be successful.
You will be of weight among the people,
  and secure in the hand of the god!
The god hates the insincere of words,
  and the hypocrite is his great loathing!
Do not covet the property of a poor man,
  and be not hungry for his bread;
a poor man's property is a choking for the throat,
  and a vomiting for the gullet.

VII

Do not injure a man with pen upon papyrus;
  it is an abomination to the god.
Do not bear witness with lying words,
  nor injure another with your tongue.

Do not make a reckoning with him that has nothing,
    and do not falsify your pen.
If you find a large debt against a poor man,
    then divide it into three parts;
    abandon two and let one remain,
    and you will find it as the ways of life!
You will sleep well; and in the morning, having passed the night,
    it will be like receiving good news!
Better is praise as one who loves men
    than riches in a storehouse!
Better is bread when the heart is happy
    than riches with troubles!

VIII

Do not make heavy the scales, nor falsify the weights,
    nor diminish the fractions of the measure.
For the Baboon sits beside the balance,
    and his heart is the plummet!
For which god is like the great god Thoth,
    who discovered these things and made them?
Make not diminished weights:
    through the power of the god, they will abound in grief!

IX

Do not lie down fearful of the morrow;
    when the earth brightens, what will the morrow be like?
    No man knows what the morrow will be like!
The god is ever in his powers,
    while man is in his deficiencies.
The words men say do pass away,
    but the deeds of the god do not.
Do not say, "We, who are blameless . . ."
    or strive to argue or justify.
As for your wrongdoing, the god has it;
    it is sealed with his finger![91]

[91] The gods know your misdeeds and have them all written and sealed. No amount of mealymouthed expression of self-righteousness and justification will do you any good.

X

Do not confound a person in the law court,
  do not pervert justice thereby.
Do not attend only to one clothed in white;
  turn not away from him who is threadbare.
Do not take the bribe of the powerful,
  nor oppress for him the weak.
As for Justice, it is the great gift of the god;
  he gives it to whom he wishes.

XI

Do not empty your belly to everybody;[92]
  do not damage thereby your prestige.
Do not spread your words about to the crowd,
  nor associate yourself with the blabbermouth.
Better is a man whose talk remains in his belly,
  than he who speaks it out to destruction.
Just as one does not run to achieve success,
  one does not throw for his own destruction!

XII

Do not laugh at a blind man,
  nor jeer at a dwarf,
  nor disturb the course of the lame.[93]
Do not jeer at a man who is in the hand of the god,[94]

---

[92] For the connotation of "belly" see note 83. The general point of this section is that he who blabs about his inmost life and feelings to everyone ends, at best, by demeaning himself, and could very well work his own destruction.

[93] This ethical precept is remarkable, in view of the fact that in most of the ancient Mediterranean world misshapen and otherwise physically and mentally handicapped persons were objects of sport, derision, and abuse. The pygmies imported from Nubia for the entertainment of the nobility and the figures of Thersites and of the limping Hephaestus in Homer are cases in point.

[94] Not only in the ancient world, but until comparatively recently, it was believed that madmen and idiots were, as we would say in the same vein, "touched," that is, from above (or below, as the case may have been).

nor face him fiercely if he has gone astray.[95]
As for man, he is clay and straw,
  and the god is his builder!
he tears down and builds up every day!
He makes a thousand inferiors at his desire,
  or he makes a thousand men as overseers,
when he is in his hour of life,
  in his period of activity.
How joyful is he who has arrived at the West,
  now that he is safe in the hand of the god![96]

XIII

Associate with a man of your own station—
  Ra is secure far away and above![97]
Give a hand to an old man when he is sated with beer;
  honor him just as his children would![98]
Do not discover a widow if you catch her in the fields,
  nor cease being kindly to her replies.[99]
Do not turn away the stranger from your jugs,
  and let him be enhanced before your servants.
Beloved of the god is he who rejoices the humble,
  more than the one who honors the noble.

Regard these thirty chapters:[100]
  they delight, they instruct!

[95] This line might also be translated: "Nor are you favored of countenance in that he has strayed," meaning, the fact that he has "wandered off" does not make you any the superior for that.

[96] One is safe from the vicissitudes of fate only after having departed this life and gone to the Other World in the West, secure under the protection of Osiris.

[97] That is, do not try to be a social climber. Only Ra is secure way up there! Let him be!

[98] Throughout the ancient world it was considered a mark of due respect to bear up and help along home an older person in his cups.

[99] As in the Old Testament, the right of the poor and the widowed to glean from the reapings in the fields was recognized as an ancient prerogative. The point of this precept is not to call attention to a widow found gleaning in the fields, and if questioning her, to act kindly.

[100] The original text is divided into thirty chapters. Compare Proverbs 22:20.

They are the foremost of all books;
   they make the ignorant know!
If they are read out before the ignorant one,
   then will he be cleansed through them.
Come, fill yourself with them and place them in your heart!
   become a man who can expound them,
   who can explain them as a teacher.
As for the scribe who is skilled in his office,
   he will find himself worthy to be a courtier!

It has come to an end, in the writing of Shenu, son of the Father of the God, Pa-Miu.[101]

The "Schoolboy" Texts

Fortunately for us, the Egyptians had a high regard for learning and knowledge, and the education of boys, certainly among the upper classes and most probably among the various levels of the commonalty, was considered to be of the utmost importance. What is fortunate for us is that we have found, among the ruins, very many papyri, writing-boards and ostraca covered with texts which the schoolboys were set to copy as writing exercises. Thus many texts were accidentally preserved which would otherwise have been lost.

Since the priests were the repositories of learning, the schools were attached to the temples. An excellent indication of the attitude of the Egyptians to learning was their name for the school, *per-en-ankh,* "the house of life." The schoolboy learned reading and writing and reckoning, with important emphasis on

---

[101] The scribe Shenu (or Senu, depending on the reading of the hieratic text) made the copy of the text that has come down to us. His father, Pa-Miu, was a "Father of the God," one of the higher ranks of the priesthood. Compare Genesis 45:8, in which Joseph names first among the high offices conferred upon him by Pharaoh that of "Father to Pharaoh." The king, as the living Horus, had his special worship.

188

calligraphy, and studied the ancient literature. The pedagogic method used seems to have been the constant copying, by the students, of classic texts and the didactic literature, under the supervision of the priest, who was their teacher and who regularly checked their "notebooks" and corrected their mistakes (we have several actual practice exercises with erasures, crossings-out, and the teacher's corrections). In this manner the boy perfected his reading and writing, at the same time absorbing the teachings of the texts he copied. Naturally a major portion of the exercises was made up of extracts from the didactic literature, and the texts given below were obviously written specifically for the edification of the Egyptian youngsters in the schools.

A most interesting aspect of ancient Egypt is that although politically the state was an absolute, monolithic autocracy, the means whereby an individual could enter the ruling bureaucracy and advance to the various levels of the political and religious hierarchy were quite democratic for these times. It was not a closed system. Any boy of free parentage who showed any promise could enter the House of Life and learn to become a scribe. Once he received his scribal training, a good and relatively easy living was assured. If he had the intelligence and ambition, all the various higher branches of the "civil service" were open to him. He could become a priest and advance to the higher orders, or he could enter the administrative bureaucracy and eventually become a magistrate or higher, with even the possibility of being appointed vizier. We know that some of the viziers had arisen from humble backgrounds. There was also the theoretical possibility that the scribe who made good and advanced to the highest echelons could, if he married a princess of royal blood, even become king. The pharaoh Hor-em-Heb, who reigned at the very end of the Eighteenth Dynasty (1349–1319 B.C.), came of parentage unknown to us, and was previously a general of the army. Significantly, his lasting monument, one of the great masterpieces of world art, is his statue at the Metropolitan Museum in New York, showing him squatting in the scribe's cross-legged position, his papyrus scroll unrolled across his knees. Likewise, some of our best pieces of Egyptian sculpture show viziers and princes, who loved to have themselves depicted for all eternity as scribes, squatting cross-legged and holding the reed pen and papyrus scroll, their gaze directed forward in keen and intelligent attention.

The following selections, diligently copied by the schoolboys, are in the form of precepts given by father to son, comparing the advantages and opportunities accorded the scribe as against the miseries and vicissitudes involved in other occupations which he would presumably have to enter as a "dropout," and admonishing him against the various pitfalls and temptations lying in his path. Like many other aspects of ancient Egypt, all this is startlingly modern.

Advice to Schoolboys

I

I place you at school along with the children of notables, to educate you and to have you trained for this enhancing calling.

Behold, I relate to you how it fares with the scribe when he is told: "Wake up and at your place! The books lie already before your comrades! Place your hand on your clothes and look to your sandals!"

When you get your daily task, be not idle and read diligently from the book. When you reckon in silence, let no word be heard.[102]

Write with your hand and read with your mouth. Ask counsel

---

[102] Arithmetic and geometry were major subjects of instruction in the schools. Unerring calculation—and we know that the Egyptians performed some complicated processes—demanded concentration and silence in a world without calculating machines.

190

of them who are clever. Be not slack, and spend not a day in idleness, or woe betide your limbs! Enter into the methods of your teacher and hear his instructions. Behold, I am with you every day!

II

O scribe, be not idle, be not idle, or you will be soundly chastised! Set not your heart on pleasures, or you will be ruined. Write with your hand, read with your mouth, and ask counsel of them that have more knowledge than you.

Procure for yourself the calling of a magistrate,[103] that you may attain it when you become old. Fortunate is a scribe that is skilled in his calling, a master of learning. Persevere every day; thus shall you obtain mastery over the knowledge of writing. Spend no day in idleness or you will be beaten. The ear of a boy is on his back, and he hearkens when he is beaten!

Set your heart upon hearing my words; they will be profitable to you.

The kaeri[104] is taught to dance, horses are broken in, a kite is put in a nest, a hawk's wings are bound.

Persevere in asking counsel, neglect it not; and in writing, sicken not of it.

Set your heart upon hearing my words; you will find them profitable.

III

Be not a foolish man, that has no instruction.

By night you are taught, and by day you are instructed, but you do not listen to instruction, and you do after your own devices!

---

[103] Not necessarily a judge, but any of the many types of official in the elaborate bureaucracy of ancient Egypt. The more highly skilled scribe ("excellent in his fingers") could attain to the better positions, assuring greater emolument and higher status.
[104] An Ethiopian animal, also cited further on as an example of what can be accomplished by way of training.

The kaeri listens to words, when it is brought from Ethiopia. Lions are taught, horses are broken in, but you—the like of you is not known in the whole land! Know that, if you please!

IV

My heart is sick of giving you further teaching! I may give you a hundred blows, and yet you cast them all off! You are as a beaten ass unto me, that is stubborn. You are as a jabbering Nubian unto me, that is brought with the tribute![105]

The kite is put into a nest, the wings of the kite are bound; I will also make you play the man, you bad boy! Know that, if you please!

V

I am told that you forsake writing, that you give yourself up to pleasures. You go from street to street, where it smells of beer, to destruction. Beer, it will scare men from you, and it will send your soul to perdition.

You are like a broken steering-oar in a ship,[106] that is obedient on neither side. You are like a shrine without its god, and like a house without bread.[107]

You are encountered climbing a wall and breaking in; men run away from before you, for you inflict wounds upon them.[108]

Would that you knew that wine is an abomination, that you would take an oath in respect to wine, that you would not set your heart on the bottle, and would forget *terek*![109]

---

[105] Slaves were always part of the tribute of Nubia, whose tribesmen were continually harassing the southern borders. The inevitable consequence was punitive expeditions from Egypt. Naturally the Nubians had to send annual tribute after being subdued. To the Egyptians the language of the Nubian slaves sounded like aimless jabbering.

[106] In your drunkenness.

[107] An interesting observation—the drunken person is bereft of the most essential quality of a human being, reason.

[108] He has gone so far as to become criminally delinquent.

[109] Apparently some sort of drink.

You are taught to sing to the flute and to the pipe, to speak to the harp in wails,[110] and to sing to the lyre.

You sit in the house, and the girls encircle you. You sit in front of the wench and are besprinkled with oil; your garland of *ishet-penu*[111] hangs about your neck, and you drum on your paunch. Then you reel and you fall on your belly and are besmirched with dirt!

VI

I have heard that you follow pleasures. Turn not your back on my words! Do you give your mind to all manner of futile things?

I will cause your foot to stumble when you go in the streets, and you shall be beaten with the hippopotamus whip!

However, I have seen many like you, that did sit in the writing academy and that did not say "by the god"[112] without swearing: "Books are nothing at all!" Yet they became scribes, and One [113] remembered their names, to dispatch them on errands.

If you look at me myself, when I was as young as you, I passed my time with the handcuff on me,[114] and this it was that bound my limbs, when it stayed on me for three months and I was imprisoned in the temple,[115] while my father and mother were on earth and my brethren also. When it[116] left me, and my hand was free, then I surpassed what I had been before, and was the first of all my comrades and surpassed them in books.

---

[110] Egyptian rock and roll, evidently. They were modern in all respects.

[111] A type of plant or flower.

[112] As with many young hipsters today (and in all generations of human history) every phrase they uttered was punctuated with oaths and cuss words. However, as is true of many of these obnoxious juveniles, they grew out of it with maturity and fulfilled their intellectual promise.

[113] The king or the vizier was frequently referred to by this honorific indefinite form.

[114] The father, in endeavoring to encourage his son, reminds him that he was no angel in his day either, and that he ran afoul of the authorities.

[115] Being under the jurisdiction of the temple school, he was not thrown into a common jail, but was imprisoned in the temple itself, which evidently had such a place of durance for its own juvenile delinquents.

[116] That is, the handcuff. As figured in the murals, it looked like a sort of wooden pretzel hanging from the prisoner's neck, and through the holes of which the hands were locked by the wrists.

Do as I say, and your body will be healthy, and you will be found in the morning to have no superior.

VII

I am told that you forsake writing, that you have gone and run away. You forsake writing as fast as your feet can manage it, like a pair of horses.

Your heart flutters like a bird, and you are like an ass when it gets a beating.

But you are not a hunter of the desert, nor a Madjoi of the west![117]

But you are not one that is deaf, that cannot hear, and one speaks to him with the hand.

You are like a skipper's mate who does not look out for adverse winds, and searches not for the wave. If the outer rope is let go, it pulls him by the neck.[118]

[What follows is obscure. We are informed that he *plucks* flowers *on the banks,* and a probably comic description is given of his dress: *his wig with its curled locks, that reach to his feet, is of Ethiopian work,* etc. The ending is: *He has a full ear on the day of the ass and is a steering-oar on the day of the boat.*[119]]

VIII

I am told that you forsake writing, that you give yourself up to pleasures. You set your mind on work in the field, and turn your back on the Words of the God.[120] Do you not bethink you how it

---

[117] That is, you are not a wild barbarian but presumably an intelligent and civilized Egyptian, who should know better.

[118] That is, an ignoramus who stupidly bungles his job and gets all fouled up in the rigging to boot. A "schlemiel."

[119] Possibly meaning that he turns out all right despite all this, as in the previous section.

[120] The hieroglyphic characters and the "magic" of writing were considered to have been revealed to men by the god Thoth, who invented writing and who was the official scribe and registrar of the gods. Thoth was hence the patron deity of all scribes, and the characters of the writing were "the Words of the God."

fares with the husbandman,[121] when the harvest is registered?[122] The worm has taken half the grain, the hippopotamus has devoured the rest. The mice abound in the field, and the locust has descended. The cattle devour, and the sparrows steal. Woe to the husbandman!

The remainder, that lies on the threshing floor, the thieves make an end of that. The bronze harrow is destroyed, the pair of horses die at the threshing and plowing.

And now the scribe lands on the embankment and will register the harvest. The porters carry sticks, and the Nubians palm-ribs.[123] They say: "Give grain!" "There is none there." He is stretched out and beaten; he is bound and thrown into the canal. His wife is bound in his presence, his children are put in fetters.[124] His neighbors leave them, they take to flight, and look after their own grain.

But the scribe, he directs the work of all people. For him there are no taxes, for he pays tribute in writing, and there are no dues for him. Know that, if you please!

IX

Put writing in your heart, that you may protect yourself from hard labor of any kind and be a magistrate of high repute!

Do you not recall the indolent one whose name is unknown? He will be loaded like an ass, while he carries in front of the scribe who knows what he is worth.[125]

Come, let me tell you how woefully fares the soldier, according as his superiors are many—the general, the commander of the auxiliary troops, the *saket* who is at their head, the standard-bearer, the

---

[121] Various alternative occupations to that of scribe are now considered, and their shortcomings will be emphasized.

[122] All crops were strictly tallied and registered on the government rolls for purposes of taxation. The farmer had to pay as tax a percentage of the gross harvest that his land was supposed to yield, not of the net remaining after various types of loss, depredation, and so on.

[123] The government Internal Revenue man, who descends with his staff of porters to carry the taxes, and with the Nubians who were frequently employed as police. We have representations of hapless farmers, from whom the assessed grain was not forthcoming, shown being held down on the ground and bastinadoed.

[124] They will be sold as slaves for debt.

[125] The lazy good-for-nothing is reduced to being a servant and porter for the learned scribe, who is a man of position.

lieutenant, the scribe, the captain of fifty, and the commander of the expeditionary troops. They go in and out of their courts in the royal palace, they say: "Let them[126] know work!"

He is awakened when an hour has gone by, and he is driven like an ass. He works until the sun goes down under its darkness of night. He is hungry, and his body is worn; he is dead while yet alive.

X

Ah, what mean you by saying: "It is thought that the soldier is better off than the scribe?"

Come, let me tell you how the soldier fares, the often-belabored, when he is brought while yet young, to be shut up in the barracks. He receives a burning blow on his body, a ruinous blow on his eye, a blow on his eyebrow that lays him out, and his pate is cleft with a wound.[127] He is laid down and beaten, like a document.[128] He is battered and bruised with flogging.

Come, let me tell you how he goes to Syria, and how he marches over the mountains. His bread and water are borne upon his shoulder like the load of an ass; they make his neck as bent as that of an ass, and the joints of his back are bowed. His drink is stinking water. He falls out only to keep watch. When he reaches the enemy, he is like a trapped bird, and he has no strength in his limbs.

If he comes back home to Egypt, he is like wood that the worm eats. He is sick, and becomes bedridden. He is brought back upon the ass; his clothes are stolen, and his servant has run away.

O scribe, turn you away from the thought that the soldier is better off than the scribe!

XI

Turn your face by day to writing, and read by night, for you know all that the Sovereign does as touching his measures in their

---

126 That is, the common soldiers.
127 As in all armies until recently, discipline and punishment were quite corporal.
128 Like the pith of the papyrus stalk, which was beaten into thin sheets.

entirety. All the subjects are mustered, and the best are taken.[129]
The man is made into a soldier, and the stripling into a recruit. The
boy, he is only bred to be torn from the arms of his mother; if he
attains manhood, his bones are battered.

Are you an ass that is led, for it has no understanding in its body?

Acquire for yourself this great calling of a scribe; pleasant and
abounding in possessions are your palette[130] and your papyrus roll,
and blithesome are you every day!

Know that, if you please!

XII

Set your heart on being a scribe, that you may direct the whole
earth!

Come, let me tell you of a miserable calling, that of the officer of
chariotry. He is placed in the stable because of the father of his
mother,[131] with five slaves; two men of them are given him as
helpers.

He hastens to get steeds from the stall in His Majesty's presence.
When he has obtained goodly horses, he is glad and exults. He
comes with them to his town, and he tramples it underfoot[132] with
zest. He is happy when he thus tramples underfoot, but he knows
not yet how it is with him!

He expends his wealth which he had from the father of his mother[133]
that he may acquire a chariot. Its pole costs three *deben* and the
chariot costs five *deben*.[134]

---

[129] Scribes, as having special and necessary skills, were not "drafted."

[130] The scribe's writing-case, usually of wood, containing a compartment for his reed
pens and two small wells sunk into the end, in one of which he mixed black ink and
in the other, red.

[131] The chariotry was, of course, regarded as the elite division, and was chosen from
good families. It should be remembered that in ancient Egypt the descent and inheritance was through the female line.

[132] "To tread the earth" or "trample the earth under foot" was an expression for
traveling, riding, etc. Incidentally, men did not ride on horseback, and there was no
cavalry as such until later Greek times. In the Homeric epics, for example, horses
are used only to draw chariots and are never ridden upon.

[133] See the second part of note 131.

[134] A weight of measure. No coinage was used at this time.

He hastens to trample underfoot from upon it. He makes himself into one that is shod, and takes himself and thrusts himself into sandals.[135] He casts the chariot away in the thicket, and his feet are cut by the sandals and his shirt is pierced with thorns.

When one comes to muster the troops, he is grievously tormented. He is beaten upon the ground, beaten with a hundred stripes.[136]

XIII

Be a scribe who is freed from forced labor, and protected from all work. He is released from hoeing with the hoe, and he need not carry a basket.

It separates you from plying the oar, and it is free from vexation. You have not many masters, nor a host of superiors.

No sooner has a man come forth from his mother's womb, than he is stretched out before his superiors. The boy becomes a soldier's henchman, the stripling a recruit, the grown man is made into a husbandman, and the townsman into a groom. The lame [one] is made into a doorkeeper, and the nearsighted into one who feeds cattle; the fowler goes among the marshes, and the fisherman stands in the wet.

The superintendent of the stable stands at the work, while his span is left in the field. Grain is thrown down to his wife, and his daughter is on the embankment. If his span leaves him and runs away, he is carried off to the foreign troops.[137]

The soldier, when he goes up to Syria, has no staff and no sandals. He knows not whether he will be dead or alive, by reason of the fierce lions. The foe lies hidden in the scrub, and the enemy stands ready for battle. The soldier marches and cries out to his god: "Come to me and deliver me!"

---

[135] When the army gets into wild and hilly country, for example, in Syria, chariots become useless, and the charioteer has to abandon his chariot and put on heavier footgear in order to proceed over the rough terrain.
[136] Presumably, punished for not making a better showing.
[137] This paragraph seems to refer to the officer of chariotry who still has to oversee his own fields when not on duty. If his horses run away, he is put into the expeditionary force of infantry.

198

The priest stands there as a husbandman, and the *waab*-priest works in the canal;[138] he is drenched in the river. It makes no difference to him whether it be winter or summer, whether the sky be windy or rainy.

When the baker stands and bakes and lays bread on the fire, his head is inside the oven, and his son holds fast his feet. Comes it to pass that he slips from his son's hand, he falls into the blaze!

But the scribe, he directs every work that is in this land!

XIV

Let not your heart go afluttering like leaves before the wind! Set not your heart on pleasures. Alas, they profit not, they render a man no service. When he works, and it is his lot to serve the Thirty,[139] he works and conserves not his strength, for evil toil lies yet in front of him. No servant brings him water, and no women will make bread for him, whereas his companions live according to their desire, and their servants act in their stead. But the man of no sense stands there and toils, and his eye looks enviously at them.

Therefore give heed, you naughty one; you obstinate one, who will not hear when you are spoken to! Hasten to it, the calling with the happy life! It is one that directs all the Councils of the Thirty, and the courtiers of the Royal Circle.

Know that, if you please!

[138] Evidently the lower orders of the priesthood had certain unpleasant duties to perform in connection with the temple economy. We know also that the ordinary priests served in the temple during only part of the year, spending the rest of the time working their fields. This was also true in ancient Israel, at least during Second Commonwealth times, as we know from Talmudic writings.
[139] The administrative functionaries who directed the local government.

18 Social Upheaval and World-Weariness

With the breakup of the Old Kingdom, which had lasted for five centuries and which had been a period of glorious optimism, prosperity, and splendid isolation (see Chapter 3), there set in a period of political disintegration and social upheaval, a situation quite analogous to that of Europe during the Middle Ages, after the collapse of the Roman Empire. This First Intermediate period was, likewise, a period of feudalism, in which there was no central authority. Each petty noble was master in his own domain, all sorts of unscrupulous opportunists played a free hand, and "every man did what was right in his own eyes." Old, established values and social distinctions were upset, and according to the remaining representatives of the old aristocracy, misery prevailed throughout the land.

This state of affairs is reflected in the little literature that has survived from the period. The entire tone is that of a resigned pessimism, sometimes tinged with morbidity, as in *The Dispute of a Man with His Soul,* in which the author debates the eternal question of "To be or not to be." In *The Admonitions of Ipuwer,* human despair at divine injustice is goaded even to the extremity of a quarrel with the cosmic "establishment." A note of hope for the future is sounded in *The Prophecy of Nefer-Rohu.* This text probably dates from the beginning of the Middle Kingdom, when security and order had once more been established, but it indicates a vivid recollection of the chaos, injustice, and general misery that had prevailed in the previous period.

The Dispute of a Man With His Soul

... Then I opened my mouth to my soul,[1] that I might answer what it had said: "This is too much for me now, that my soul does not speak with me. My soul goes forth; let it stand and wait for me!

"Behold, my soul disobeys me because I did not hearken to it, and drag myself to death ere I have come to it, to cast myself upon the fire in order to consume myself. Rather, let it be near to me on this day of misfortune, and wait on the other side!

"My soul is foolish to hold back one wretched over life and delay me from death before I have come to it. Rather, make the West pleasant for me! Is it something bad? The period of life is limited in any case: even the trees must fall! Thoth, who contents the gods, he will judge me! Khonsu, the Scribe in Truth, he will defend me! Ra, who guides the Solar Bark, he will hear my words! My distress is heavy, and he bears it for me!"

And this is what my soul said to me: "And are you not a plain man? Yet you are as concerned as if you were a possessor of wealth!"[2]

I said: "If my soul will hearken to me, and its heart agrees with me, it will be happy. I will cause it to reach the West, like one who is in his pyramid, and at whose burial there has stood a survivor. I shall drink from the river whose water is drawn, and look down on the souls that are unsatisfied!"[3]

Then my soul opened its mouth to me, to answer what I had said: "If you are calling burial to mind, that is a distress of the heart; it is a bringing of tears, it is making a man sorrowful. It is haling a man from his house and throwing him upon the hill.[4] Never shall you go up above to behold the sun. They who built in granite and fashioned pyramids—fine things of good work—when the builders

[1] The beginning of the text is lost. Apparently the soul has delivered what it considers a final argument and has turned away in refusal to continue further, as if to say: "Go ahead and commit suicide if you want to, but don't expect me to stick by you."

[2] Meaning, "and therefore in a hurry to take it with you to the Other World, where you would always have it." In these parlous times, a wealthy man can well lose his wealth if he keeps on living, but if he should die while still ahead of the game, he could secure it for all eternity by means of the magic spells and rituals performed during the funerary rites.

[3] Probably because they have been wicked.

[4] The tombs were situated on the hills at the edge of the desert.

have become gods,[5] their offering tables are as empty as those of
the wretches who die on the riverbank—part of their bodies held by
the water and part by the heat of the sun, and the fish of the bank
hold converse with them! Listen, then, to me; lo, it is good to listen
to people! Follow the happy day and forget care!

"Take the case of a poor man who plows his field and then loads
his harvest on to a boat, and hurries to tow the boat since his feast
day approaches. He sees a flood coming on in the night, and keeps
vigil when Ra goes down. He comes forth with his wife, but his children perish upon the water, dangerous with crocodiles in the night.
At last he sits down, when he can regain his voice, and says: 'I do
not weep for that girl; there is no coming forth into the West for
her. I am troubled for her children that are broken in the egg, that
behold the face of the crocodile-god before they had lived.' "[6]

Then I opened my mouth to my soul, that I might answer what
it had said:

"Behold, you make my name reek,
    lo, more than the stench of carrion
    on days in summer, when the sky is hot.

"Behold, you make my name reek
    lo, more than a fisherman
    on the day of the catch, when the sky is hot.

"Behold, you make my name reek
    lo, more than the stench of bird droppings,
    more than the hill of willows with the geese.

"Behold, you make my name reek
    lo, more than the odor of fishermen,
    more than the shores of the swamps when they have fished.

"Behold, you make my name reek
    lo, more than the stench of crocodiles,
    more than sitting among crocodiles.

[5] Namely, when they were dead.
[6] That girl can never have eternal life, as she could never be mummified, and so on,
having been devoured by the crocodiles. The grief is rather for her unborn children.

202

"Behold, you make my name reek
  lo, more than that of a woman
  when lies are told about her to her man.

"Behold, you make my name reek
  lo, more than that of a lusty boy
  against whom it is said, 'He belongs to his hated one!'[7]

"Behold, you make my name reek
  lo, more than a treacherous city,
  more than a traitor who turns his back.[8]

"To whom shall I speak today?
  One's fellows are evil;
  the friends of today do not love.

"To whom shall I speak today?
  Men are rapacious;
  every one seizes his neighbor's goods.

"To whom shall I speak today?
  Gentleness has perished;
  insolence has access to all men.

"To whom shall I speak today?
  The evil have a contented countenance;
  good is rejected in every place.

"To whom shall I speak today?
  He who by his evil deeds should arouse wrath
  moves all men to laughter, though his iniquity is grievous.[9]

"To whom shall I speak today?
  Men rob;
  Every man seizes his neighbor's goods.

---

[7] Meaning that he is really a bastard, hating his real father as the cause of his illegitimacy.

[8] Possibly a topical allusion here.

[9] That is, they chuckle at his cleverness in getting away with it, instead of being wrathful with him.

"To whom shall I speak today?
  The foul man is trusted,
  but one who was a brother to him has become an enemy.

"To whom shall I speak today?
  No one remembers yesterday;
  no one now requites good to him who has done it.

"To whom shall I speak today?
  Brothers are evil;
  a man is treated as an enemy for his uprightness.

"To whom shall I speak today?
  Faces are not seen;
  every man's face is downcast toward his brethren.[10]

"To whom shall I speak today?
  Hearts are greedy;
  the man on whom men rely has no heart.

"To whom shall I speak today?
  There are no righteous onces;
  the land is given over to the doers of evil.

"To whom shall I speak today?
  There is lack of a trusty friend;
  one must go to an unknown in order to complain.

"To whom shall I speak today?
  There is none that is peaceable;
  the one with whom one went no longer exists.[11]

"To whom shall I speak today?
  I am laden with misery,
  and lack a trusted friend.

"To whom shall I speak today?
  The evil which treads the earth,
  it has no end.

[10] That is, no man can look his fellow in the eye.
[11] Good and trusty friends are all dead.

204

"Death is in my sight today
   as when a sick man becomes whole,
   as when one goes out after an illness.

"Death is in my sight today
   as the odor of myrrh,
   as when sitting under sail on a breezy day.

"Death is in my sight today
   as the odor of lotus flowers,
   as when sitting on the riverbank getting drunk.[12]

"Death is in my sight today
   as a well-trodden path,
   as when a man returns home to his house from war.

"Death is in my sight today
   as a clearing of the sky,
   as a man discerning what he knew not.

"Death is in my sight today
   as when a man longs to see his home again
   after he has spent many years in captivity.

"Nay, but he who is Yonder[13]
   will be as a living god,
   inflicting punishment for evil upon him who does it.

"Nay, but he who is Yonder
   will stand in the bark of the Sun-god
   and will assign the choicest things therein to the temples.

"Nay, but he who is Yonder
   will be a man of knowledge,
   not hindered from petitioning Ra when he speaks."

This is what my soul said to me: "Set aside lamentation, you who

---

[12] Getting drunk was regarded as one of the greatest pleasures by the Egyptians, and they were quite frank about it.
[13] In the Other World, where he becomes Osiris.

are mine, my brother! Although offered up on the brazier,[14] still you shall cling to life, as you say. Whether I remain here if you reject the West, or whether you reach the West and your body is joined with the earth, I will alight after you go to rest. Then we shall make an abode together!"

The Admonitions of Ipuwer

I

Ah, but the face is pale, the bowman is ready. The plowman goes to plow with his shield. The wrongdoer is everywhere. There is no man of yesterday![15]

Ah, but the Nile is in flood, yet no one plows. Doorkeepers say: "Let us go and plunder!"

Ah, but the washerman refuses to carry his load. Birdcatchers have made themselves ready for battle. A man looks upon his son as an enemy!

Ah, but the virtuous man goes in mourning because of what has happened in the land. Foreigners have become people[16] everywhere. Every man says: "We know not what has happened throughout the land!"

Ah, but women are barren, and there is no conception. Khnum[17] fashions men no more because of the condition of the land!

Ah, but paupers now possess fine things. He who once made for himself no sandals now possesses riches!

Ah, but the heart is violent. Plague stalks through the land, and blood is everywhere!

Ah, but many dead men are buried in the river. The stream is a sepulcher, and the Pure Place[18] is become a stream!

[14] Since he is going to burn himself up, he will be as a burnt-offering.
[15] A man like those of former times, when all was well.
[16] The word meaning "men, people" was applied only to Egyptians. Foreigners were not considered to be people. The same notion is found among many other cultures. For example, among the ancient Greeks, non-Greeks were called *barbaroi*, "babblers," since they did not speak the language "people" speak, namely, Greek.
[17] A creator-god, believed to have fashioned mankind on his potter's wheel.
[18] The place of embalming. The corpses have become too numerous and are thrown into the river.

Ah, but the highborn are full of lamentations, and the paupers are full of joy. Every town says: "Let us drive out the powerful from our midst!"

Ah, but men look like *gem*-birds.[19] Squalor is throughout the land. There is none whose clothes are white in these times!

Ah, but the land turns round as does a potter's wheel. The robber possesses riches!

Ah, but the river is blood. If a man drinks thereof, he rejects it as human and thirsts for water!

Ah, but the crocodiles are glutted with what they have carried off. Men go to them of their own accord![20]

Ah, but men are few. He that lays his brother in the ground is everywhere to be seen![21]

Ah, but the son of the highborn is no longer to be recognized. The child of his lady is become the son of his handmaid![22]

Ah, but the Red Land[23] is spread abroad throughout the country. The nomes are destroyed. The foreigners from without are come into Egypt. There are no people anywhere!

Ah, but gold and lapis lazuli, silver and turquoise, carnelian and bronze are hung about the necks of slave girls. But noble ladies wander through the land, and mistresses of houses say: "Would that we had something to eat!"

Ah, but laughter has perished and is no longer made. It is grief that walks through the land, mingled with lamentations!

Ah, but great and small say: "I wish I were dead!" Little children say: "He ought never to have caused me to live!"

Ah, but they who were in the Pure Place, they are cast forth upon the high ground. The secret of the embalmers lies open![24]

Ah, but that has perished which was still seen yesterday. The land is left to its weariness, as when one has pulled up the flax![25]

[19] A kind of heron, which may have had a dirty appearance.
[20] They commit suicide by jumping into the river.
[21] Gravediggers are everywhere.
[22] There is no longer a distinction between his chief wife's child and that of his slave girl.
[23] The desert, and by extension, foreign lands in general.
[24] Tombs are broken open and robbed, the mummies of the nobles being thrown out on the ground after the robbers have finished with them.
[25] No stubble is left on the flax field.

207

Ah, but the entire Delta is no longer hidden. The confidence of the North Land is now a trodden road.[26] What is one to do? The inaccessible place belongs now to them who knew it not as to them who know it, and strangers are versed in the crafts of the Delta!

Ah, but the magistrates are hungry and suffer need. The irascible man says: "If I knew where the god is, I would make offering to him!"[27]

Ah, but all cattle, their hearts weep. The herds lament because of the state of the land!

Ah, but the children of princes, men dash them against the walls. The children that have been fervently desired, they are laid upon the high ground. Khnum complains because of his weariness!

Ah, but insolence has come to all men throughout the land. A man slays his brother by the same mother!

Ah, but the roads are ambushed and the streets are watched. Men sit in the bushes until the benighted traveler comes, in order to take his load from him. What is upon him is stolen. He gets blows of the stick to smell, and is slain wrongfully!

Ah, but that has perished which was still seen yesterday, and the land is left over to its weariness. Would that there might be an end to men, no conception, no birth! O that the earth would cease from noise and strife be no more!

Ah, but grain has perished everywhere. People are stripped of clothing, perfume, and oil. Everyone says: "There is no more!" The storehouse is bare, and he that kept it lies stretched out on the ground. Would that I had lifted up my voice at that moment, that it might have saved me from the pain in which I am![28]

Ah, but the splendid judgment hall, its writings are taken away; its secret place is laid bare!

Ah, but magic spells are divulged and are now ineffectual, for the people have them in mind![29]

---

[26] The natural boundaries of Egypt have no longer sufficed to keep out foreigners.
[27] The bitter cynicism of one angered by divine failure.
[28] Perhaps if he had come forward to admonish the king when it all began, it might not have come to this.
[29] The profane have had access to the highly "classified" government archives and divulged their contents. The powerful magic spells were valuable government secrets.

Ah, but the public offices are opened, and their lists are taken away. Serfs become lords of serfs. Woe is me because of the misery in such a time!

Ah, but the scribes of the grain sacks, their writings are destroyed. That whereon Egypt lives is a "When I come, it's brought me!"[30]

Ah, but the laws of the judgment hall are placed in the vestibule. Yea, men walk upon them in the streets, and the rabble tear them up in alleys!

Ah, but they who builded tombs have become field laborers, and they who were in the god's bark are yoked together.[31] Priests are buried with their produce, and princes are embalmed with their resin, as far as the land of Keftiu,[32] and now they come no more!

Ah, but Elephantine and the Thinite nome and Upper Egypt, they pay taxes no more by reason of the unrest.[33] To what purpose is a treasury without its revenues? But glad is the heart of the king when the truth comes to him! What can we do about it? All goes to ruin!

Ah, but the rabble have attained to the condition of the Divine Ennead! That procedure of the House of the Thirty is divulged![34]

Ah, but the great judgment hall is a "go out, that he may come in."[35] The rabble go and come in the Great Houses!

Ah, but the children of magistrates are thrown on to the streets. He that has knowledge says: "Yea." The fool says: "Nay." He that has no knowledge, to him it seems good![36]

---

[30] The records of grain distribution in the government granaries are destroyed, and the stores are "come-and-get-it."

[31] Only the nobility could build tombs. The inhabitant of the tomb represented himself as sailing with Ra-Atum-Khepri in his Solar Bark. These nobles are now yoked together in the field gang.

[32] Keftiu is Crete (the Caphtor of the Old Testament). Egypt apparently had spheres of influence in Crete at this early period, and the princes and priests stationed there would return to Egypt to be buried in their tombs.

[33] The southernmost provinces take advantage of the confusion.

[34] The rabble now have the privileges of the gods. The Ennead was the group of nine principal gods of Egypt. There was a larger group of thirty gods called the Great Ennead.

[35] There is such a mob there that one can get in only when someone else leaves.

[36] Evidently referring to the weak and inept king, who denies that these things are so. Ipuwer quite boldly calls attention to the king's blind and foolish optimism.

II

Behold, the fire mounts up on high! Its burning goes forth against the enemies of the land!

Behold, a thing has been done which happened not aforetime; it has come to this that the king has been taken away by the rabble![37]

Behold, he that was buried as a falcon[38] lies only on a bier. What the pyramid hid will become empty!

Behold, it has come to this, that the land is despoiled of kingship by a few foolish men!

Behold, it is come to this, that men display enmity against the uraeus-serpent,[39] the defender of Ra, which caused the Two Lands to be in peace!

Behold, the secret of the land, whose limits were unknown, is divulged. The Residence is overturned in an hour.

Behold, this has happened among men: he that could not build himself a chamber now possesses a walled enclosure!

Behold, ladies lie on mats, and magistrates in the storehouse. He that could not sleep on a board now possesses a bed!

Behold, the rich man sleeps thirsty. He that once begged him for his dregs now has beer that bowls one over!

Behold, he who had no knowledge of harp playing now possesses a harp. He to whom one never sang now praises the goddess of music!

Behold, he who had nothing now possesses wealth. The noble man praises him!

Behold, the poor of the land have now become rich. He who possessed something is now one who has nothing!

Behold, he who had no bread now owns a barn. That wherewith his storehouse is provided is the property of another!

Behold, the bald head that used no oil now owns jars of pleasant myrrh!

---

[37] The king is wholly under the influence of his unscrupulous upstart advisers. As is evident from the next verses, this has led even to the spoliation of the royal tombs.
[38] The king was identified with the god Horus, who was represented as a falcon.
[39] The cobra-goddess head on the king's diadem, considered to defend Egypt from its enemies.

Behold, she who had no box now possesses a coffer. She who looked at her face in the water now owns a mirror!

Behold, he who slept unwed now finds women galore!

Behold, a man is happy when he just eats his food: "Spend your possessions in joy and without holding yourself back! It is good for a man to eat his food, which the god whom he praises assigns to him!"[40]

Behold, he who knew nothing of his god now makes offering to him with the incense of another!

Behold, noble and great ladies, who possessed goodly things, their children are given to the beds![41]

Behold, no office is any longer in its right place: they are as a frightened herd without herdsmen!

Behold, the cattle rove about and there is none who cares for them. Each man fetches for himself thereform and brands it with his name!

Behold, a man is slain beside his brother. He leaves him in the lurch in order to rescue himself!

Behold, he who had no yoke of oxen now owns barns. He who fetched for himself corn-doles now himself causes them to be dispensed!

Behold, he who had no slaves now owns serfs. He who was a notable now himself executes behests!

Behold, no craftsman works. The enemy despoils the land of its crafts!

Behold, the mighty ones of the land, no one reports to them the condition of the people. All goes to ruin!

III

Remember how fumigation is made with incense, and water offered from an ewer in the early morning![42]

---

[40] One might as well "go hell-for-broke."

[41] Possibly meaning that they are prostituted.

[42] In these verses, beginning "Remember," Ipuwer may be either recalling to the king the traditional temple observances of the past, or what is more likely, reminding him that there exists a little group of devoted priests (probably including himself) who are faithfully observing the ancient precepts, so that all is not necessarily lost if the king will but rouse himself to right action.

Remember how fat geese are brought, and geese and duck and the divine offering made to the gods!

Remember how natron is chewed, and white bread prepared on the day the head is moistened![43]

Remember how flagstaffs are erected[44] and offering-slabs carved, how the priest purifies the temples and the house of the god is whitened like milk, how the Horizon[45] is perfumed and the offering-bread perpetuated!

Remember how the ritual regulations are observed, and the sacred days adjusted, and how bad priests are removed!

IV

It is said: He[46] is the herdsman of all men. No evil is in his heart. Though his herd is diminished, yet he has spent the day in order to tend them. Ah, that he had perceived their nature in the first generation! Then he would have smitten down evil; he would have stretched forth the arm against it, and destroyed the seed thereof and their inheritance! . . . But men always desire to produce offspring, and seed issues from the women, although oppression is on every side. There is no pilot in their time! Where is he today? Does he sleep, then? Behold, his might is not seen. When we were thrown into mourning, I found you not!

True command, intelligent perception, and true justice are with you, but it is confusion which you set throughout the land, together with the noise of men who contend. If three men journey upon a road, they are found to be two men; the greater number slays the lesser. Is there a herdsman who loves death?

But you will command that a reply be made! Lies are told you, the land is tinder, mankind is destroyed, and all these years are confusion. A man is slain even on his roof, when he is on the watch in the

---

[43] The priests cleansed their mouths with natron water and washed their heads as purificatory rites.

[44] Before the pylons of the temples.

[45] The temple.

[46] Referring to the king. As a divinity, he has the real interests of the people at heart, but he has been ill-advised. If only he had foreseen the evil, he would have destroyed it. But he wanders, and his flocks seek him in vain.

boundary house. Only if he be strong and save himself does he remain alive. If one walk on the road, what is upon him is stolen. He gets blows of the stick to smell and is slain wrongfully.

Would that you might taste some of these miseries yourself! Then would you say. . . .[47]

V

It is good, however, when ships sail upstream![48]

It is good, however, when the net is drawn in and the birds are made fast!

It is good, however, when the hands of men build pyramids and dig canals and make groves of trees for the gods!

It is good, however, when men are drunken,[49] and when they drink *miyet* and are glad of heart!

It is good, however, when rejoicing is in men's mouths, and the nobles of the district stand and look on at the jubilation in their houses, clad in fine raiment!

It is good, however, when beds are stuffed and the headrests of the nobles are protected with amulets, and every man's wish is satisfied with a bed in the shade, behind a closed door, and he need not sleep in the bushes!

VI

This is what Ipuwer said when he answered the majesty of the Lord of All: "To be ignorant of it is something that is pleasant to the heart. You have done what is good in their hearts, you have kept alive the people among them, but they still cover their faces for fear of the morrow.[50]

"There[51] was once a man who was old and stood in the presence

[47] A rather bold thing to say to the king, but perhaps even Ipuwer is permitting himself a little of the general *lèse-majesté* to a good purpose. Unfortunately, the rest of this section is fragmentary.
[48] This section is evidently a wish-fulfilling vision of the happy future.
[49] See note 12.
[50] To be sure, it is pleasant to close your eyes to all that is going on and please your favorites. But even they are fearful of the morrow!
[51] Ipuwer here begins to relate to the king either an illustrative parable or an actual injustice which the king committed.

213

of death, and his son was still a child and without understanding . . .
and opened not yet his mouth to speak unto you. You took him away
through a deathly doom. . . ."

[The remaining two columns of the papyrus are quite fragmentary.]

The Prophecy of Nefer-Rohu

Now it happened when the Majesty of King Seneferu, True of
Voice,[52] was beneficent king in this whole land—on one of these days
it came to pass that the officials of the Residence[53] entered into the
Great House[54] (life, prosperity, health!)[55] to offer greeting to the king,[56]
and they came forth again that they might offer further greeting, as
was their daily observance. Then said His Majesty to the treasurer
who was at his side: "Go and bring to me the officials of the Residence
who have gone forth hence today in order to offer greeting."

They were led in unto him forthwith and lay on their bellies in the
presence of His Majesty a second time. And His Majesty said unto
them: "My friends, I have caused you to be summoned, in order that
you may seek out for me a son of yours who has understanding, or a
brother of yours who excels, or a friend of yours who has performed
some noble act, one who will speak to me some fine words, choice
speeches, in hearing which My Majesty may find diversion."

They said before His Majesty: "There is a chief lector-priest[57] of

---

[52] A phrase regularly following the name of a deceased person, referring to his justification before Osiris in the Other World.

[53] The residence-city of the king.

[54] The palace of the king. In Egyptian it is *Per-aa,* the origin of the word "Pharaoh"
in the Old Testament. In the Eighteenth Dynasty, the term was used to refer to the
king himself, as we sometimes use "the White House" in referring to the President.

[55] A stock phrase repeated after every mention of the name of the king, "His
Majesty," the palace and/or its portals, and so forth, and meaning "may he live,
prosper, and be healthy." In this, as in many other texts, this is repeated in the above
context throughout, but we are giving it here at the first instance only.

[56] The daily reports of the high officials to the king and his aides.

[57] Literally, "he who bears the ritual-scroll." The members of this grade were among
the most learned of the priests, thoroughly familiar with the sacred writings and magic
spells, and directed the religious ceremonials.

Bastet,[58] O Sovereign our Lord, named Nefer-Rohu; he is a commoner,[59] valiant of arm, and a scribe excellent of his fingers; he is a lordly person, who is richer than any of his equals. Oh that he might see Your Majesty!"

Then said His Majesty: "Go and bring him to me!" And he was led in unto him forthwith, and he laid himself on his belly in the presence of His Majesty. Then said His Majesty: "Come now, Nefer-Rohu, my friend, and speak to me some fine words, choice speeches, in hearing which My Majesty may find diversion!"

And the lector-priest Nefer-Rohu said: "Shall it be of that which has happened, or of that which is going to happen, O Sovereign my Lord?" Said His Majesty: "Nay, of that which is going to happen. If anything has happened even today, pass it by!"

Then he[60] stretched out his hand to the box of writing materials, and took him a scroll and a pen-and-ink case, and then he put it in writing.

What was spoken by the lector-priest Nefer-Rohu, the wise man of the East, he who belongs to Bastet at her appearances, the child of the nome of Heliopolis, while he brooded over that which would come to pass in the land, and thought of the condition of the East, when the Asiatics would come in their might, and would afflict the hearts of the harvesters, and take away their yokes of cattle when plowing.

He said: "Rise, O my heart, and bewail this land whence you are sprung! Rest not; behold, it lies before your face: rise up against that which is before you! The great ones are in the same condition as the land. That which has been made is as if it never had been made, and Ra must begin to found the land anew. The whole land

---

[58] Bast, or Bastet, was the cat-goddess who embodied the charming and sensual attributes of the feline (in contrast to Sekhmet, the lion-goddess of war and destruction), whose home was Bubastis (*Per-Bastet*, "the house of Bastet") in the eastern Delta.

[59] The Egyptian word denotes anyone not a member of the nobility, not necessarily a peasant. Any commoner could, potentially, attain to the highest honors (like Winston Churchill in our time). See The "Schoolboy" Texts.

[60] The commentators take this to refer to the king, as taking down Nefer-Rohu's prophecy. We know that the king and the nobility in general were quite literate, having received a good scribe's education in the temple schools.

215

has perished, there is nothing left; not even the black of the nail survives of what should be there![61]

"The land is ruined; no one concerns himself about it any more— no one speaks, and no eye weeps. How fares this land? The sun is veiled, and will not shine that men may see. None can live when the storm veils it; all men are dulled through want of it.

"I will speak of what is before me; I do not foretell what has not come![62]

"The river of Egypt is empty, and men cross over the water on foot. Men shall search for water upon which the boats may sail; its road has become a bank, and the bank has become water.[63] The south wind will oppose the north wind; the sky will no longer be of a single wind!

"A foreign bird will be born in the marshes of the Delta,[64] having made its nest at the side of people.[65] And people will allow it to approach, in their distress!

"Indeed those good things are ruined, the fish ponds which were resplendent with catches of fish and wild fowl. All good things have passed away, and the land is laid low by reason of that food of the Asiatics who traverse the land![66]

"Foes are in the East; Asiatics have come down down into Egypt, and there is no helper who hears! One will be attacked by night, and men shall force their way into houses. Sleep shall be banished from mine eyes, and I will lie there and say: 'I am awake!'

"The wild beasts of the desert shall drink from the rivers of Egypt, that they may cool themselves upon their banks, for there is none to

---

[61] Not even a tiny amount.

[62] "I can only tell what is before me in my vision." Note that most of the prophecy is in the vivid present tense.

[63] Things are topsy-turvy.

[64] Evidently referring to the infiltrators from Syria who had established themselves in the Delta region, among the dwellers in Lower Egypt.

[65] The only "people" are Egyptians. See note 16. In their confusion and misery, the Egyptians will allow these foreigners to become entrenched in the land.

[66] Meaning either that the Asiatics are a bitter food which Egypt must taste, or rather, in view of the context, that the foreign hordes will seize the fish and fowl for themselves.

scare them away! The land is seized and taken, and none knows
what the issue will be—it is hidden, and one cannot say, see, or hear it!

"I show you the land in lamentation and distress. That which never
happened before has happened. Men shall take up weapons of war,
that the land may live on uproar. Men shall fashion arrows of bronze,[67]
that they may ask bread for blood. Men will laugh with the laughter
of sickness.[68] Men will not weep because of death, men will not sleep
hungry because of death;[69] a man's heart shall follow after himself
alone!

"Men do not make mourning today, for the heart is entirely averted
from it. One remains seated in his corner, thinking of himself alone
while one slays another! I show you the son as an enemy and the
brother as adversary, and a man murdering his own father!

"Every mouth is full of 'Love me!'[70] and all good things have
departed. The land is destroyed; that which was made is as though it
had not been made. Men take the goods of a goodly man and give
them to one from without. I show you the possessor in deprivation,
and the outsider contented. He whose granary was filled for him is
now denuded.

"And hatred reigns among the townsmen; the mouth that speaks
is brought to silence.[71] If a speech is answered, the hand reaches out
with a stick, and people have to say 'Don't kill him!' A thing spoken
is as fire from the heart, and what a mouth utters is not endured!

"The land is diminished, but its governors are multiplied. The field
is bare, but the taxes are great. Little is the corn but great is the tax
measure, and it is measured to overflowing![72]

[67] It has been shown that metal arrowheads were first used in Egypt in the Eleventh
Dynasty (about 2100 B.C.).
[68] Of hysteria or delirium.
[69] Death will be such a common occurrence, and so little notice will be taken of it,
that even the mourning customs will not be observed. Everyone will be preoccupied
with his own preservation.
[70] Erman asks whether this might have been the regular cry of the beggar; hence the
sense would be that only beggars are left in the land, in agreement with the second
part of the verse.
[71] If anyone protests the harshness of the new masters, he is cruelly beaten, as in the
next verse.
[72] The taxcollector's grain measure, probably larger than it should be.

"The sun separates himself from men; he rises but for an hour! None will know that it is midday since his shadow will not be distinguished.[73] No face will be bright that beholds him, and the eyes will not be moistened with water. He will be in the sky as the moon, although he deviates not from his former course, and his rays are in men's faces after his former wise![74]

"I show you the land in lamentation and distress. He who was weak of arm now has a strong one. Men salute him who formerly saluted others. I show you the undermost turned to the uppermost. Men live in the cemeteries. Paupers will acquire riches, and nothings eat the offering-bread. The nome of Heliopolis will no longer be the land of birthplace of every god![75]

"Then, indeed, shall a king come from the South—Ameni, True of Voice, is his name.[76] He is the son of a woman of Nubia,[77] and born in Upper Egypt. He shall receive the White Crown, and wear the Red Crown.[78] He shall unite the Two Powerful Ones;[79] he shall delight the Two Lords[80] with what they love. That which encircles the fields shall be in his grasp, and the oar in his hand![81]

"Rejoice, O people of his time! The son of a man of degree will make himself a name for all eternity. They who are disposed toward evil and devise hostility, they have subdued their mouthings for fear

---

[73] The gloom will not permit the shadow of the gnomon to fall on the sundial.

[74] Meaning probably that the sun's withdrawal and the consequent gloom are illusions resulting from the general hysteria and despair.

[75] The final, culminating catastrophe. The most ancient sanctum of Egypt, Heliopolis, the scene of the first appearance of Ra, from whom all the great gods of Egypt issued, will be as nothing. The fortunes of Egypt have fallen to their lowest possible depths. Now is the time for the savior-king to appear.

[76] *Ameni* is a shortened form of *Amen-em-hat* ("Amen to the fore"). The "true of voice" epithet, applied only to the names of the deceased, was obviously inserted by the Eighteenth Dynasty copyist.

[77] We have no knowledge of the origins of Amen-em-hat's mother.

[78] The tall white crown of Upper Egypt and the low red crown of Lower Egypt.

[79] The respective goddesses of the two crowns.

[80] Horus and Set, as the two tutelary divinities of the two lands of Egypt.

[81] Probably alluding to one of the coronation ceremonies, during which the king ran around the sacred enclosure holding an oar in one hand and what seems to be some cult object in the other.

of him! The Asiatics shall fall before his slaughter, and the Libyans[82] shall fall before his flame. His enemies will succumb before his wrath, and the rebels to his might. The uraeus-serpent that is on his brow, it quells for him the traitors!

"There shall be built the Wall of the Ruler,[83] and the Asiatics shall not again be suffered to go down into Egypt. They shall again beg for water as they used to do, that they may be able to give to their cattle to drink.

"And Justice shall come again to its place, and Iniquity will have been cast forth. He will rejoice who shall behold this, and who shall be in the service of the king!

"A man of learning shall pour out water for me, when he sees that what I have spoken is fulfilled!"[84]

---

[82] The Egyptians had constant trouble from the Libyans, even from Old Kingdom times.

[83] A series of fortifications along the northwestern frontier at the gateway to Syria, built by Amen-em-hat. It is mentioned in *The Story of Sinuhe*.

[84] Another learned scribe will pour out libations of water at my tomb, in honor of a deceased colleague.

219

19   The Goodness of Life:
Lyric Poetry and Song

One frequently finds that in moods of pessimism and despair there is an undercurrent of hedonism. Whether this tendency to hedonism is man's natural, unconscious, built-in antidote to suicidal desperation, or a consciously pragmatic rationale of handling the existential dilemma is hard to say. We find, however, as far back as ancient Egypt, and reflected also in the Biblical book of Ecclesiastes, the pragmatic view that since life and the world are "absurd" (to use a contemporary term) in that they are full of misery, pain, and ultimate injustice, the only sensible thing to do is to enjoy whatever good things life has to offer while we are here, and to abandon ourselves to whatever pleasures of the moment we can glean from an existence in a callously indifferent universe.

This hedonistic pragmatism in the face of the "irrational" injustice of the world and of fate is expressed in several texts inscribed on the walls of the tombs of the Egyptian nobles, most of them dating from the New Kingdom. They are represented as being sung by the harpers who accompany the dancing girls at the sumptuous banquets which the deceased is enjoying in the World of Eternity, and for this reason they are referred to as "Songs of the Harper" or "Banquet Songs." The cynicism of these songs may have originated during the chaos and upheaval of the First Intermediate period, but their main burden is an ultimate triumph, a wonderful expression of the optimism and love of sheer living felt by the ancient Egyptians.

Another expression of the triumph of life and its joys we find in the collections of delightful love lyrics which have survived. In the lushness and vivid color of their oriental imagery, in their graphic similes (sometimes startling to us), and above all in the intensity of their passion, they immediately call to mind The Song of Songs of the Bible, which is also a collection of passionate songs of love which generations of bleakly pious commentators have attempted to sublimate into stultifying allegory and have failed dismally. Both the Biblical collection and the Egyptian love lyrics are part of the same ancient tradition of erotic verse which we find in the cultures of the Fertile Crescent, and the thread of which we may trace all the way through *The Thousand and One Nights* and beyond. As in the Biblical love songs, the youth will speak in one poem and the girl in another, addressing either the beloved or their own "hearts." Similarly, the lovers call each other "brother" and "sister."

By way of contrast, and to indicate the pragmatic optimism and acceptance of whatever good things life may afford, which seem to have pervaded the life-view of even the most humble classes in ancient Egypt, we have included a few of the songs sung by peasants and serfs in the fields, herdsmen and palanquin bearers. These songs are inscribed over the representations of these scenes in the tombs of the noblemen and were in all probability actual rhythmic chants in common use.

The Songs of the Harper

I

Well is it with this good prince,
   Though goodly destiny may suffer hurt.[1]
Bodies pass away and others remain

---

[1] Meaning that reversal of fortune cannot really harm him, since he views human life as transitory and so gets the most out of existence while upon this earth.

221

Since the time of them who were before.[2]
The gods[3] who were aforetime rest in their pyramids,
  and likewise the noble and glorified,
    buried in their pyramids.
They that build houses,
  their habitations are no more.
    What has been done with them?

I have heard the discourses of Imhotep and Herdedef,[4]
  with whose words men speak everywhere.
    What are their habitations now?
Their walls are destroyed,
  their habitations are no more,
    as if they had never been!

None comes from thence
  that he may tell us how they fare,
    that he may tell us what they need,
      that he may set our heart at rest,
        until we also go to the place whither they are gone!

Be glad,
  that you may cause your heart to forget
    that men will one day beatify you.[5]
Follow your desire
  so long as you shall live.

---

[2] Generations come and go, as is also the refrain of the Book of Ecclesiastes.
[3] The ancient kings.
[4] Famous and brilliant men of Old Kingdom times. Imhotep was the vizier of King Zoser, founder of the Third Dynasty. He was the Leonardo da Vinci of his time. He was an architect and engineer, having designed and built Zoser's Step Pyramid and its complex, reputedly a great physician, and the author of a collection of wise sayings as well as an excellent administrator. He was so greatly regarded as an outstanding genius that he was later deified (the only mortal to whom this honor was accorded in ancient Egypt, the king being a god by birth) and considered to be a son of Ptah, the craftsman and creator god. Herdedef was a son of King Cheops (see "King Cheops and the Magicians").
[5] An essential ritual of the funerary ceremonials was the "beatification," in which the deceased was rendered a glorified immortal.

Put myrrh on your head,
  clothe yourself in fine linen,
    and anoint yourself with the genuine marvels
      of the things of the god!

Increase yet more the delights which you have,
  and let not your your heart grow faint;
    follow your desire and do good to yourself!
Do what you require upon earth,
  and vex not your heart
    until that day of lamentation[6] comes upon you.
Yet He with the Quiet Heart[7] hears not their lamentation,
  and cries deliver no man from the Other World!

REFRAIN: Spend the day happily and weary not thereof!
            Lo, none can take his goods with him!
              Lo, none who has departed can come again!

II

How quiet is this righteous prince!
  The goodly destiny has come to pass.[8]
Bodies pass away since the time of the god,[9]
  and a generation comes in their place.
Ra shines forth in the morning,
  and Atum[10] goes down in Manun.[11]
Men beget, women conceive,
  and every nose breathes air.
Day dawns, and their children go one and all to their places![12]

---

[6] The day of your decease.
[7] Osiris, Lord of the Other World and the deceased therein. "Quiet" here is understood in the sense of "satisfied, content," as in the first line of the next song.
[8] He is now with Osiris in the Other World.
[9] A frequently encountered phrase in texts, meaning since primeval time, when the gods reigned upon earth.
[10] Atum, meaning "he who completes" is one of the aspects of Ra-Atum-Khepri, the primal god, as the setting sun.
[11] A mythical region in the West.
[12] The next day sees them already in their tombs.

Spend the day merrily, O priest!
  Put unguent and fine oil together to your nostrils,
    and garlands and lotus flowers
      on the body of your sister[13] whom you favor
        as she sits beside you!
Set singing and music before your face;
  cast all evil behind you,
    and bethink you of joy,
Until the day comes when one reaches port[14]
  in the land which loves silence.[15]

Spend the day merrily, Nefer-hotep,
  you excellent priest with clean hands!
I have heard what came to pass;
  their walls are destroyed,
    their places are no more,
      they are as if they had never been
        since the time of the god.
Be mindful of the day when you shall be taken;[16]
  there is none who has returned.

REFRAIN: Spend the day merrily!

III

All ye excellent nobles,
  and ye gods of the Mistress of Life,[17]
Hear ye how praises are rendered to this priest,
  and homage done to this excellent noble's lordly soul,
    now that he is a god living forever,
      magnified in the West.

---

[13] The regular term for the beloved in the love poetry of the ancient Near East, as exemplified in the Egyptian love lyrics (which see) and in the Song of Songs in the Bible.

[14] One of the several Egyptian euphemisms for the day of decease.

[15] The domains of Osiris. One of the appellations of Osiris was "Lord of Silence."

[16] That is, to the land of the dead.

[17] The Other World at the West, where there is eternal life, sometimes personified as a goddess.

So may they become a remembrance in after days,
   and for everyone who comes to this tomb.

I have heard these songs
   that are in the tombs of ancient time;
What they say when they extol the life upon earth
   and belittle the region of the dead.
To what purpose do they act thus toward the Land of Eternity,
   the just and the right, where no terrors are?
Wrangling is its abhorrence,
   and there is none who girds himself against his fellow.

This land that has no foe,
   all our kindred rest in it since the earliest day of time.
And they who shall be in millions of millions of years,
   they shall come hither every one!
There is none that may tarry in the land of Egypt;
   there is none that does not pass yonder.
The duration of that which is done upon earth
   is as a dream.
Soon "Welcome, safe and sound!" is said
   to him who has reached the West.

Love Lyrics

I

Is there anything sweeter than this hour?
   for I am with you, and you lift up my heart—
   for is there not embracing and fondling when you visit me
   and we give ourselves up to delights?
   If you wish to caress my thigh,
   then I will offer you my breast also—it won't thrust you away!

Would you leave because you are hungry?
      —are you such a man of your belly?
Would you leave because you need something to wear?
      —I have a chestful of fine linen!

225

Would you leave because you wish something to drink?
>   Here, take my breasts! They are full to overflowing, and
>   all for you!
Glorious is the day of our embracings;
I treasure it a hundred thousand millions!

II

Your love has gone all through my body
>   like honey in water,
>   as a drug is mixed into spices,
>   as water is mingled with wine.
Oh that you would speed to see your sister
>   like a charger on the battlefield, like a bull to his pasture!
For the heavens are sending us love like a flame spreading through
>   straw
>   and desire like the swoop of the falcon!

III

Troubled is the pool of my tranquillity—
>   For the mouth of my only sister is a lotus-bud;
>   Her breasts are perfumed incense, and her arms clasp tight!
>   Her forehead is a snare of willow, and I am a wild duck;
>   To my eyes her hair is the lure in the snare—and I am entrapped!

IV

Beginning of the beautiful songs of delight of your sister,
the beloved of your heart, as she comes from the fields:
>   O my brother, my beloved,
>   my heart follows your love;
>   Just think of anything, and I say, "See, it is done!"
>   I have just set my snares with my own hands.
>   All the birds of Punt[18] alight in Egypt, perfumed with myrrh.
The most beautiful will come first and snatch my bait;
>   his fragrance is of Punt, and his talons are filled with balsam.

---

[18] A land on the southern shores of the Red Sea, and a favorite source of spices, incense, perfumes, and gold and other good things.

226

My heart's wish for you is: let's set them free together,
   and I'll be alone with you! And I'll let you hear the
   shrill cry of my myrrh-anointed one!
How lovely it would be if you were there with me when I set
   the snare,
O beautiful one who comes to the meadows of his beloved!
The bird is caught by the worm and is crying plaintively,
   but the love of you restrains me and I can't set it free![19]

I might as well take away my nets.
What shall I say to my mother, to whom I come every evening,
   laden with captive birds?—
"I didn't set any traps today?"
It is I who am captured—by the love of you!
The wild goose soars, hovers, and plunges into the net;
Flocks of birds are circling round—
   but I am bemused, all alone with my love.
My heart yearns for your breast, and can never part from your beauty.
O my beautiful, my heart's desire is to care for you as mistress of
   your house,
   your arm resting in my arm, enfolding me with your love!
I will say to my inmost heart, "If my elder brother is away from
   me this night
   I am like one who is in the tomb."
For are you not health and life, you who return the joy of health
   to my heart which seeks you?

V

My god, my brother, my husband—
How sweet it is to go down to the lotus pond
   and do as you desire—
   to plunge into the waters, and bathe before you—
   to let you see my beauty in my tunic of sheerest royal linen,
   all wet and clinging and perfumed with balsam!

[19] According to the literal construction of the text here and of the lines following,
the girl is saying: "Like the bird, it is I who am caught, but the love of you restrains
me from freeing myself of it."

I go down into the water to be with you,
  and come up again to you with a red fish
  lying so fine and splendid within my fingers;[20]
  and I place it upon my breast—
  Oh, brother! look and see!

VI

I see my sister coming—
  My heart is in joy, and my arms are opened wide to embrace her;
  And my heart rejoices within me without ceasing—
    Come to me, O my mistress!
When I embrace her and her arms enlace me,
  it is as if I were in Punt,
  drenched in her fragrance!
When I kiss her with her lips opened,
  ah, then I am drunk without beer!
Hasten to prepare the bed, handmaiden!
Place the finest linen for her limbs,
  perfumed with precious unguents!
O would that I were her Negro slave girl who bathes her,
  then I would always see the color of all her limbs!
O would that I were the one who washes her linen,
  to rinse the perfumes which pervade her garments!
O would that I were the ring upon her finger,
  so that she would cherish me as something which adds beauty to
    her life!

VII

Beginning of the words of the great bringer of joy to the heart:
O unique one, sister-beloved without compare,
  more beautiful than all women!
Behold, she is like the star-goddess[21]

---

[20] The *double-entendre* is of course quite evident.
[21] The brilliant star Sirius, whose rising above the horizon together with the sun, about the middle of July, began the Egyptian New Year. The Egyptian name for the star, *Sepdet,* has the feminine ending (*t*) and the goddess determinative.

resplendent at the beginning of the happy year;
Luminous and perfect, of gleaming skin;
Lovely are her eyes when she glances,
Sweet are her lips when she speaks,
    and her words are never too many!
Her neck is long, and her nipple is radiant,
    and her hair is deep sapphire.
Her arms surpass the brilliance of gold,
    and her fingers are like lotus blossoms.
Her buttocks curve down languidly from her trim belly,
    and her thighs are her beauties.
Her bearing is regal as she walks upon the earth—
        she causes every male neck to turn and look at her.
Yes, she has captivated my heart in her embrace!
In joy indeed is he who embraces all of her—
    he is the very prince of lusty youths!
See how she goes forth—like that one and only Goddess![22]

VIII

My brother-beloved troubles my heart with his voice;
    he causes illness to lay hold of me.
He is a neighbor of my mother's house,
    but I cannot go to him.
It is good of my mother to forbid me to go to see him,
    for my heart is disturbed when I think of him.
Love of him has seized me captive.
            "But he's out of his mind!"
            "Yes, and so am I—as much so as he!"
Oh, he doesn't know how much I desire to embrace him—
        if he did, he would send to my mother for me!
O brother! I am decreed unto you by the Golden One of women![23]
Come to me, so that I may look upon your beauty!
My father and mother will rejoice,
            and everyone will make festival for you together!
They will make festival for you, O brother!

[22] Hathor, of course,
[23] Hathor is frequently called the Golden One.

IX

I passed by the vicinity of his house
  and I found the door open.
My brother was standing beside his mother,
  and all his brothers and sisters were with him.
Love of him captivates all who pass—
  such a splendid youth, without equal, a beloved of choice virtues!
He looked at me as I passed,
  and I was alone with my joy.
How my heart has exulted in jubilation, O brother,
  since we saw each other!
If only your mother had known my heart,
  she would have gone to her own quarters immediately!
O Golden Goddess! put this into her heart,
  and then I'll hasten to my brother;
  I'll kiss him before his companions;
  I'll not weep in shame at the presence of others,
    but will rejoice that they see that you know me.
I will make a festival to my Goddess!
My heart is fluttering to the point of springing forth,
  at the thought that I may see my brother in dreams this night;
How beautifully, then, would the night pass!

X

Seven days have I not seen my sister.
A sickness has crept into me,
  my limbs have become heavy, and my body does not know itself.
  Even should the master physicians come to me,
  my heart would not be soothed by their remedies.
As for the magician-priests, there is no resource in them;
  my illness cannot be diagnosed.
But to say to me, "Here she is!"—
  that will make me live again!
Her name is what will revive me;

the coming and going of her messengers is what will give life to
my heart.
She is better for me than the entire Collection![24]
For me her coming would be the Sound Eye of Horus![25]
When I see her, then I am well;
   when she opens her eyes, my limbs are young again;
   when she speaks, then I am strong;
   when I embrace her, she banishes evil from me.
But she is gone from me for seven days!

XI

Hurriedly scampers my heart
   when I recall my love of you—
It does not allow me to go about like other mortals—
It seems to have been uprooted from its place.
It doesn't even let me put on my tunic
   or even take my fan—
I am not able to paint my eyes
   or anoint myself with perfume.
"Don't linger thus! Get back to yourself!"
   I say when I think of him,
"Don't cause me silly pain, O my heart—
Why do you play the madman?
Just sit cool and he'll come to you,
   and everyone will see!
Let not people say of me,
   'There's a girl fallen hopelessly in love!'
Stand firm when you think of him, O my heart!
   don't bound about so!"

[24] The compendium, or "United Formulary" of the medical writings.
[25] Namely, "my health, my salvation." Horus's Eye, which had been torn out in his
epic struggle with Set, was made sound and restored to him by Thoth. Sacred amulets
in the form of the Eye of Horus, called the *wedjat*, "the Sound (Eye)" were worn for
good health and well being.

XII

I adore the Golden One,
  I exalt the Mistress of Heaven.
I give praise unto Hathor
  and glory to my Divine Lady!
For I implored her
  and she hearkened unto my prayer.
She commanded me unto my mistress,
  and she came of her own accord to see me.
How grand is that which has happened to me!
I exult, I rejoice, I'm the greatest!
From the moment when it was said, "Look! Here she is!"
For lo! she came, and all the hot youths fell headlong
  in their great love of her.
I made petition unto my Goddess
  and she has given me my sister as a gift!

Work Songs

Songs of the Peasants in the Fields

I

Thresh for yourselves, thresh for yourselves, oxen!
  thresh for yourselves, thresh for yourselves!
Straw to eat and barley for your masters;
  give yourselves no rest, it is cool today!

[Another version:]
Work for yourselves, work for yourselves, ye oxen!
  Work for yourselves!
The chaff for yourselves, the barley for your masters!

II

It is a good day
  and it is cool.

232

The sky does as we want it to do—
   let us work for the nobleman!

The song which they answer and say:
   This good day has come forth on the land,
     the north wind has come forth.
The sky does as we want it to do—
   let us work as our hearts may be set!

Song of the Herdsman
The herdsman is in the water among the fish.
He speaks with the shad,
   and greets the *khat*-fish.
O West! Whence is the herdsman?
   A herdsman of the West.

Song of the Palanquin Bearers
Better is it when it is full
   than when it is empty!
Happy are they who bear the chair!
Better is it when it is full
   than when it is empty!

Come down to them that are rewarded, hail!
   Come down to them that are rewarded, health!
O reward of Ipi,[26] be it as great as I desire!
Better is it when it is full
   than when it is empty!

[26] Their master.

233

V
Tales of Ancient Egypt: Magic, Adventure, and Humor

Folktale and Fiction in Ancient Egypt   The art of the storyteller was man's first form of entertainment, a recreation that enabled him to escape for a while from his everyday world of toil and care into a world of fantasy—a world in which magic and sorcery, marvelous monsters and startling incident, miraculous transformations and high adventure were of regular occurrence and in which the gods walk upon earth.

It is only natural that in ancient Egyptian literature, the oldest literature in the world, we should find the earliest written examples of the folktale and the novel (or rather, novelette) already developed as a sophisticated art form. The reader will have already noticed many elements and motifs of the art of fiction in the texts of the ancient cosmic myths in the first part of our collection. Here are the beginnings, over four thousand years ago, of the fairy tale, the ghost story, the novel of miraculous adventure and the picaresque, with the earliest traditions and plot-motifs which appear again and again throughout the stream of world literature, from the Bible through *The Odyssey,* the *Arabian Nights, Don Quixote,* and into our own times.

In these stories the reader will see the ancient Egyptians vividly revealed, as in all other forms of their art, in all their intense joy of life, their wide-awake sophistication, their excellent sense of humor, and their pragmatic skepticism—in other words, in all their essential humanity.

20 The Contendings of Horus and Set

This story is one of the most remarkable in all literature. It is a sort of mythological novelette of the picaresque. In its episodic, exciting adventure, bizarre and risqué (and even downright bawdy), and in its use of the everyday, almost slangy language of the people, it is the very prototype of the picaresque, and the magnificent beginning (to the best of our knowledge) of a vigorous and lusty tradition exemplified by such later high points of prose fiction as *The Satyricon* of Petronius, *The Golden Ass* of Apuleius, and in more modern times the works of Cervantes, Le Sage, and Kerouac.

In *The Contendings,* however, the characters are all deities. The essential plot, if such an episodic "romance" can have a plot, is the ancient contest of Horus against Set, who had usurped the prerogatives of Horus's father Osiris—the Royal Myth of Egypt, which we have already presented in selections from the *Pyramid Texts,* in Chapter 10. But here the gods are represented with the entire gamut of human feelings and affections, and with those of not very edifying humans at that! In fact, the entire story seems to be a colossal burlesque of the gods, full of what to us might seem unseemly levity and irreverence. This might not appear to agree with our quite justified concept of the ancient Egyptians as a profoundly religious people, but an interesting parallel, also in eastern Mediterranean culture, comes to mind when we remember *The Frogs* of Aristophanes, in which the great god Dionysus is hilariously burlesqued and even held up to ridicule. And the ancient Greeks were certainly a religious people. To the present writer, at least, the explanation seems to be an obvious one: when you believe the gods to be always with you and about you, and your relationship with them is as close and intimate as it is with your parents, you can occasionally indulge in a little banter and "kidding around" with them as you do with your parents. The occasions of banter endear them to you even more.

The papyrus dates from the reign of Ramesses V, of the Twentieth Dynasty (about 1160 B.C.). I have tried to make the translation as literal as possible in an attempt to preserve the feeling-tone of the original. It was not always easy.

Thus went the trial of Horus and Set, gods mysterious of forms, the greatest and most powerful princes who ever were:

Now Horus the Divine Child was sitting before the Lord of All[1] for the purpose of demanding the royal office of his divine father Osiris, beautiful of appearings, son of Ptah[2] who lightens the West[3] with his brilliance; while Thoth was presenting the Eye of Horus to the Mighty Prince who is in Heliopolis.[4]

Then spoke Shu,[5] son of Ra, before Atum, the Mighty Prince who is in Heliopolis: "Justice is master over force! Perform you justice by saying, 'Give the office to Horus!'" And Thoth said to the Divine Ennead: "Right a million times!"

[1] Ra-Atum-Khepri, here often referred to as *Ra-Her-Akhety,* "Ra-Horus of the Two Horizons."
[2] This view of Ptah as father of Osiris shows the influence of the Memphite theology. See Chapter 6.
[3] The Other World.
[4] Thoth, as scribe of the gods and "Clerk of the Court," presents the sacred Eye of Horus to the Lord of All, possibly as part of the hieratic ceremonial of the divine tribunal and as symbol of justice. The Eye of Horus was invested with many levels of magic significance as far back as the *Pyramid Texts* (see page 49). Also, the Eye may here be symbolic of the royal crown of Egypt, which is the object of the contention, pending the outcome of the litigation, and is entrusted to Ra presumably as the impartial judge.
[5] Personified god of the air, who together with Tefnut, "moisture," was created by Ra-Atum-Khepri out of himself. See page 56.

238

Then Isis uttered a great cry, and she rejoiced exceedingly. And she rose up before the Lord of All, and she said: "North-wind, go to the West and gladden the heart of Wen-nefer,[6] may he live, prosper, and be healthy!"

Then said Shu, son of Ra: "Present the Divine Eye to Horus! It is the justice of the Ennead."

But the Lord of All said: "What is this action of yours, this taking counsel on your own!"

Then the Ennead said: "He has already assumed the royal cartouche of Horus, and the White Crown has been placed upon his head."[7]

Then the Lord of All was silent for a great while, for he was angry at the Divine Ennead.

Thereupon Set, the son of Nut, said to Ra: "Let him be sent outside with me, and I'll let you see how my hand will prevail over his hand before the Divine Ennead. That is the only way to dispossess him."[8]

Then Thoth said to Ra: "We would not discern the guilty one that way. Now then, should the office of Osiris be given to Set while his son Horus is standing here?"[9]

Then Ra-Her-Akhety[10] was very, very angry, for it was the desire of Ra to give the office to Set, great of force, the son of Nut.[11] Then

[6] The North-wind was believed to bring health and happiness. *Wen-nefer*, literally, "the Beautiful Being," is a frequent appellation of Osiris.

[7] Apparently what had been said by Shu and Thoth was immediately done, and so the crowning of Horus was now regarded by the Ennead as a *fait accompli*.

[8] Set, wild and impetuous, wants Ra to have Horus "step outside" with him and settle it that way. Rather a modern touch.

[9] Thoth, as advocate, upholds strict legality. Horus has presented his claim before the divine court of justice. Settling the issue by a fist fight is no way to determine the respective merits of the case. Furthermore, as long as Horus stands on his case in court, he cannot be deprived of his office without due process of law.

[10] Ra-Horus of the Two Horizons is not to be confused with Horus Son of Isis. This is the Elder Horus, one of the primordial deities of Egypt who, like Ra, was associated with the sun, and thus was frequently identified with him.

[11] Ra's favoring Set is curiously reminiscent of Isaac in his favoring of Esau in the Old Testament. Strikingly parallel also is the fact that Esau is described as red (Genesis 25:25), wild, and a hunter (Genesis 25:27), all distinctive attributes of Set. Note also that in the Canaanite mythological texts of Ugarit, the old primordial god Il favors Mot against Baal.

239

Onuris[12] uttered a great cry before the Divine Ennead, saying: "What are we going to do about it?"

Thereupon Atum, the Mighty Prince who is in Heliopolis, said: "Let there be summoned Ba-Nebdedet, the Great Living God,[13] that he may judge the two youths."

Thereupon they brought Ba-Nebdedet, the great god who is within Setit,[14] before Atum, together with Ptah-Tenen.[15] And Atum said to them: "Judge the two youths and make them stop this behavior of theirs, wrangling every day."

Ba-Nebdedet, the Great Living God, answered him: "Let us not decide this in our ignorance. Let a letter be sent to Neith, the Great Goddess and Divine Mother.[16] Whatever she says, that we will do."

Then the Divine Ennead said to Ba-Nebdedet, the Great Living God: "A judgment was already made between them in the primordial time in the hall "Unique of Truths."[17] And the Ennead said to Thoth[18] before the Lord of All: "Come, make a letter to Neith, the Great Goddess and Divine Mother, in the name of the Lord of All, the Bull who is in Heliopolis!"

[12] In Egyptian, *In-Heret*, "he who brought the distant one," alluding to his having brought back a lioness-goddess who had gone off to the Nubian desert.

[13] The goat- or ram-god of Mendes in the Delta, who was considered the living manifestation both of Ra and Osiris, combining the powerful fertility aspects of both. Ba-Nebdedet was pre-eminently a god of generation and as such would be qualified to determine the legitimacy of Horus and of Set.

[14] An island in the Nile, at the First Cataract. Here the attempt is made to identify Ba-Nabdedet with the ram-god Khnum, naturally a powerful, generative deity, who was worshiped in that region.

[15] In one New Kingdom text Ptah-Tenen is described as changing himself into Ba-Nebdedet, and by copulating with the queen, giving generation to the king.

[16] Neith, goddess of Saïs in the Delta, was an old war, fertility, and mother-goddess, usually depicted with her symbol of two crossed arrows upon her head. Being a very ancient goddess, she was sometimes regarded as mother of Ra. The crocodile-god Sebek was also her son, and later in this text Isis, although daughter of Nut, also calls her "mother." An interesting parallel of the warrior-goddess who serves as judge and arbiter is found in the Greek myth of Athena in the *Oresteia* of Aeschylus. This was called to my attention by my student Phyllis Kriegel.

[17] We know nothing of such an earlier judgment. Also, the Ennead appears to appeal to this earlier judgment, which was presumably in favor of Horus, because of their doubt as to what Neith's decision might be.

[18] As scribe of the gods.

And Thoth said: "I will do it, I will do it indeed!"

Then he sat down to make the letter, and in it he said: "The King of Upper and Lower Egypt, Ra-Atum, beloved of Thoth, Lord of the Two Lands, God of Heliopolis, the divine Sun-disk which illumines the Two Lands with its brilliance, Divine Nile mighty in repletion, Ra-Horus of the Two Horizons (while Neith the Great Goddess and Divine Mother is healthy and youthfully flourishing), the Divine Living Spirit of the Lord of All, the Bull in Heliopolis in his capacity as Divine and Good King of the Beloved Land,[19] regarding the following: This thy servant spends the night in pre-occupation over Osiris, while Sebek remains unperturbed forever![20] What are we going to do about these two who for eighty years now have been before the court, and no one knows how to judge between them? Come now, advise us as to what we are to do about it!"

And then Neith, the Great Goddess and Divine Mother, sent a letter to the Divine Ennead, saying: "Give the office of Osiris to his son Horus. Do not perform heinous iniquities, which would be out of place. Otherwise, I shall be angry, and the sky will crash down to the ground! And tell the Lord of All, the Bull who is within Heliopolis: 'Double Set in his possessions, give him Anath and Astarte, your two daughters,[21] and place Horus in the seat of his father Osiris.' "

The letter of Neith, the Great Goddess and Divine Mother, reached the Ennead while they were sitting in the great hall called

---

[19] The Beloved Land was a usual designation of Egypt. All these resounding titles were used in the usual titularies of the Pharaoh.

[20] Ra has to be concerned with the affairs of Osiris and of Egypt, whereas Sebek, Neith's other son, remains firm and tranquil, with nothing to bother him.

[21] Anath and Astarte were the two great goddesses of ancient Syria and Canaan. During the cosmopolitan period of the Empire, they were incorporated within the Egyptian pantheon with the other chief Syrian deities, and are frequently mentioned in the texts of the period. Anath and Astarte were made daughters of Ra, as here, or of Ptah. Set was, among other things, quite a lascivious deity, and giving him both of these highly desirable and sensual Syrian goddesses would tend to mollify him. The Egyptians also equated Baal, the deity of the Syrian Hyksos invaders, with Set, the villain of the gods. Therefore giving him the Syrian goddesses would be rather logical.

"Horus, Foremost of Horns,"[22] and the letter was given into the hand of Thoth. And then Thoth read it out aloud before the Lord of All and before the entire Ennead. And they said with one voice: "The goddess is right!"

But the Lord of All was angry at Horus, and he said to him: "You are feeble in limbs and body, and this office is too great for you, a brat with a foul taste still in his mouth!"[23]

Then Onuris was angry, and likewise the entire Ennead, even the Thirty,[24] may they live, prosper, and be healthy! And the god Baba[25] got up, and he said to Ra-Her-Akhety: "Your shrine is empty!"[26]

And Ra-Her-Akhety was aggrieved at this reply which had been given him, and he laid himself down on his back, and his heart was very miserable indeed. Then the Ennead went forth and they uttered a great cry in the face of the god Baba, and they said to him: "Get out of here! You have committed a very heinous offense!" And they went forth to their dwellings.

And then the Great God spent a whole day lying on his back in his pavilion, and his heart was very miserable indeed, and he was all alone. Now, after a long time came Hathor, the Lady of the Southern Sycamore,[27] and she stood before her father, the Lord of All, and she uncovered her vulva before his face. And the Great God laughed at seeing this.[28] Thereupon he rose up, and he went

[22] As embodiments of the fertility principle, the great deities of the ancient Near East were commonly associated with the bull (or cow, in the case of the goddesses) and were frequently depicted with horns. Isis and Hathor were frequently represented with cow's horns.

[23] Horus's mother Isis had been impregnated by Osiris after the latter had been slain and later temporarily revived to a feeble state by Isis's magic. Consequently, Horus was considered to be a prematurely born weakling. Ra taunts him in addition with being a mere sniveling child with the stale taste of his mother's milk still in his mouth.

[24] As comprising a sort of grand jury. The terrestrial judicial councils of Egypt were composed of thirty magistrates.

[25] A minor deity, a sort of monster who was supposed to devour the hearts of the wicked at the Judgment of the Dead.

[26] That is, "Nobody takes you seriously; nobody worships you any more." This, of course, is the supreme insult, and Ra just can't take it.

[27] Hathor, goddess of love and beauty, was one of the most powerful fertility goddesses, like Ishtar in Mesopotamia and Anath in Syria.

[28] An analogous story is told in Greek myth, in connection with the goddess Demeter. Greatly saddened by the futile search for her daughter Persephone, who had been

242

and sat with the Great Ennead, and he said unto Horus and Set: "Speak your piece!"

Then Set, great of strength, son of Nut, said: "Me, I'm Set, great of strength within the Ennead! I'm the one who slays the enemy of Ra daily when I'm in the prow of the Bark of Millions,[29] and no other god can do it. I will take the office of Osiris!"

Thereupon they said: "Set, son of Nut, is right!"

Then Onuris and Thoth gave a great cry, saying: "Shall the office be given to the mother's brother while a son of the divine body is present?"[30]

Then said Ba-Nebdedet, the Great Living God: "And then shall the office be given to this young fellow while Set, his elder brother, is present?"

Then the Ennead uttered a great cry in the face of the Lord of All, and they said to him: "Behold these words which you have spoken, which should never have been heard!"[31]

Then spoke Horus, son of Isis: "It would not be fair at all if I were cheated in the presence of the Ennead, and that the office of my father Osiris should be taken away from me!"

---

abducted by Hades, ruler of the infernal regions, Demeter (in the guise of an old woman) came to Eleusis, near Athens, and was kindly received at the court of King Celeus. As she sat there downcast in mourning, one of the women of the palace (her name is variously given as Iambe or Baubo) roused Demeter from her depression by her jests and by exposing her genitals. When understood psychologically, the purpose of this becomes clear: revelation of the most private parts of the body is a sharing of the most personal intimacy. This serves as a drastic means of enticing out the psyche, which in a state of depression has become intensely withdrawn into itself, and establishing a bond of communication, thus lifting the psyche out of its depression. For this psychological interpretation, I am indebted to Dr. H. L. Newbold, psychiatrist and novelist, and my sometime student in Greek mythology.

[29] The Solar Bark in which Ra makes his daily journey across the sky. Set is frequently represented as slaying with a spear the great serpent Apophis, who threatens to devour the sun.

[30] There were two traditions regarding the family relationship of Horus and Set. According to one, Osiris, Set, Isis, and Nephthys were children of Geb and Nut. Horus, as son of Osiris, would precede his uncle, Set, in the inheritance. According to the other tradition, Set was the elder brother of Horus, and thus would precede him. The two conflicting traditions are utilized here for the sake of argument.

[31] Namely, Ra's unceasing opposition to the claims of Horus, which have led to this impasse.

And Isis was furious against the Ennead, and she swore an oath by the gods in the presence of the Ennead, saying: "By the life of my mother Neith, and by the life of Ptah-Tenen, High of Plumes, who curbs the horns of the gods, these words shall be put before Atum, the Mighty Prince who is in Heliopolis, and likewise before Khepri, who is within his Divine Bark!"[32]

Then the Ennead said to her: "Do not be angry; his rights will be given to him who is in the right, and all that you have spoken shall be done."

Thereupon Set, son of Nut, was furious against the Ennead, because they had said these words to Isis the Great, the mother of the god. And Set said to them: "I will take my forty-five-hundred-pound scepter and I'll kill one of you every day!"

And then Set made an oath by the Lord of All, saying: "I will not argue in this tribunal while Isis is in it!"

Then Ra-Her-Akhety said to them: "Cross over to the Island-in-the-Midst,[33] and judge there between them. And tell Anty the Ferryman: 'Do not ferry across any woman who looks like Isis!' "

Then the Ennead crossed over to the Island-in-the-Midst, and they sat there and ate bread.

And then Isis came, and approached Anty the Ferryman as he was sitting by his boat. She had changed herself into an old woman, and walked along with her back all bent; and on her finger was a little gold signet ring. And she said to him: "I'm here to ask you to ferry me across to the Island-in-the-Midst, for I have come with this jar of meal for my little boy. He has been taking care of some cattle in the Island-in-the-Midst for five days, and he is hungry."

And he said to her: "They told me not to ferry across any woman."

Then she said to him: "Whatever they told you, wasn't it only regarding Isis?"

---

[32] Ra, Atum, and Khepri were, of course, one and the same. Does this mean that she will make him "eat his words"? The great goddesses have proven themselves to be quite formidable to the old god Ra; for examples, see Chapters 7 and 8. Likewise in the Ugaritic myths, Anath threatens the old god Il with bodily harm.
[33] In the midst of the Nile, no doubt; at any rate, a mythical island.

244

And he said to her: "What will you give me if I ferry you across to the Island-in-the-Midst?"

Then Isis said to him: "I will give you this loaf of bread."

And he said to her: "What is your loaf of bread to me? Should I ferry you across to the Island-in-the-Midst when I was told not to ferry any woman across—all for your loaf of bread?"

Thereupon she said to him: "I will give you this gold signet ring on my finger."

And he said to her: "Give me the gold signet ring." And she gave it to him. Thereupon he ferried her across to the Island-in-the-Midst.

And then, while she was walking beneath the trees, she looked up and saw the Ennead as they were sitting and eating bread before the Lord of All in his pavilion. And Set looked, and saw her as she was coming in the distance. Then she uttered an incantation with her magic, and changed herself into a young girl beautiful of body, and there was none like her in the entire land. And he fell in love with her very sorely indeed. Thereupon Set rose up from where he sat eating bread with the Great Ennead, and went to get in front of her; and no one had seen her except himself. And he stood behind a tree and called to her and said: "I'd like to stay here with you, little beauty!"

And she said to him: "But see, my great lord! I was the wife of a herdsman, and I bore him an only male child. Then my husband died, and my boy came to look after the cattle of his father. And then a stranger came and sat himself down in my byre, and spoke in this manner to my little boy: 'I will beat you and take away your father's cattle and drive you out!' Thus he spoke to him. I would like you to become his champion."

Thereupon Set said to her: "Shall the cattle be given to a stranger, while the husbandman's boy is alive?"

Then Isis changed herself into a kite-bird, and she flew and perched on top of an acacia tree and cried out to Set, saying: "Weep over yourself! You yourself have said it! Your own cleverness has condemned you! What do you want now?"[34]

---

[34] Compare Isis's parable and its effect with the analogous parable spoken by Nathan the prophet to David regarding Uriah and Bathsheba (II Samuel 12:1–7).

Thereupon he began to weep, and he went to the place where Ra-Her-Akhety was, and he wept. And Ra-Her-Akhety said to him: "What do you want now?"

And Set said to him: "That bad woman came against me again, and once more she has given me aggravation! She changed herself into a beautiful young girl before my face, and she said to me: 'As for me, I was the wife of a herdsman, and he died. And I had borne to him an only male child. He was looking after some cattle of his father's, when a stranger came to my boy in the byre, and I gave him bread. Many days after, the intruder said to my boy: "I will beat you and take away your father's cattle, and they shall become mine!" That's how he spoke to my boy.' So she said to me."

"And what did you say to her?" said Ra-Her-Akhety.

Then Set said: "I said to her, 'Shall the cattle be given to a stranger, while the husbandman's boy is alive?' And I added: 'The face of this intruder shall be beaten with a stick, and he shall be driven out. Then shall your boy be put in his father's seat.' That's what I said to her."

Then Ra-Her-Akhety said to him: "Well, then, see! You have convicted yourself! What do you want now?"

Thereupon Set said to him: "Let Anty the Ferryman be brought, and let him be punished severely, saying, 'Why did you let her get across!' So should it be said to him."

Thereupon Anty the Ferryman was brought before the Ennead, and they took off the toes of his feet.[35] Then Anty abjured gold unto this day in the presence of the Great Ennead, saying: "Gold has been made an abomination for me and for my city."

Then the Ennead crossed over to the western bank of the Nile, and they sat upon the mountain. When evening came, Ra-Her-Akhety and Atum, Lord of the Two Lands in Heliopolis, sent to the Ennead, saying: "What are you doing, still sitting there? Are you going to make the two youths end their lives in the tribunal? When my letter

---

[35] Meaning that he was well bastinadoed, or else to account for the fact that Anty, whose name means "he-of-the-claws," was considered to have claws on his feet. The claws would have replaced his toes.

reaches you, you shall set the White Crown on the head of Horus the son of Isis and proclaim him in the place of his father Osiris!"

And Set was sorely angry indeed. Then the Ennead said to Set: "What are you angry about? Shall one not do as Atum, the Lord of the Two Lands in Heliopolis and Ra-Her-Akhety has said?"

Thereupon they established the White Crown upon the head of Horus the son of Isis.

Then Set uttered a great cry in the face of the Ennead, and he was furious as he said: "Shall the office be given to my young brother while I, his elder brother, am alive?" And he made an oath, saying: "The White Crown shall be removed from the head of Horus son of Isis and he shall be thrown into the water, that I may contend with him over the office of Ruler!" Thereupon Ra-Her-Akhety did accordingly.

And Set said to Horus: "Come, let us change ourselves into two hippopotamuses, and let us plunge into the waters of the Great Green.[36] He who shall emerge within three months of days, to him shall the office not be given.[37]

And Isis sat weeping, and said: "Set has killed my boy Horus."

Thereupon she brought a quantity of yarn, and she made a rope. And she took a pound of copper, and melted it into a weapon of the water[38] and tied the rope to it, and she threw it into the water where Horus and Set had plunged in.[39] And the barb bit into the body of her son Horus. Thereupon Horus uttered a loud cry, saying: "Come to me, my mother Isis, my mother! Call unto the barb, that it let loose from me! I am Horus son of Isis!"

Then Isis gave a great cry, and she said to the barb: "Let loose from him! Lo, he is my son Horus, my boy!" Then her barb let loose from him.

And then again she threw the harpoon into the water, and it bit

[36] The sea.
[37] The idea being to see who could stay under water longest.
[38] A harpoon.
[39] The Egyptians used to hunt the hippopotamus with harpoons attached to ropes, very much as whales were hunted in the days of *Moby Dick*. When several harpoons had been launched into the animal's hide, they would haul it in by means of the ropes.

into the body of Set. And Set uttered a loud cry, saying: "What are you doing to me, my sister Isis? Come, call unto the barb that it let loose from me! I am your brother, from your own mother, O Isis!"

Then her heart felt for him very greatly. And Set called to her and said: "Do you wish evil to your own brother Set?"

Then Isis called out to her harpoon, saying: "Let loose from him! Behold it is the brother of Isis, from her own mother, whom you have bitten!" Then the harpoon let loose from him.

Thereupon Horus was furious against his mother Isis. He went out of the water, and his face was wild and savage like that of the leopard of Upper Egypt, and in his hand was his sixteen-pound battle-ax. He cut off the head of his mother Isis,[40] and carrying it in his arms, he went up onto the mountain. Thereupon Isis changed herself into a statue of flint which has no head.

Then Ra-Her-Akhety said unto Thoth: "Who is this woman who has come without a head?"

And Thoth said to Ra-Her-Akhety: "O my good lord, this is Isis the Great, the mother of the god! Her son Horus has removed her head."

Then Ra-Her-Akhety uttered a great cry, and said unto the Ennead: "Let us go and inflict a great punishment upon him!"

Thereupon the Ennead went up these mountains to look for Horus the son of Isis. Now as for Horus, he was lying under a *shenusha* tree in the oasis country.

And Set found him, and he laid hold of him and threw him on his back upon the mountain. And he took out his two eyes from their places, and he buried them on the mountain, where they illumined the earth.[41] And his eyeballs became two bulbs, and they grew into lotuses.

---

[40] According to another text, Thoth by his magic replaced the decapitated head of Isis with that of a cow. This was evidently intended to explain why Isis was often represented as cow-headed—actually a fusion of Isis with the attributes of Hathor.

[41] The motif of the mutual mutilations of Horus and Set goes back to the *Pyramid Texts* (see pages 85–86), where we have the concept of the Magic Eye of Horus. Here, Set tears out both the eyes of Horus, and they become the sun and the moon. This is usually predicated of the two eyes of Horus of the Two Horizons.

Then Set returned, and he said unto Ra falsely: "I did not find Horus," although he had found him.

Thereupon Hathor, the Lady of the Southern Sycamore,[42] went and she found Horus. And he was lying and weeping upon the mountain in the desert. And she seized a gazelle and she milked it, and she said to Horus: "Open your eyes, that I may put this milk therein."

And he opened his eyes, and she put the milk therein. She put it into his right eye and she put it into his left eye, and she said to him: "Now open your eyes!"

And he opened his eyes, and she looked at him, and found him restored. Then she went and said to Ra-Her-Akhety: "I found Horus, and Set had deprived him of his eyes. Then I raised him up again, and behold he is come."

Thereupon the Ennead said: "Let Horus and Set be called, and let them be judged!" And so they were brought before the Ennead.

And the Lord of All said to Horus and Set in the presence of the Great Ennead: "Go forth, and hearken unto what I say to you! Eat, drink, and let us be at peace; only stop this quarreling every day after day!"

Then Set said to Horus: "Come on, let's have a good time in my house!"

And Horus said to him: "I'll do it; certainly, I'll be most glad to do it!"

And so when evening came, the bed was spread for them, and the two of them lay down together. And then in the night Set made his penis stiff, and he thrust it between the thighs of Horus. But Horus put his hands between his thighs, and caught the semen of Set. And then Horus went, and said to his mother Isis: "Come here, my mother Isis! See what Set has done to me!"

And he opened his hand, and showed his mother the semen of Set. She uttered a loud cry, and she cut off his hands and threw them into the water. Then she provided him with hands equally as

---

[42] Hathor (in Egyptian, *Het-Her*) means "the house of Horus." Although usually regarded as the wife of Horus, she is sometimes mentioned as his mother. With our knowledge of depth psychology, this association of the unconscious mythopoeic mind does not seem strange.

good. Then she took a little sweet ointment, and put it on the penis of Horus. And she made it get stiff, and inserting it into a pot, made his semen run down into it.

In the morning, Isis went with Horus's semen to the garden of Set, and she said to Set's gardener: "What sort of vegetable do you grow here for Set to eat?"

The gardener replied: "Set eats nothing from here but lettuces."[43] Thereupon Isis put the semen of Horus on them.

And then Set came, as was his wont every day, and he ate the lettuces as he usually did. And he rose up pregnant with the semen of Horus.[44] And Set went and said to Horus: "Come, let us go, and I'll contend with you in the tribunal."

And Horus replied: "I'll do it; certainly, I'll be most glad to do it!"

And so, both of them went to the tribunal and they stood before the Great Ennead, who said to them: "Say what you have to say."

Thereupon Set said: "Let the office of Sovereign (may he live, prosper, and be healthy) be given to me! As to Horus here, I have subjected him to the usages of war."[45]

Thereupon the Ennead uttered a loud cry, and they spat and vomited before the face of Horus.

Then Horus laughed at them. And Horus swore by the god, saying: "Everything that Set has said is false! Let the semen of Set be called, and we'll see from where it will answer! Then let my own be called, and we'll see from whence it will answer!"

[43] The Egyptian variety of lettuce (*Lactuca sativa*) mentioned in the text was closely associated with the powerfully phallic god Min, no doubt because of the fertility symbolism inherent in its milky sap. For these reasons, the Egyptians regarded lettuce as an aphrodisiac. Knowing the sexual proclivities of Set as we do, we are not surprised that he would be rather addicted to it.

[44] The notion that pregnancy can be induced by swallowing something is widespread among children and in primitive folklore. A well-known example is the myth of the birth of Athena from the head of Zeus after the latter had impregnated and then devoured Metis. The entire concept illustrates the "displacement from below upward" in dreams and myths, as observed by Freud.

[45] In various cultures it was the custom to assault sexually enemies defeated in battle. It was also a token of their complete subjection and humiliation. For example, the case of T. E. Lawrence ("of Arabia") which has recently been published and has added to his posthumous fame. Just so, Set believes that he has caused Horus utter loss of face and dishonor. See also the Addendum to this tale.

Thereupon Thoth, Lord of the Divine Words, the Scribe of Truth of the Ennead, placed his hand upon the arm of Horus and said: "Come forth, O semen of Set!" And it answered to him from the waters in the marsh.

Then Thoth placed his hand on the arm of Set and said: "Come forth, O semen of Horus!"

And it said to him: "Where shall I come forth?"

Thereupon Thoth said to it: "Come forth from his ear!"

But it answered: "Shall I come out of his ear, I who am a divine fluid?"[46]

Then Thoth said to it: "Come forth from his forehead!" Thereupon it came forth as a sun-disk of gold upon the head of Set.

And Set was very, very furious indeed, and he put forth his hand to seize the sun-disk of gold. But Thoth took it away from him, and he placed it as an ornament upon his own head.[47]

Then the Ennead said: "Horus is right, and Set is wrong!"

And Set was very furious indeed, and he bellowed aloud when the Ennead said: "Horus is right, and Set is wrong!"

And Set swore a great oath by the life of the god and said: "The office shall not be given to him until he is put outside with me! We will make for ourselves ships of stone, and both of us will have a sailing race. Then whoever is the winner, let him be given the office of Sovereign (may he live, prosper, and be healthy!)."

Thereupon Horus made himself a ship of cedar, and he plastered it over with gypsum, and he cast it upon the water in the evening; and no one in the entire land had seen it. And Set saw the ship of Horus, and thought it was stone. So he went to the mountain and cut off a rocky peak, and he made himself a stone ship one hundred and thirty-eight cubits long.

Then they went down into their ships in the presence of the

[46] Probably because it would be a form of *lèse majesté*. As mentioned previously, in dreams and myths the upper orifices of the body take the place of the lower because of the censorship imposed by the unconscious mind—the "displacement from below upward."

[47] According to a more ancient version of the myth, Thoth was himself born from the head of Horus. This, of course, puts it in complete parallelism to the birth of Athena, including the fact that Thoth, Metis, and Athena were deities of wisdom.

251

Ennead. And the ship of Set sank into the water. Then Set changed himself into a hippopotamus and caused the ship of Horus to founder. Then Horus took his harpoon, and threw it at the body of Set.[48] Thereupon the Ennead said to him: "Don't throw it at him!"

Thereupon he took his harpoons and put them in his ship, and fared downstream to Saïs.[49] And he spoke to Neith, the Great Goddess and Divine Mother: "Let judgment be made between me and Set, for we have been before the tribunal for eighty years, and no one seems to be able to judge us! He has never been declared justified against me, but a thousand times have I been justified over him every day. He never regards anything that the Ennead says. I wrangled with him in the Hall of the Way of Truths, and I was justified over him. I wrangled with him in the Hall of Horus Foremost among Horns and was justified over him. I wrangled with him in the Hall of the Field of Reeds and was justified over him. I wrangled with him in the Hall of the Pool in the Field and was justified over him!"

And the Ennead said to Shu, the son of Ra: "Justified in all that he has said is Horus, the son of Isis!"

Then Thoth said to the Lord of All: "Let a letter be sent to Osiris, and let him judge between the two youths!"

And Shu the son of Ra said: "Right a million times is that which Thoth has said to the Ennead!"

And the Lord of All said to Thoth: "Sit down and make a letter to Osiris, and let us see what he will have to say!"

And so Thoth sat down and wrote out a letter to Osiris, as follows: "The Bull,[50] Lion Who Hunts for Himself; The Two Goddesses,

---

[48] The hippopotamus was often considered an animal of Set, and Horus was represented as hunting it as such.

[49] In the Delta; the ancient city of Neith.

[50] Ra, the sender of the letter, is identified by the following resounding titles in the same manner as the ruling Pharaoh. In New Kingdom times, the formal titulary of the king consisted of his five royal names: his Horus name (usually as "Powerful Bull"), his Two Goddesses name, his Horus of Gold name, his name as King of Upper and Lower Egypt, and his name as Son of Ra. It will be noticed that here his last name is given as Son of Ptah, as was that of Osiris at the beginning, again indicating a possible Memphite origin of the story.

Who Protects the Gods and Contains the Two Lands; The Horus of
Gold, The Inventor of Mankind in the Primeval Time; King of
Upper and Lower Egypt, The Bull Who is in Heliopolis (may he
live, prosper, and be healthy!); Son of Ptah, Glorious One of the
Two Countries, Rising as the Father of His Ennead, Who Eats
Gold and All Sorts of Precious Stones[51] (may he live, prosper, and
be healthy!). Come now, advise us as to what should be done
about Horus and Set, so that we may not take some action in our
ignorance!"

And so, after due time the letter reached the Divine King, the
Son of Ra, Great in Overflowing Abundance, Lord of Sustenance.[52] And he uttered a great cry when the letter was read out
before him. And very quickly he sent answer to where the Lord of
All was with the Ennead, saying: "Why, indeed, should my son
Horus be defrauded? It is I who make you strong. It is I who produce the barley and the wheat to nourish the gods as well as living
creatures after the gods, and no other god finds himself able to do
it!"[53]

And the letter of Osiris arrived at the place where Ra-Her-Akhety
was, and he was sitting with the Ennead at high noon in Khasu.[54]
And so it was read out before him and the Ennead. And Ra-Her-
Akhety said: "Come, answer me this letter very quickly to Osiris, and
say to him: 'What if you had never come into being; what if you
had never been born? The barley and the wheat would still exist!' "

And the letter of the Lord of All reached Osiris, and it was read
out before him. Then he sent to Ra-Her-Akhety again, saying: "Very
good indeed is everything you have done, you who truly invented
the Ennead! Meanwhile, Justice has been allowed to sink down into
the Nether World! But regard this matter yourself: This land of mine

---

[51] Many texts represent the flesh of the gods as being made of gold, lapis lazuli, and
turquoise. The concept of the powerful supreme deity devouring the other gods and
thereby assimilating their qualities is found in the *Pyramid Texts* and is often met
with in myth.
[52] Osiris as embodiment of the teeming and nourishing fertility principle.
[53] Osiris was regarded as the source of the nourishing grain, who vouchsafes of his
bounty to all beings.
[54] Khasu, or Xois, in the Delta is mentioned as one of the cult centers of Ra.

is full of messengers fierce of countenance, who do not fear any god or goddess. I can have them go forth and fetch the heart of anyone who does evil, and they will remain here with me![55] What indeed is the meaning of my resting here in the West, while all of you are without, even though none of you is stronger than I, and despite the fact that you have found out how to perform injustice! It is this: When Ptah the Great One South of His Wall and Lord of Memphis, the Life of the Two Lands, made the heavens,[56] did not he say to the stars which are in it: 'You shall go to rest every night in the West, where Sovereign Osiris is. And after the gods, both nobles and populace shall go to rest in the place where you are!' Thus did he say to me."[57]

After due time the letter of Osiris reached the place where the Lord of All was, together with the Ennead. And Thoth received the letter, and read it aloud before Ra-Her-Akhety and the Ennead. And they said: "True, quite true, is all that has been said by the King, Great of Overflowing Abundance, Lord of Sustenance, may he live, prosper, and be healthy!"

Thereupon Set said: "Let us be taken to the Island-in-the-Midst, that I may contend with him!"

And he went to the Island-in-the-Midst, and there too Horus triumphed over him.

And then Atum, Lord of the Two Lands in Heliopolis, sent to Isis, saying: "Bring Set, fastened with fetters!"

And Isis brought Set, fastened with fetters like a prisoner. Then Atum said to him: "Why didn't you let judgment be pronounced between you, instead of seizing for yourself the office of Horus?"

And Set said to him: "Nay, on the contrary, my good lord! Let Horus, son of Isis, be called, and let the office of his father Osiris be given to him!"

---

[55] Osiris's "messengers" who execute his commands are parallel to the "angels" of the Bible. "Angel" is the Greek word *angelos,* which means "messenger," and which is in turn an exact translation of the Hebrew word *mal'akh* as used in the Old Testament.
[56] For Ptah as creator of the universe, see The Theology of Memphis, in Chapter 6.
[57] Osiris's claim to ultimate authority is that the stars, the gods, and all humanity are eventually destined to come to the Other World, his domain in the West.

Thereupon they brought Horus, son of Isis, and they put the White Crown upon his head, and they placed him in the seat of his father Osiris, and they said to him: "You are the good King of Egypt, the Beloved Land! You are the Good Lord (may you live, prosper, and be healthy) of every land, forever and unto all eternity!"

And Isis cried out to her son Horus and said: "You are the beautiful king! My heart is in joy, that you illumine the earth with your splendor!"

Then said Ptah, the Great One South of His Wall, Lord of Memphis, the Life of the Two Lands: "What now shall be done for Set, now that Horus has been placed in the seat of his father Osiris?"[58]

And Ra-Her-Akhety said: "Let Set, son of Nut, be given to me, and be as my son. His voice shall thunder in the sky, and he shall be feared."[59]

Thereupon they went and said to Ra-Her-Akhety: "Horus, son of Isis, has risen as Ruler, may he live, prosper, and be healthy!"

And Ra rejoiced very greatly indeed, and he said to the Ennead: "Acclaim him and jubilate! Bow to the ground for Horus, son of Isis!"

And Isis said: "Horus has risen as Ruler, may he live, prosper, and be healthy! The Ennead is in festival, and the heavens are rejoicing!"

And they took garlands when they saw Horus, son of Isis, risen as Ruler of Egypt, may he live, prosper, and be healthy! The hearts of the Ennead were content, and the entire land was in jubilation when they saw Horus, son of Isis, when he was awarded the office of his father Osiris, Lord of Djedu.

> IT HAS COME TO A HAPPY ENDING IN THEBES,
> THE PLACE OF TRUTH.

---

[58] Note that Ptah speaks only at the end, and to clear up a final point. As the most supreme deity, he is far and above all this.

[59] Set was, among other things, god of thunder and storm, and is referred to as "roaring" in the *Pyramid Texts* (verse 1150). For this reason, the Hyksos equated him with their Canaanite storm and fertility god Baal. See note 21.

ADDENDUM: Set's attempted sexual assault of Horus has various levels of significance which cannot be enlarged upon here. It may be of interest, however, to quote a parallel text, which is unfortunately fragmentary, but in which we have another reference to the magic power of the semen of Set, which Isis is anxious to obtain. It is quite possible that both *The Contendings* and the text of which the following fragment was a part are the words of a mystery ritual of initiation. There are several analogous texts referring to the initiation rituals of the Mysteries of Dionysus.

The text is in F. Llewellyn Griffith, *The Petrie Papyri, Hieratic Papyri from Kahun and Gurob* [(London, 1898), I, 4; II, Plate III]. The text is rather fragmentary, and only the following portion (with Griffith's restorations) admits of something like a consecutive rendering:

The Majesty of Set said to the Majesty of Horus: "How beautiful are your buttocks! Come spread your legs."

The Majesty of Horus said: "Be careful! I'll tell my mother Isis!"

When they had come to the palace, the Majesty of Horus said to his mother Isis: "Set came to sodomize me!"

And she said to him: "We'll fight against him. Go in unto him with this scheme. When he propositions you again, say to him: 'It's embarrassing and difficult for me, but you are stronger than I, and can overcome me.' Thus shall you speak to him. And then, when he will offer you violence, then thrust your fingers between your buttocks. He will give his semen, and it will be most sweet to him. Then bring me the semen which flows from his penis, but do not allow the sun to see it."[60]

And so afterward the Majesty of Set said to him: "Come, don't be afraid! I only want to do that for which I have been created. . . ."

[The text breaks off here.]

---

[60] So that it may not dry and lose its magic force?

21 King Cheops and the Magicians

This story is probably the oldest of the popular tales. The papyrus itself, known as the Papyrus Westcar, dates from the Hyksos period (1730–1580 B.C.), but its prototype was no doubt much older, antedating the Middle Kingdom. The form of the narrative is that of the "chain story," a group of tales told within the framework of an over-all story. This device is familiar from such well-known examples as *The Thousand and One Nights* and Boccaccio's *The Decameron*.

King Cheops (in Egyptian, *Khufu*), who reigned about 2600 B.C. and built the Great Pyramid, is being entertained by some of his sons, who spin various yarns dealing with wonders performed by famous magicians. Tales of magic and the supernatural have always had a strong fascination. These *Tales of the Magicians* certainly have this, and in addition they show a keen insight into the quirks and foibles of human nature.

I

Then the Prince Khafra stood up to speak and said: I will let Your Majesty hear a wonder which took place in the reign of your father King Nebka,[1] True of Voice, when he went to the Temple of Ptah, Lord of Ankh-tawy.[2]

---

[1] "Father" was often used throughout the ancient world, as it frequently is today, in the sense of "forefather." King Nebka reigned during the preceding dynasty, the Third, and he was a remote ancestor, if at all, of Cheops.
[2] "Life of the Two Lands," site of the temple of Ptah in Memphis.

His Majesty went to confer with the Chief Lector-priest Weba-aner. Now Weba-aner's wife had fallen in love with a certain townsman.[3] And she sent him a box of beautiful clothes by a handmaid, and he came back with the handmaid.

Now when some days had passed by—now there was a garden house by Weba-aner's lake[4]—then the townsman said to Weba-aner's wife: "Why, there is a garden house by Weba-aner's lake; see, let us make a time in it!"[5]

And Weba-aner's wife sent a message to the steward who was in charge of the lake, saying: "Let the garden house which is by the lake be made ready." And she spent the day there, drinking and eating with the townsman until the sun went down. Now when evening had come, he went down to the lake to bathe. And the handmaid went to the steward and reported to him what had happened with Weba-aner's wife.

Now when the earth brightened,[6] and a second day had come, the steward went to the Chief Lector-priest Weba-aner and related the whole of this matter to him.

Then Weba-aner said: "Bring me my box of ebony inlaid with gold." And he modeled a crocodile of wax, seven fingers long. And he recited a magic spell over it, and said to it: "Whoever comes to bathe in my lake, seize him for me!"

Then he gave it to the steward, and said to him: "Now when the townsman goes down to the lake according to his daily habit, then you must throw the crocodile into the water after him." The steward went off, taking the crocodile with him.

Then Weba-aner's wife sent to the steward in charge of the lake, saying: "Let the garden house be made ready, for I am coming to sit in it." And the garden house was made ready with all good things. Then they[7] went off and made a happy day with the townsman.

---

[3] The Egyptian word denotes a person not a member of the nobility or the priesthood, what we would call a commoner.

[4] On the estates of the wealthy Egyptians there was usually a rectangular pool, called a lake, surrounded by trees and gardens, with a little pavilion, or garden house, near it.

[5] Literal translation!

[6] The regular idiomatic Egyptian expression for "dawn."

[7] Weba-aner's wife and her handmaiden, who was already an accomplice in the affair.

Now when evening had come, the townsman came to the lake according to his daily habit. Then the steward threw the wax crocodile after him into the water; and it became a crocodile seven cubits long, and it seized the townsman and carried him off.

Now Weba-aner was detained with His Majesty King Nebka, True of Voice, for seven days, the townsman being kept in the deepest place of the lake, without breathing. And when the seven days had passed, King Nebka, True of Voice, proceeded to the Temple. Then the Chief Lector-priest Weba-aner placed himself in the royal presence, and said to His Majesty: "May Your Majesty go and see this wonder that has come to pass in Your Majesty's reign to a townsman!" And His Majesty went with Weba-aner.

Then Weba-aner called the crocodile, saying: "Bring back the townsman here!" And the crocodile came forth, bringing the townsman, to the place where they were. And the Majesty of King Nebka, True of Voice, said: "Certainly, this is a terrible crocodile!" Then Weba-aner stooped down and took it up, and it was a wax crocodile in his hand.

And the Chief Lector-priest Weba-aner reported to His Majesty King Nebka, True of Voice, this thing that the townsman had done with his wife in his house. Then His Majesty said to the crocodile: "Take to yourself what is your own!" And the crocodile went down to the depth of the lake, and no one knew where he went with the townsman.[8]

Then the Majesty of King Nebka, True of Voice, had Weba-aner's wife brought to a piece of land north of the Residence, and he set fire to her, and her ashes were thrown into the river. Lo, that is a wonder which came to pass in the reign of your father, King Nebka, True of Voice, a feat of the Chief Lector-priest Weba-aner!

And the Majesty of King Cheops said: "Let a thousand loaves of bread, and a hundred jugs of beer, and an ox, and two measures of incense, be offered to King Nebka, True of Voice; and also let one cake, and one jug of beer, and a large haunch of meat, and one

---

[8] It is interesting to note that the punishment of the townsman, like that of Weba-aner's wife, is ordained by the king, and not by Weba-aner.

measure of incense be given to the Chief Lector-priest Weba-aner,[9] for I have seen an example of his learning!

And it was done, according to all that His Majesty commanded.

II

Then Prince Baufra stood up to speak and said: I will relate to Your Majesty a wonder that came to pass in the time of your father Seneferu, True of Voice[10]—one of the deeds of the Chief Lector-priest Djadja-em-ankh.

One day King Seneferu was sad. So he assembled the officers of the Palace in order to seek for him a diversion, but he found none. Then said he: "Go, bring me the Chief Lector-priest, the Scribe of the Book, Djadja-em-ankh!" And he was brought to him straightway.

And his Majesty said to him: "I had assembled the officers of the Palace together in order to seek for me a diversion, but I could find none."

And Djadja-em-ankh said to him: "If Your Majesty would but betake you to the lake of the Great House! 'Man' a boat with all fair damsels from the inner apartments of your palace. Then will the heart of Your Majesty be diverted when you see how they row to and fro! Then, as you view the pleasant nesting places of your lake, and view its fields and its pleasant banks, your heart will be diverted thereby."

His Majesty said unto him: "I will do this. Get you back to your house, but I will go boating. Have brought to me twenty paddles of ebony inwrought with gold, their handles being of *sekeb*-wood inwrought with fine gold. Have brought to me twenty women, of those with the fairest limbs, and with beauteous breasts and braided tresses, such as have not yet given birth. And moreover have brought to me twenty nets, and give these nets to these women, after their clothes have been taken off!" And it was done according to all that His Majesty commanded. And they rowed to and fro, and the heart of His Majesty was glad when he beheld how they rowed.

[9] These are mortuary offerings, to be placed in the tombs of King Nebka and of Weba-aner.

[10] Seneferu was the father of Cheops, and the founder of the Fourth Dynasty.

Then one of them, she who was at the stern,[11] became entangled
with her braided tresses, and a fish pendant of new turquoise fell
into the water. And she became silent and ceased rowing, and her
side became silent and ceased rowing.

Then said His Majesty: "Aren't you rowing?" And they said: "Our
leader is silent and has stopped rowing." And His Majesty said to
her: "Why don't you row?" She said: "It is the fish pendant of new
turquoise that has fallen into the water." He had another one brought
to her and said: "I give you this one instead." And she said: "I want
my pot down to its bottom!"[12]

Then said His Majesty: "Go and bring me the Chief Lector-priest
Djadja-em-ankh!" And he was brought straightway. And His Majesty
said: "Djadja-em-ankh, my brother, I have done as you said, and the
heart of My Majesty was diverted when I beheld how they rowed.
But a fish pendant of new turquoise belonging to a leader fell into
the water, and she was silent and rowed not, and so she spoiled her
side. And I said unto her: "Why don't you row?" And she said to
me: "Because a fish pendant of new turquoise has fallen into the
water." And I said to her: "Row on, and I will replace it." And she
said to me: "I want my pot down to its bottom!"

Then the Chief Lector-priest Djadja-em-ankh said what he said,
words of magic, and he placed the one side of the water of the lake
upon the other,[13] and found the fish pendant lying on a potsherd.
And he brought it and gave it to its mistress. Now as for the water,
it was twelve cubits deep in the middle, and it reached twenty-four
cubits after it was turned back. Then he said what he said, words of
magic, and he brought the waters of the lake back to their place.

And His Majesty spent the whole day in merriment with the entire

---

[11] The ancient Egyptian pleasure boats had two sets of rowers, one set on each side,
each rower at the end serving as "stroke," or coxswain. In Seneferu's crew of girls in
fish net, it is the "coxswain" of her side who loses her pendant. In one tomb painting,
a woman is shown in a pleasure boat with just such a turquoise fish jewel in her
hair. In this story, the fish pendants charmingly add to the marine motif of the fish
nets on Seneferu's girls.

[12] Evidently a popular expression meaning something like "I want my own and all
of my own." The pertness of the spirited girl is an excellent touch.

[13] Compare Moses dividing the waters of the Red Sea. Dividing the waters was
apparently something of an Egyptian specialty in the magic art.

palace, and he rewarded the Chief Lector-priest Djadja-em-ankh with all good things.

Lo, this is a wonder which came to pass in the time of your father King Seneferu, True of Voice, one of the deeds of the Chief Lector-priest, the Scribe of the Book, Djadja-em-ankh.

And the Majesty of King Cheops said: "Let there be offered to the Majesty of King Seneferu, True of Voice, a thousand loaves of bread, a hundred jugs of beer, one ox, and two measures of incense, and let there be given to the Chief Lector-priest, the Scribe of the Book, Djadja-em-ankh, one cake, one jug of beer, and one measure of incense, for I have seen an example of his learning!" And it was done according to all that His Majesty commanded.

III

Then Prince Dedef-Hor[14] stood up to speak and said: "Hitherto you have heard only examples of what they knew who have gone before us, and we know not the truth from falsehood. But even in your own time there is a great magician, one who is unknown to you!"

Then said His Majesty: "Who is that, Dedef-Hor, my son?" And Prince Dedef-Hor said: "There is a townsman,[15] Djedi is his name, and he dwells in Djed-Seneferu. He is a townsman of one hundred ten years, and he eats five hundred loaves of bread, a haunch of beef in the way of meat, and drinks one hundred jugs of beer unto this very day.[16] He knows how to put on again a head that has been cut off, and he knows how to make a lion follow after him with its leash

---

[14] In this story, note the play on the root *djed* in the proper nouns Dedef (or Djedef)-Hor, Djedi, Redjedet, Djed-Seneferu, a device that, like paranomasia, was much favored by the Egyptians, and to which they attached much significance. The hieroglyphic biliteral *djed,* the "column of Osiris," when used as a word means "to be firm, enduring, and so on."

[15] See note 3.

[16] This and the following sentence describe some of the miraculous qualities of Djedi. One hundred and ten was the Egyptian round figure for a good old age. In perfect keeping with the Egyptian background of the Biblical story, Joseph lives to the age of one hundred and ten (Genesis 50:26).

trailing on the ground.[17] He knows the number of secret chambers in the sanctuary of Thoth!"[18]

Now the Majesty of King Cheops, True of Voice, was always seeking for himself the secret chambers of the sanctuary of Thoth, to make for himself the like thereof for his Horizon.[19]

Then said His Majesty: "You yourself, Dedef-Hor, my son, shall bring him to me!"

And ships were made ready for Prince Dedef-Hor, and he voyaged upstream to Djed-Seneferu.[20] Now when the ships were moored to the bank, he went journeying by land and sat in a litter of ebony, the poles of which were of *sesenem*-wood and overlaid with gold. And when he came to Djedi, the litter was set down. And he stood up to salute him, and he found him lying on a mat at the threshold of his house, and a slave held his head and was stroking it for him, and another was rubbing his feet.

And Prince Dedef-Hor said: "Your condition is like life before growing old and before old age, the occasion of decease, of enwrapping and of burial.[21] You are still one who sleeps on into the daylight, free from sickness, and without the hacking cough of old age. Greetings, revered one! I have come hither to summon you on behalf of my father Cheops, True of Voice, that you may eat the dainties that the King gives, the victuals of them that are in his service, that he may bring you after a happy life to your fathers, who are in the realms of the dead."

Said this Djedi: "In peace, in peace,[22] Dedef-Hor, O King's son,

[17] That is, of its own accord, without being led by its keeper.

[18] Thoth was the ibis-god of writing, learning, and magic, all of which, to the Egyptians, were intimately related. As patron deity of learning and as scribe of the gods, Thoth and his mysteries would be especially known to such a high adept in the sacred books as Djedi.

[19] The tomb-sanctuary of the king, into which he "sets" in repose, like the sun in the horizon.

[20] Near the pyramid of Seneferu, at Meidum.

[21] That is, you are as hale and hearty as one who has not yet attained such a great age. You sleep the whole night through, unlike most old people. In the Egyptian text, the language of these greetings is, as Battiscombe Gunn says, "very high-falutin and difficult to translate."

[22] A usual expression of greeting in Egyptian. Compare Hebrew *shalom*, Arabic *salaam*, "peace."

whom his father loves! May your father Cheops reward you! May he
advance your station among the elders! May your *ka* contend with
your adversary![23] May your soul know the ways leading to the
portal of Hebesbag![24] Greetings, O King's son!"

And Prince Dedef-Hor held out his hands to him and helped him
up; and then he went with him to the riverside, giving him his hand
the while. And Djedi said: "Let a ship be given me, that it may bring
my children, together with my books." And two vessels with their
crews were put at his service; but Djedi voyaged downstream in the
ship in which was Prince Dedef-Hor.

Now when he reached the Residence, Prince Dedef-Hor entered in
to make report to the Majesty of King Cheops, True of Voice. And
Prince Dedef-Hor said: "O Sovereign my Lord. I have brought Djedi."
Said His Majesty: "Go, bring him to me!" Then His Majesty proceeded to the pillared hall of the Palace, and Djedi was brought in
unto him.

And His Majesty said: "How is it, Djedi, that I have never seen
you before?" And Djedi said: "It is he who is summoned who comes.
The Sovereign summoned me, and lo, I have come."

And His Majesty said: "Is it true what is said, that you can put on
again a head that has been cut off?" And Djedi said: "Yea, that I
can, O Sovereign my Lord."

And His Majesty said: "Have brought unto me a prisoner that is
in the prison, that his punishment may be inflicted." And Djedi said:
"But not on a man, O Sovereign my Lord! Lo, it is forbidden to do
such a thing to the Noble Herd!"[25]

Then a goose was brought in unto him, and its head was cut off,
and the goose was placed on the western side of the hall and its head
on the eastern side of the hall. And Djedi said what he said, words
of magic, and thereupon the goose stood up and waddled, and its
head likewise. Now when one part had reached the other, the goose
stood up and cackled. And he had a duck brought unto him, and there

[23] That is, may your Divine Essence successfully overcome the malevolent demons
who impede the passage of the deceased to the blessed realms of the Other World.
[24] One of the guardians of the portals of the Other World.
[25] Human beings, in Egyptian texts, are sometimes referred to as the "Noble Herd,"
and the "Flock of the God," a concept not innovated by monotheism. Note also the
essential humaneness of Djedi.

was done unto it the like. And His Majesty had an ox brought to him, and its head was made to tumble to the ground. And Djedi said what he said, words of magic, and the ox stood up behind him, while its tether fell to the ground.

IV

And King Cheops said: "It has been said that you know the number of the secret chambers in the sanctuary of Thoth." And Djedi said: "So it please you, O Sovereign my Lord, I know not the number thereof, but I know the place where it is."[26] And His Majesty said: "Where is that?" And Djedi said: "There is a chest of flint in the chamber named 'The Inventory' in Heliopolis.[27] Lo, it is in the chest. But Sovereign my Lord, it is not I who will bring it to you." And His Majesty said: "Who, then, will bring it to me?" And Djedi said: "It is the eldest of the three children who are in the belly of Redjedet that will bring it to you."

And His Majesty said: "With pleasure. But as for what you are saying—who is she, this Redjedet?" And Djedi said: "She is the wifc of a priest of Ra, Lord of Sakhebu;[28] she is pregnant with three children of Ra, Lord of Sakhebu.[29] He has told her that they will exercise this Excellent Office[30] in this entire land, and that the eldest of them will be Great Seer[31] in Heliopolis."

Then His Majesty's heart grew sad thereat.[32] And Djedi said: "Pray, what is this mood, O Sovereign, my Lord? Is it because of the three children? Then I say unto you: after you, then your son, then his son, and then one of them."[33]

[26] That is, where the number is written and hidden. Number is of great importance in magic, and it is of prime significance in various mystical systems where it is the basis of elaborate metaphysical constructions, for example the Kabbalah.
[27] The chamber was presumably in the temple of Ra.
[28] A town near Heliopolis, the great ancient seat of Ra.
[29] Throughout the ancient world, of course, the gods begot on human mothers children who became illustrious and/or royal. The kings of Egypt began to add the "Son of Ra" name to their titularies during the Fifth Dynasty.
[30] The kingship.
[31] One of the titles of the high priest of Ra in Heliopolis.
[32] Because Ra will establish a new line, replacing that of Cheops.
[33] Before this happens, you and your grandson will reign after you. Cheops was succeeded by his son Khaf-Ra, and the latter's son Men-Kau-Ra, or Mycerinus. Shepses-Kaf, the last king of the Fourth Dynasty, is not mentioned here.

And His Majesty said: "When will she give birth, pray, this Redjedet?"

"She will give birth on the fifteenth day of the first month of the second season."[34]

And His Majesty said: "Then the sandbanks of the Canal of the Two Fishes[35] are uncovered; otherwise, I myself would have set foot there, to see the Temple of Ra, Lord of Sakhebu." And Djedi said: "Then will I cause the water to stand four cubits deep over the sandbanks of the Canal of the Two Fishes."

Then His Majesty betook himself to the Palace. And His Majesty said: "Let Djedi be assigned to the house of Prince Dedef-Hor, that he may dwell with him. Fix his allowance at a thousand loaves of bread, a hundred jars of beer, an ox, and a hundred bunches of leeks." And it was done according to all that His Majesty commanded.

Now on one of these days it came to pass that Redjedet suffered the pangs of childbirth. Then said the Majesty of Ra, Lord of Sakhebu to Isis, Nephthys, Meskhenet, Heket, and Khnum:[36] "Up, go ye and deliver Redjedet of the three children that are in her womb, that will exercise this Excellent Office in this entire land. They will build your temples, they will furnish your altars with victuals, they will replenish your libation-tables, and they will make great your offerings."

Then these deities went, when they had taken on the forms of dancing-girls, and Khnum was with them, carrying their things.

And they came to the house of Ra-weser,[37] and found him stand-

[34] The Egyptian year was divided into three seasons of four months each. The first season, called *Akhet,* was that of the inundation of the Nile, and began in midsummer. The second season, *Peret,* began about the middle of November, when the waters receded. *Peret* is usually translated "winter," but Egypt has no winter as we know it. The third season was *Shemu,* possibly meaning "dry."

[35] Evidently a canal leading to Sakhebu. It would be rather dry when the Nile flood receded, making navigation difficult.

[36] Isis and Nephthys are the two great goddesses, the children—with Osiris and Set—of Geb and Nut. Meskhenet is the special goddess of childbirth. Heket is an ancient fertility goddess, appropriately represented as frog-headed. She is associated with Khnum, the god who fashions human beings on his potter's wheel. Ra himself, who has fathered Redjedet's triplets, sends these powerful deities to effectuate the birth.

[37] Redjedet's husband, the aforementioned priest of Ra. The name means "Ra is powerful."

ing with his loincloth hanging down.[38] Then they presented to him
their *menit*-collars and their rattles.[39] And he said: "My mistresses,
behold there is a lady here who is in travail!" And they said: "Let
us see her, for we understand midwifery." And he said unto them:
"Come."

Then they entered in before Redjedet, and shut the door of the
room upon them and her. And Isis placed herself in front of
her, and Nephthys behind her, and Heket hastened the birth.
And Isis said: "Be not lusty in her womb, in this your name of
Weser-eref!"[40] This child slipped forth on to her hands, a child of
one cubit with strong bones. The royal titulary of his limbs was
of gold, and his headcloth of real lapis lazuli.[41] They washed him,
cut his navel cord and laid him on a sheet upon a brick. And
Meskhenet drew near unto him, and she said: "A king who will
exercise the Kingship in the entire land." And Khnum gave health
to his body.

[The birth of the two other children is then related, both times in
the same words and in the same detail. But the adjurations are, of
course different:] "Draw not near in her womb, as truly as you are
named Sah-Ra!"[42] [and] "Be not dark in her womb, as truly as you
are named Keku!"[43]

---

[38] All flustered, and caught *en déshabillé.*
[39] The word translated as "dancing-girls" in the preceding paragraph actually denotes those priestesses whose sacred function was that of making music and singing
and dancing in the ritual of the deity. The *menit* (a sort of collar with a large
pendant in the back—feminine and masculine symbols combined) and the rattle were
ritual objects primarily associated with the great fertility-goddess Hathor. Extending
these objects to a person was a token of the grace of the goddess.
[40] Personal names as plays upon words are familiar from the Bible, where the names
of children, for example, those of Jacob's wives, are built upon utterances of their
parents when they are born. *Weser-eref* means "more powerful than he." Actually,
the name of the first king of the Fifth Dynasty was *Weser-Kaf,* "powerful is his *ka*
(his divine essence)."
[41] The royal and divine infants are born as represented in their statues, with their
titularies inlaid in gold on their arms, and their headcloths fashioned of lapis lazuli.
[42] The root *sah* means "draw near" and "endow." The second king of the Fifth
Dynasty was *Sahu-Ra,* "endowed of Ra."
[43] *Keku* means "darkness," but the third Fifth Dynasty king was *Ka-ka-i,* which may
possibly mean something like "my divine essence is a divine essence," or "he of
the double divine essence," neither of which seems, at least to us, to make too much
sense. He is better known by his other name of *Nefer-ir-Ka-Ra,* "well performs the
Divine Essence of Ra."

And these divinities went forth, after that they had delivered Redjedet of the three children. And they said: "Let your heart be glad, Ra-weser! Behold, three children are born unto you!" And he said unto them: "My mistresses, what can I do for you? I pray you give this measure of barley to your porter, and use it for yourselves as payment, to prepare beer."[44] So Khnum loaded himself with the barley.

Now when they had gone their way to the place whence they had come, Isis said unto these deities: "What means it, that we have come and yet have worked no wonder for these children, that we may make report to their father who sent us forth?" So they fashioned three royal crowns, and they placed them in the barley.

And they caused storm and rain to come in the sky,[45] and they went back to the house. And they said: "We pray you, let us lay the barley here in a sealed chamber until we return from dancing in the north." And they laid the barley in a sealed chamber.

And Redjedet purified herself with a fourteen days' purification.[46] And she said to her handmaid: "Has the house been provisioned?" And she said: "It has been provisioned with every good thing, save for pots, which have not been brought." And Redjedet said: "Why, pray, have not pots been brought?" And the handmaid said: "There is nothing here with which to make beer, except for the barley belonging to the dancing-girls, and that is in a chamber bearing their seal." And Redjedet said: "Go down and fetch some of it, and Ra-weser will recompense them for it after he returns."

So the handmaid went and opened the chamber. And she heard in the chamber the sound of singing, music, dancing, rejoicing, and all that is done in a King's honor. Then she went and told Redjedet

---

[44] Ra-weser, of course, does not know their real identity, and seeks to reward them as humans. The motif of the divinity appearing in human guise in order to aid favored mortals is found in the Biblical stories connected with Abraham. There, it is not the deity who appears in human form, but his messengers ("angels") as an accommodation with monotheism.

[45] As a pretext for returning to Ra-weser's house. The barley would be spoiled by the rain.

[46] In early societies, and in aboriginal societies today, a woman who has given birth is considered unclean, and consequently taboo until she has undergone a period of isolation and/or rituals for the purposes of purification (see Leviticus 12:2–8).

all that she had heard. And Redjedet went round the chamber, but could not find the place where it was being done. Then she laid her temple to the grain sack, and she found that it was in this [the grain sack]. And she put it [the grain sack] in a chest, put the chest in another locker, corded it with hide, put it in a closet which contained her pots, and sealed the door upon it.

And Ra-weser came in from the field, and Redjedet related to him this matter. And he rejoiced greatly, and they sat them down and made a happy day.[47]

Now after some days had passed by, Redjedet was enraged with her handmaid about a matter, and had her punished with blows. And the handmaid said unto the people who were in the house: "How can she do this? She has borne three kings. I will go and tell it unto the Majesty of King Cheops!"[48]

So she went, and found her eldest brother binding yarn of flax on the threshing floor. And he said to her: "Whether are you bound, little girl?" Then she related unto him this matter. And her brother said to her: "And so you have come even to me, and am I to take part in the betrayal?" And he took a bundle of flax to her, and dealt her a grievous blow. Then the handmaid went to fetch her a handful of water, and a crocodile seized her.

Then her brother went to tell it to Redjedet, and he found Redjedet sitting with her head upon her knees[49] and her heart heavy more than anything. And he said unto her: "Mistress, why are you so troubled?"

And she said: "It is this girl, who has grown up in the house. Lo, she is even now gone forth, saying: 'I will go to reveal it'!"

And he hung down his head and said: "My mistress, she came and told me the affair, and I dealt her a grievous blow. And she went to draw her some water and a crocodile seized her."

[The papyrus breaks off here.]

---

[47] A frequent expression for having a good time.
[48] So that he will "liquidate" this threat to his dynasty.
[49] One of the usual Egyptian attitudes of mourning. See below, "The Story of Sinuhe," third paragraph, where the courtiers, at the death of the king, sit "with heads bent down upon their laps."

22 The Tale of the Two Brothers

Also a tale of magic and sorcery, this story has as its underlying motif that of the married woman who is carnally attracted to a youth serving in her household. She attempts to seduce him, but he remains adamantly chaste out of loyalty to his master and refuses to succumb to her wiles. Then, with all the "fury of a woman scorned," she accuses the youth to her husband of having attempted to rape her, and the expected violent consequences ensue. This motif is one of the most frequently encountered in the folktale, the most well-known examples in our culture being the story of Joseph and Potiphar's wife in the Bible, and that of Hippolytus and Phaedra, referred to by Homer and used by Euripides as the subject of one of his greatest tragedies. The Egyptian tale is characteristically amplified and embellished with incidents of magic and transformation.

The extant copy of the story is on a papyrus dated to about 1220 B.C., during the Nineteenth Dynasty.

It is told that there were once two brothers, of one father and one mother. Anubis was the name of the elder, and Bata was the name of the younger.

Now Anubis had a house and a wife, and his younger brother lived with him like a son. It was he who made clothes for him and drove his cattle to the fields. And it was he who did the plowing and harvested for him, and it was he who did all the work that there is in the fields. Now the younger brother was a comely youth. There

270

was none his like in all the land; and the might of a god was in him.

And Anubis's younger brother tended his cattle as was his daily wont, and he went home to his house each evening laden with all manner of herbs of the field, and with milk and wood, and all good things of the fields, and set them down before his elder brother, who was sitting with his wife. And he drank and ate, and went out to sleep in his cow house, alone among his cattle.

Now when it had dawned and another day had come, the younger brother brought food which had been cooked, and set it down before his elder brother, who gave him provisions for the fields. And he collected his cattle to pasture them in the fields, and he drove them out. And they said to him: "The grass of such and such a place is good." And he understood all that they said, and took them off to the good place with the grass that they wanted. And the cattle that he tended became very fine, and they increased their calving very, very much.

Now at the time of plowing his elder brother said to him: "Make ready for us a good team of oxen for plowing, for the land has come forth [after the inundation],[1] and it is a good time for plowing. Also come to the field with seed, for we shall be busy plowing tomorrow." So he said to him. And his younger brother did just as his elder brother had told him to.

Now when it had dawned and another day was come, they went to the field with their seed and busied themselves with plowing, and they were very happy in their work at the beginning of their labors.

Now some time after this they were in the field, and they were held up for shortage of seed. And Anubis sent his younger brother, saying: "Go and fetch us seed from the village."

And Bata found his elder brother's wife sitting and doing her hair. And he said to her: "Get up and give me some seed, that I

[1] The annual inundation of the Nile occurred around mid-July. This event, so important to the Egyptian agricultural economy, together with the coincidental appearance of the brilliant star Sirius above the horizon just before sunrise, was the beginning of the Egyptian year. (See King Cheops and the Magicians, note 34.) The year had three seasons of four months each: Akhet, "inundation"; followed by Peret, "coming forth"—the emergence of the fields from the water when the Nile had subsided—to which Anubis is referring here; and Shemu, possibly meaning "deficiency of water."

may go back to the field, because my brother will be waiting for me. Don't make me wait."

And she said to him: "Go and open the granary and take what you want. Don't make me interrupt my hairdressing!"

Then the youth went into his cow house and brought a large vessel, wishing to take away much seed, and he loaded himself up with barley and wheat and came out with them.

And she said to him: "How much is that on your shoulder?" And he told her: "It's three bushels of wheat and two bushels of barley—five bushels in all which are on my shoulder." Thus he spoke to her.

Then she talked with him, saying: "There is great strength in you! I see your feats daily!" And she desired to know him as a man is known.

And she stood up and took hold of him and said to him: "Come, let us spend an hour lying down together. It will be well for you, and I will make you fine clothes!"

Then the youth became like a panther of southern Egypt for great anger at the evil speech that she had uttered to him, and she was very much afraid. And he talked with her, saying: "But see, you are like a mother to me, and your husband is like a father to me! He, who is older than I, it is he who brought me up. What is this great crime which you have said to me? Do not say it to me again, and I will not tell it to anyone. I will not let it come out of my mouth to any man."

And he lifted up his burden and went off to the field. And he reached his elder brother, and they busied themselves at their labors.

Now afterward, at evening time, his elder brother went home to his house, while Bata tended his cattle and loaded himself with all manner of things of the field, and brought his cattle back before him to put them into their cow house in their village for the night.

Now his elder brother's wife was afraid because of the speech that she had uttered, and she brought fat and grease,[2] and made as if

---

[2] To smear on her "bruises." She could also use it as an emetic to bring on the vomiting which was another part of her act.

she had been beaten, with the intent to say to her husband, "It is your younger brother who has beaten me!"

And her husband came back in the evening, as was his daily wont. And he reached his house, and found his wife lying down pretending to be in pain. She did not pour water over his hands according to his wont, nor had she lighted the lamp before he came in. His house was in darkness, and she was lying there vomiting.

And her husband said to her: "Who has been speaking with you?" Then she said to him: "No one has been speaking with me except your younger brother. When he came to fetch seed for you and found me sitting alone, he said to me: 'Come, let us spend an hour lying down together. Put on your wig!'[3] he said to me, and I did not listen to him. 'Am I not your mother, and is not your brother like a father to you?' I said to him. And he was afraid, and he beat me to prevent me from reporting it to you. Now if you let him live, I will kill myself! See, when he comes back, do not speak to him, because if I were to accuse him of this evil thing, he would turn it into an injury."[4]

And his elder brother became like a panther of southern Egypt. And he sharpened his spear, and took it in his hand, and he stood behind the door of his cow house to kill his younger brother when he returned in the evening to drive his cattle into the cow house.

Now when the sun had set, Bata loaded himself with all manner of herbs of the field, according to his daily wont, and came back. And the foremost cow entered the cow house, and said to her herdsman: "See, your elder brother is standing in front of you with his spear to kill you! Flee before him!"

And he understood what his foremost cow had said. And the next one went in and said the same thing. And he looked under the door of the cow house, and saw the feet of his elder brother as he stood behind the door with his spear in his hand. And he

---

[3] The elaborate wig of ringlets worn by Egyptian women when they wanted to be prettied-up. Both men and women of ancient Egypt shaved the hair of their entire bodies for the purpose of cleanliness, and they wore either wigs or closefitting skullcaps both for aesthetic reasons and to protect their heads from the sun.
[4] That is, he would make a self-righteous denial.

273

set his burden down on the ground and betook himself to speedy flight. And his elder brother went after him with his spear.

Then his younger brother prayed to Ra, the Horus of the Double Horizon, saying: "My good Lord, thou art he who judges between the evil doer and the just man!"

Then Ra heard all his pleas, and created a great water between him and his elder brother, full of crocodiles. And one of them found himself on one side, and one on the other. And the elder brother struck twice on the hands[5] because he had not killed him.

And the younger brother called to him from the other side, saying: "Stay here until dawn, and when the sun rises you and I will be judged before him, and he will deliver the evildoer unto the just. For I will never live with you again, nor be in any place where you are. I will go to the Valley of Cedar!"

Now when it had dawned and another day was come, Ra, the Horus of the Double Horizon, arose, and they saw one another. And the youth spoke with his elder brother, saying: "Why did you pursue me to kill me wrongfully before you heard what I had to say? For I am indeed your younger brother, and you are like a father to me, and your wife is like a mother to me—is it not so? Now when you sent me forth to fetch seed for us, your wife said to me: 'Come, let us spend an hour lying together!' But see, to you she has turned it into the opposite!"

And he informed him of everything that had happened between him and his wife, and he swore by Ra, the Horus of the Double Horizon, saying: "Your coming with your spear to kill me wrongfully was at the bidding of a filthy whore!"

And he took a reed knife and cut off his phallus, and threw it into the water, and a shad swallowed it.[6] And he grew faint, and became weak. And his elder brother was very sorry for him and stood

[5] As a gesture of anger or frustration.
[6] An obvious parallel motif is found in the Osiris and Set myth. Set, after cutting up the body of Osiris, scattered the dismembered portions throughout the nomes of Egypt, but he threw the phallus into the Nile, where it was devoured by an oxyrhinchus-fish.

weeping aloud for him. He was not able to cross the water to where his younger brother was, because of the crocodiles.

And his younger brother called to him, saying: "Though you remember one bad thing, do you not remember one good one, or anything that I have done for you? Go home and collect your cattle, for I will not stay in any place where you are! I will go to the Valley of the Cedar. Now what you can do for me is to come to help me. For I shall take out my heart, and place it on top of the flower of the cedar. And if the cedar is cut down, and my heart falls to the ground, and you come to seek it—do not be discouraged if you spend seven years in seeking it. And if you find it and put it into a jar of cold water, then I shall come to life, and I will take vengeance for being sinned against! And you will know if anything is wrong with me when a pot of beer is given into your hand and it foams up. Then do not delay. It will certainly happen to you!"

And he went off to the Valley of the Cedar.

And his elder brother went off to his house with his hand laid on his head, which was smeared with dust.[7] Then he arrived at his house, and he killed his wife and threw her to the dogs. And he dwelt in mourning for his younger brother.

Now, some time after this, Bata was in the Valley of the Cedar, no one being with him. And he spent his days hunting the beasts of the desert, and in the evening he came back to lie down under the cedar, on the top of whose flower his heart was.

And some time after this, he built himself a castle with his own hands in the Valley of the Cedar, full of all good things, in order to set up a home for himself. Then he came out of his castle, and he encountered the Ennead walking and ordering the affairs of the whole world. And the Ennead told one of themselves to say to him: "Hail, Bata, Bull of the Ennead, are you here alone, having left your town, fleeing from the wife of Anubis your elder brother? See, he has killed his wife, and you are avenged upon him for all the injuries done to you!" And they were very sorry for him. And Ra, the Horus

---

[7] As a token of grief.

of the Double Horizon, said to Khnum:[8] "Do you fashion a spouse for Bata that he may not dwell alone!"

And Khnum made him a spouse, who was more beautiful than any woman in all the world; the seed of every god was in her. And the Seven Hathors came to see her; and they said with one voice, "She will have a sharp death!"[9]

And he loved her very, very much. And she dwelt in his house, and he spent his days hunting the beasts of the desert, bringing them and laying them before her. And he said to her: "Do not go outside, lest the Sea carry you off![10] For you shall not be able to save yourself from him, being only a woman. Now my heart lies on top of the flower of the cedar, and if anyone else finds it I shall fight with him." And he revealed everything to her concerning his heart.

Now some time after this Bata went to hunt, after his daily wont. Then the girl went out to walk about under the cedar which was beside her house. Then the Sea saw her, its waves beating after her, and she betook herself to flight before it and went into her house. And the Sea brought away a lock of her hair.

And the Sea brought it to Egypt, and laid it at the place of the launderers of Pharaoh (may he live, prosper, and be healthy!).[11] And the smell of the lock of hair entered into Pharaoh's clothes. And the King quarreled with Pharaoh's launderers saying: "There is a small of unguent in Pharaoh's clothes!" And they quarreled thus every day, and they did not know what to do.

And Pharaoh's head launderer walked to the riverbank, and his

---

[8] A ram-headed god, frequently represented as fashioning all living creatures on a potter's wheel.

[9] The Seven Hathors presided at the birth of children and announced their destiny. Here they foretell her death by the sword.

[10] The powerful and villainous Yam, Syro-Canaanite god of the sea, and in the ancient Canaanite texts the violent opponent of Baal. Along with other Canaanite deities, Yam was "adopted" into the Egyptian pantheon during the very cosmopolitan New Kingdom period. We have an Egyptian papyrus, unfortunately in quite a fragmentary condition, describing Yam's attempt to carry off Astarte, another Canaanite goddess, here represented as a daughter of Ptah.

[11] The regular formula following every mention of the king, the palace, and so on. It would be tiresome to repeat it at every point in the translation here.

heart was very wretched as a result of the daily quarrels. And he stopped still and stood on the bank looking at the lock of hair, which was in the water. And he made a man go down, and he brought it to him. And he found its odor very sweet, and he took it to Pharaoh.

And they fetched the scribes and learned men of Pharaoh. And they said to Pharaoh: "This lock of hair belongs to a daughter of Ra, the Horus of the Double Horizon, in whom there is the seed of every god! It is a present to you from another country. Send messengers to every foreign land to seek her, but as to the messenger who goes to the Valley of the Cedar, send many people with him to bring her back." Then His Majesty said, "What you have said is very, very good." And the people were sent forth.

Now many days after this, the people who had gone to the foreign lands came back to make report to His Majesty. But those who had gone to the Valley of the Cedar did not return, for Bata had killed them. But he spared one of them to make report to His Majesty.

Then His Majesty sent many soldiers and charioteers to fetch her back; and among them was a woman into whose hands had been given all beautiful feminine adornments. This woman came back to Egypt with her, and there was rejoicing over her in all the land. And His Majesty loved her very, very much, and he named her as Great Favorite.

And he spoke to her to get her to talk about her husband. And she said to His Majesty: "Have the cedar cut down and destroyed!" And he sent soldiers with their weapons of bronze to cut down the cedar. And they reached the cedar and cut down the flower on which was Bata's heart. And he fell down dead at that very moment.

Now when it had dawned and another day had come, and the cedar had been cut down, Anubis, the elder brother of Bata, went into his house and sat down to wash his hands. And a pot of beer was given to him, and it foamed up; and another, of wine, and it turned sour. And he took up his staff and his sandals, also his clothes and his weapons, and set forth to journey to the Valley of the Cedar.

And he entered the castle of his younger brother, and found him lying on his couch dead. And he wept when he saw his younger

277

brother in a state of death, and went to search for his heart under the cedar under which his younger brother went to sleep in the evening. And he spent three years seeking it, and he did not find it. And when he had entered upon the fourth year, he longed to return to Egypt. And he said: "I will go away tomorrow." So he said in his heart.

Now when it had dawned and another day was come, he fell to walking under the cedar, and spent the day seeking the heart. And he went back in the evening, all bent on seeking it again. And he found a berry, and he went back with it. Now, it was his younger brother's heart. And he fetched a jar of cold water, and threw it into it, and he sat down as was his daily wont.

Now when night had come, his heart had absorbed the water, and Bata quivered in all his members. And he began to look at his elder brother while his heart was in the jar. Then Anubis, his elder brother, took up the jar of cold water in which was his younger brother's heart, and made Bata drink it. And his heart stood in its place, and he became as he had been.

And they embraced one another, and spoke to each other. And Bata said to his eldest brother: "See, I will become a great bull, with all beautiful markings, but whose true nature will not be known.[12] And you shall sit on my back until the sun rises and we are in the place where my wife is, that I may take vengeance. And you shall take me to the place where the King is, for all good things will be done for you, and you will be rewarded with my weight in silver and gold for having taken me to Pharaoh. For I shall become a great wonder, and they will rejoice over me in all the land. Then will you go away to your village."

Now when it had dawned and another day had come, then Bata changed himself into the form which he had told his brother about, and Anubis, his elder brother, sat on his back until dawn. And he reached the place where the King was, and His Majesty was informed about him. And he came to see him, and he was very glad about him. And he made a great feast because of him, saying: "This

[12] The sacred bulls of ancient Egypt were recognized and distinguished by their particularly peculiar and beautiful markings and colors.

278

is a great marvel that has happened!" And they rejoiced over him in all the land.

And the King gave his weight in silver and gold to his elder brother, who went to dwell in his village. And the King gave him many people and much property, and Pharaoh loved him very much, more than anybody else in all the land.

Now some time after this, the bull went into the domestic quarters of the Palace and stood where the Favorite was. And he fell to talking with her, saying: "See, I am still alive!" And she said to him, "Who, pray, are you?" And he said to her: "I am Bata! I know that when you had the cedar destroyed for Pharaoh it was on my account, so that I should not live. But see, I am still alive, and I am a bull."

And the Favorite was very frightened at what her husband had said to her, and she went out of the domestic quarters.

And His Majesty sat down to spend a happy day with her, and she poured out wine for His Majesty, and the King was very happy with her. And she said to His Majesty: "Swear to me by a God, saying, 'What the Favorite may say, I will do her pleasure.'" And he hearkened to all that she said. "Let me be allowed to eat some of the liver of this bull, for he will be of no use," she said to him. And the King was very much vexed at what she had said, and the heart of Pharaoh was very much pained for him.

Now when it had dawned and another day was come, the King announced a great feast with the sacrifice of the bull, and the King sent one of his chief butchers to slaughter the bull. And afterward he was slaughtered; and while he was borne on the men's shoulders he shook his neck, and cast two drops of blood beside the two door jambs of His Majesty. One of them fell on one side of the Great Portal of Pharaoh, and the other on the other side, and they grew into two large persea trees, and each of them was very fine.

And they went to tell His Majesty: "Two large persea trees have grown up, a great marvel for His Majesty, in the night, beside His Majesty's Great Portal!" And they rejoiced over them in all the land, and the King made offering to them.

Now some time after this, His Majesty appeared at the Lapis Lazuli Window, with a garland of all manner of flowers at his neck.

And he was mounted in a golden chariot, and he came out of the Palace to see the persea trees. And the Favorite came out with the entourage following Pharaoh. And His Majesty sat down under one of the persea trees, and the Favorite under the other. And Bata spoke with his wife, saying: "O you traitress, I am Bata, and I am alive in spite of you! I know that you caused the cedar to be cut down for Pharaoh on my account, and I became a bull and you had me killed!"

Now some time after this, the Favorite stood pouring out wine for His Majesty, and the King was happy with her. And she said to His Majesty: "Swear to me by a God, saying: 'What the Favorite may tell me I will do her pleasure.' So you shall say." And she said: "Have these two persea trees cut down, and made into beautiful furniture!"

And the King obeyed all that she said, and immediately His Majesty sent cunning carpenters, and Pharaoh's persea trees were cut down. And the King's wife, the Favorite, watched it done. And a splinter flew up and entered the Favorite's mouth, and she swallowed it. And she conceived and became pregnant in the space of a moment. And the King did everything that she fancied with the trees.

Now some time after this, she gave birth to a male child.[13] And they went to tell His Majesty: "A male child has been born to you!" And he was fetched, and a nurse and female attendants were given him, and the people rejoiced over him in all the land. And the King sat making holiday, and the people were in jubilation. And His Majesty loved him at once, very much, and made him Royal Son of Kush [viceroy of Nubia]. And many days after this, His Majesty made him Crown Prince of the entire land.

Now some time after this, when he had spent many years as Crown Prince of the whole land, His Majesty flew up to heaven.[14] And the new King[15] said: "Let my great royal officials be brought to

[13] The final incarnation of Bata.
[14] A frequent euphemism for the death of the king. He was the living Horus, whose usual form is a falcon.
[15] Now Bata himself, of course.

me, that I may inform them of everything that has happened to me." And also his wife was brought to him, and he and she were judged before them. And the judges agreed with him.[16]

And his elder brother was brought to him, and he made him Crown Prince of the entire land. And he spent thirty years[17] as King of Egypt, and then passed on to life.[18] And his elder brother arose in his place on the Day of Mooring.[19]

It has come to an end happily and in peace. By the Ka of the Scribe of the Treasury Ka-Gabu,[20] of the Treasury of Pharaoh (may he live, prosper, and be healthy!), and of the Scribe Hori and of the Scribe Mer-em-Ipet. Made by the Scribe Inena, the master of this manuscript. As for him who says anything against this manuscript, Thoth will be his adversary!

---

[16] And naturally condemned her to the death by the sword foretold by the Seven Hathors. With a fine delicacy, the Egyptians were reluctant to mention death sentences, and in the texts we find them euphemized or to be inferred, as here.

[17] Thirty years was a round number approximating a generation. The great *Heb-Sed* Festival, the king's jubilee, was originally held in the thirtieth year of his reign.

[18] That is, passed on to life eternal, another euphemism for dying.

[19] Still another euphemism for the day of death, found also at the end of the story of Sinuhe.

[20] Ka-Gabu was chief scribe of the Royal Treasury. Hori and Mer-em-Ipet were probably either subordinate supervisors or fellow scribes of Inena. Since Ka-Gabu evidently ordered the copy to be made, it is considered as having been done by his "spirit."

23   The Shipwrecked Sailor, or the Isle of the Serpent

This tale is one of the classics of the Middle Kingdom, specifically the Twelfth Dynasty (1990–1780 B.C.). Unfortunately the beginning of the story is lost, but the unbroken part of the papyrus begins at the "story within a story," which is that of the adventures of the shipwrecked sailor who is washed ashore on the island ruled by the fabulous and kind serpent. Evidently the story is told by a marine officer to his captain as they are returning from some unsuccessful expedition. The captain seems to be in great fear of having to face the king with the story of his failure, and the officer tells him this story to cheer him up and to emphasize the point that things are never as bad as they seem, that "all's well that ends well," and so forth. The captain, however, with characteristic Egyptian skepticism, does not seem to be impressed.

. . . Said the excellent Retainer:[1]

Let your heart be easy, O Chief![2] See, we have reached the Residence-city![3] The mallet has been taken, the mooring post has been driven, and the prow rope placed on shore. Give praise and adore the god, for all our men are embracing each other! Our crew has arrived safely, and there are none of our expedition missing.

---

[1] Literally, "follower." A courtly rank denoting an attendant upon the king.

[2] A title of rank of the lower nobility, held by local princes and chieftains, somewhat analogous to "count."

[3] The city in which the king was residing at the time, not necessarily the capital.

We reached Wawat and passed Senmut.[4] See now, we have returned in peace; we have reached our land.

Listen to me, Chief! I am not given to exaggeration. Wash yourself; pour water over your fingers. Then you will reply when you are addressed, and will speak to the king. You will have your wits about you, and will speak without faltering. A man's mouth can save him; his words obtain indulgence for him! But do as you please—I have become weary, telling you these things.

But I will tell you something similar to this which happened to myself when I set out for the mines of the Sovereign. I went down to the sea[5] in a ship of the length of one hundred and twenty cubits and forty cubits in breadth.[6] There were one hundred and twenty sailors in it, of the choice of Egypt. Whether they scanned the sky or whether they scanned the earth, their hearts were stronger than lions! They foretold a storm before it had come, and a tempest before it had arisen!

A storm broke forth while we were on the sea, before we could reach land. We carried the wind, but the storm redoubled, and it made a wave eight cubits high. I was struck by a beam of wood. Then the ship perished. Of those in it, not one survived.

Then I was cast upon an island by a wave of the sea. I passed three days with my heart alone as a companion, lying under the shelter of a tree, and embracing the shade. Then I stretched my legs to find out what I might put in my mouth.

I found figs and grapes there, and all sorts of fine greens. There were two sorts of sycamore fruit, and cucumbers like those cultivated. There were fish there, and birds; there was nothing which was not in it!

Then I stuffed myself, and put the rest of the food on the ground, as it was too much for my hands to carry. I carved out a fire drill and made a fire, and made a burnt-offering to the gods.

---

[4] Both Wawat and Senmut were down at the southern border of Egypt, not far from what is now Aswan.

[5] Literally "the Great Green."

[6] These impossibly large dimensions (and the huge crew) are part of the marvelousness in the tale.

283

Then I heard a noise like thunder. I imagined it was a wave of the sea; the trees were breaking and the earth was shaking. When I uncovered my face, I found that it was a serpent which was coming! He was thirty cubits long, and his beard was longer than two cubits! His body was overlaid with gold, and his eyebrows were of real lapis lazuli. He coiled himself forward, and opened his mouth at me. I was on my belly before him.

"Who has brought you," he said to me, "who has brought you, O little one? If you delay in telling me who has brought you, I will cause you to find yourself as ashes, and reduced to nothing!"

I answered: "You speak to me, but I hear it not! I am helpless before you—I do not know myself!"

Then he placed me in his mouth and took me off to his lair. He set me down without hurting me. I was sound; nothing had been taken from me. He opened his mouth at me while I was on my belly before him. Then he said to me:

"Who has brought you, who has brought you, O little one? Who has brought you to this island of the sea, whose borders are surrounded by water?"

Then I answered him, my arms bent before him, and I said:

"I am one who went down to the mines on a mission for the Sovereign, in a ship of the length of one hundred and twenty cubits and forty cubits in breadth. There were one hundred and twenty sailors in it, of the choice of Egypt. Whether they scanned the sky or whether they scanned the earth, their hearts were stronger than lions! They foretold a storm before it had come, and a tempest before it had arisen. Each one was strong of heart, and stronger of arm than his fellow; there was no poltroon among them. A storm came while we were on the sea, before we could reach land. We carried the wind, but the storm redoubled, and it made a wave eight cubits high. I was struck by a beam of wood. Then the ship perished. Of those in it, not one survived except me—behold me at your side! Then I was brought to this island by a wave of the sea."

"Fear not," he said to me, "fear not, O little one! Strengthen your countenance, for it is to me that you have come! See, a god

has caused you to live; he has brought you to this island of Ka.[7]
There is nothing which is not within it; it is full of all good things.
Lo, you shall spend month after month here until you complete
four months on this island. And then a ship will come from the
Residence with sailors in it whom you know. You will go with them
to the Residence, and you will die in your own city.

"How happy is he who relates what he has experienced after he
has already gone through painful things! I will relate to you something similar which happened on this island. I dwelt in it together
with my brethren, and there were children among us. We num-
bered seventy-five serpents—I will not include a little daughter
brought to me as result of a prayer.

"Then a star fell,[8] and all these went forth in the fire which it
brought. It happened that I was not there when they were burned;
I was not among them. And then I perished for them, when I
found them all as one corpse. If you are valiant, subdue your fears.
You will fill your embrace with your children. You will kiss your wife,
and you will see your own house—this is better than anything! You
will reach the Residence, and you will be in it among your
brethren."

Then I extended myself upon my belly and touched the ground
before him. Then I said to him:

"I will relate your might to the king, and will cause him to
know your greatness! I will cause to be brought to you all rare
and fragrant spices, and official incense of the temples, wherewith
every god is made content. I will relate what happened to me, and
what I have seen of your power. The god shall be praised in your
name in the city, in the presence of the magistrates of the entire
land. I will slaughter for you oxen for burnt-offerings, and will
sacrifice fowl for you. I will have brought to you ships laden with all
the best things of Egypt, as is done for a god who loves men, in a
far-off land which men do not know!"

[7] The *ka* was the divine and immortal essence of both gods and men. As a name
for the fabulous island, it may have indicated its paradisiacal abundance.
[8] A meteor or comet?

Then he laughed at me, knowing that what I said was foolishness, and he said to me:

"You have no abundance of myrrh and other rare spices. You have mere ordinary incense! But as for me, I am a ruler of Punt.[9] I have plenty of myrrh—I live in it! As for the other rare spices, they are an abundant product of this island. And when you depart from this place, you will never see it again. It will become water!"

And indeed the ship did come, as he had foretold. I went and placed myself upon a high tree, and I recognized those who were in it. Then I went to report it to him, and I found that he already knew it. And he said to me:

"Safely, safely, little one, to your home! You will see your children again. Praise my name in your city, for indeed it is my due of you!"

Then I placed myself upon my belly, my arms bent before him. And he gave me a load of myrrh and other rare and fragrant spices, eye-paint, giraffe tails, a large bundle of incense, elephant tusks, hounds, monkeys, apes—all good and noble things. Then I loaded it on this boat, and I placed myself on my belly to praise the god in his name.

Then he said to me: "Lo, you shall reach the Residence in two months, and you shall fill your embrace with your children. You shall flourish in the Residence, and there you shall be buried."

Then I went down to the shore where the ship was. I called to the soldiers who were in this ship. I gave praise on the shore to the lord of this island, and those in the ship did likewise. We made our voyage northward to the Residence of the Sovereign. We reached the Residence in two months, according to all he had foretold. I went in to the presence of the Sovereign, and presented to him the tribute which I had brought from within this island. And he praised the god in my name before the officers of this entire land.

Then I was made a Retainer and was given two hundred men. Look at me now, after I had reached land, after all that I saw and

[9] A land on the southwestern shores of the Red Sea, approximately the region of Somaliland. The Egyptians sent many expeditions there to bring back rare spices, incense, and other good things.

286

had undergone! Hearken, then, to my speech, for it is good to listen to people!"

Then he said to me: "Do not play the superior to me, my friend! Who gives water at dawn to a bird which he is going to kill later in the morning?"[10]

It has come from its beginning to its end, as found in the writing. The scribe excellent of his fingers, Amen-Aa ["Amen is great"] son of Ameny, may he live, prosper, and be healthy!

---

[10] Evidently a proverb or folk saying of rather pessimistic import. This, the chief's only speech in the text as we have it, indicates that the sailor's story has not lessened his gloomy forebodings.

287

24   The Story of Sinuhe the Egyptian

Sinuhe is the great classic of Egyptian belles-lettres, admired by all scholars for its style and use of language, and as the culmination of the culture of the Middle Kingdom. In its use of suspense and in its variety of colorful incident interlaced with poetry, the author (the story purports to be told by Sinuhe himself) has produced one of the masterpieces of world literature. The fact that several manuscripts and many fragments of the work, both on papyrus and on ostraca, have been discovered, is evidence of the fact that it was very popular among the Egyptians themselves. As a classic of style, and as a work of sustained interest, it was used as one of the standard texts set for copying by schoolboys. The reader will recognize several motifs of the folktale in the story, among them the victorious fight with the boastful, overconfident giant, recalling David and Goliath. And, of course, it is this text which Mika Waltari used as the basis for his excellent novel, *The Egyptian.*

There is an element of mystery at the beginning of the story. Sinuhe tells us that he was accompanying a military expedition to Lybia led by the royal prince and heir apparent, Sen-Wesret (the later Senusret I, who reigned from 1960 to 1936 B.C.). As the expedition was returning, after a successful campaign, secret messengers from the capital arrived to meet it, and upon hearing the news they bore, the prince immediately

288

rushed back to the capital with only a few attendants, leaving his army behind. Sinuhe happened to overhear what the news was: that the reigning king, Amen-em-Hat (Amenemhat I, the founder of the Twelfth Dynasty, and who ruled from 1990 to 1960 B.C.), was dead. He tells us that he was seized with a paralyzing terror, and stood in fear of imminent death. He managed to hide behind some bushes, and then he stole away and fled from land to land, finally ending up in Palestine, where he lived for many years. Why should Sinuhe, who evidently stood in well with Prince Senusret, be seized with terror at the news of the king's death, and why did he run away in fear of his life? We shall never know, as Sinuhe does not tell us.

All we can do is make an educated guess. Amenemhat may have perished as the victim of a palace conspiracy, as we might infer from *The Instruction of King Amen-em-Hat* (Chapter 17). If this were the case, the only possible reason for Sinuhe's fear would be that he was somehow implicated (or believed that he would be implicated) in the conspiracy. Possibly he would be accused of "guilt by association," since he occupied an important position in the palace. Be that as it may, we later learn that all of his fears were quite groundless, and that the king and the royal children were most happy to see him back many years later.

Apparent above all is Sinuhe's love of Egypt. No matter how prosperous he became in the land of his adoption, and even though he had raised a family there and accumulated wealth, he regarded the place as nothing better than a wilderness. When he was brought back to Egypt he returned to "civilization," achieving the supreme happiness of having his tomb built there, complete with an endowment of funerary offerings when he should enter the World of Eternity.

The Hereditary Prince and Chief, Treasurer of the King, and Unique Courtier, Administrative Dignitary of the districts and estates of the

289

Sovereign in the lands of the Syrians, Actual Acquaintance of the King and beloved of him, the King's Retainer[1] Sinuhe says:

I was a retainer who followed his lord, a servant of the Royal Harem and of the Princess great of praise, the wife of King Sen-Wesret and daughter of King Amen-em-Hat, namely, Neferu,[2] Lady of Reverence.[3]

In the year 30 of his reign, in the third month of the season of Inundation, the god ascended unto his horizon; the King of Upper and Lower Egypt, Amen-em-Hat, was taken up to heaven and united with the sun. The body of the god was united with him who made him.[4] The city of royal residence[5] was silent, all hearts were in grief, and the great Double Gates were sealed. The courtiers sat with heads bent down upon their laps, and the people were in mourning.

Now His Majesty had sent a great army to the land of the Lybians,[6] with his eldest son in command of it, namely, the beautiful god Sen-Wesret. He had been sent to smite the foreign lands, to strike down the dwellers in Lybia. Indeed, even now was he returning, bringing living prisoners from among the Lybians and all kinds of cattle without limit.

The courtiers of the palace sent to the western border, advising the King's son of what had come about in the Palace. The messengers found him on the road, having reached him at the time of

---

[1] "Unique Courtier," "Actual Acquaintance of the King," and "Retainer" were titles assumed by those high in the inner councils of the court and trusted henchmen of the sovereign.

[2] Literally, "Beauties."

[3] Note that Sinuhe was actually in the service of the Princess Neferu, daughter of Amen-em-Hat I, and wife of the latter's son Sen-Wesret, whom Amen-em-Hat had already elevated to the co-regency.

[4] One of the king's titles was "Son of Ra," and at his death he rejoined his father in the sky. He was also the living Horus, and at his death he became his father Osiris; but in mythic thinking, as in dreams, logical consistency is irrelevant. The historical date is probably 1962 B.C.

[5] Wherever the king happened to make his residence at the time, and not necessarily the actual capital.

[6] The Lybians to the northwest and the Nubians on the south had been harassing the borders of Egypt ever since Old Kingdom times, and these were notorious trouble spots.

evening. Not a moment at all did he delay: The Falcon[7] flew with his attendants, not letting his army know what had happened.[8]

Now those others of the King's sons who were following him in this expedition were sought out, and one of them was called aside.[9] And lo, I happened to be standing near by, and heard his voice as he was speaking. My heart was distraught, my arms flung apart, and trembling seized all my limbs. I sprang bounding away to seek myself a place to hide. I placed myself between two bushes to hide from the passers-by. I certainly had no intention of returning to the Residence, for I expected civil strife to break out, and I did not think I would live after the King's death.

I crossed Lake Maati near Nehet and landed at the island of Senefru. I passed the day at the edge of the fields, and at dawn the next morning I set forth again. I met a man standing on the road. He was frightened of me, and stood in awe.[10] When it was time for supper, I reached the town of Negau. I crossed the river on a barge without a rudder, with the aid of a westerly wind. I passed eastward of the quarry, above the temple of Hathor, Lady of the Red Hill. I gave road to my legs and went northward.

I arrived at the Walls of the Ruler,[11] which were made to repel the Syrians and to defeat the Sand-crossers. I took up a crouching position under a bush, in fear lest the watch of the day standing on the wall would see me. At the time of late evening I journeyed on, and when the sun came forth again I reached Peten, and halted at the island of Kem-Wer. A great attack of thirst overtook me. My throat was hot and dry, and I said, "This is the taste of death."

Then I lifted up my heart and pulled my limbs together, for I heard the sound of the lowing of cattle and I spied some Syrians. A distinguished chieftain among them, who had been in Egypt, recognized me. Then he gave me water and cooked milk for me. I proceeded with him to his tribe, and they treated me well.

[7] The king was the incarnate Horus, who was always represented as a falcon.
[8] Evidently the utmost secrecy had to be maintained, until Sen-Wesret could consolidate his position.
[9] It has been suggested that possibly this other son of the king may have been a pretender to the throne, put forward by the conspiratorial anti-Sen-Wesret party.
[10] Possibly because of Sinuhe's wild appearance.
[11] A fortress on the northeastern border of Egypt, built by Amen-em-Hat I.

Land gave me to land. I went forth to Byblos, and then I turned back to Kedem. There I spent a year and a half. Then Amu-nenshi, a ruler in Palestine, fetched me. He said to me, "You will fare well with me; here you will hear the speech of Egypt." He said this since he knew my character and had heard of my capacities. The Egyptians who were there with him bore witness for me.

He said to me, "For what reason have you come to this place? What is it? Has something happened at the Residence?"

Then I said to him, "King Amen-em-Hat has proceeded to the Horizon. No one knows what can happen because of it." But I added, untruthfully:

"I was returning from an expedition to the land of the Lybians when it was reported to me. My mind became unquiet. My heart was not in my body, and it drew me to the desert roads. I had not been accused of anything, no one had spat in my face, and no wretched remarks had been heard about me. My name had not been heard in the mouth of the herald.[12] I do not know what brought me to this land. It is like the dispensation of some god; or like a dream in which a man of the Delta might see himself in Nubia!"

Then he said to me, "What, then, will the land be without him, that excellent god, the fear of whom pervaded the foreign lands like Sekhmet[13] in a year of pestilence?"

I spoke to him in reply, "Indeed his son has entered into the Palace and has assumed the heritage of his father.

For he is a god; there is none his equal,
    and there is none other who surpasses him.
He is a master of understanding, excellent in plans and beneficent
                              of decrees;
    and going and coming are according to his commands.
He it was who subdued the foreign lands while his father was
                          within the palace;
    and he reported to him that what he was ordered had been
                                  done.

[12] He had not been proclaimed a malefactor.
[13] The lioness-headed goddess of war, violence, and destruction.

Mighty indeed is he, achieving with his strong arm;
    a valiant one, and there is not his equal!
He slakes his wrath by smashing skulls;
    and no one can stand up about him.
He is robust of heart at the moment of attack;
    and does not let sloth rest upon his heart.
Bold of countenance is he when sees the mêlée;
    to attack the barbarian is his joy.
He girds his shield and crushes the foe;
    and does not strike twice in order to kill!
But he is lord of charm and great of sweetness;
    and through love has he conquered!
His city loves him more than itself;
    it rejoices in him more than in its god;
    men and women salute and rejoice with him now that he is King!
He conquered while still in the egg,
    and his face was turned to royal deeds since he was born.
He makes multiply those who were born with him;
    he is unique, the gift of the god.
He is one who makes wide the boundaries;
    he will seize the southern countries, and the northern ones with
                                             ease,
    having been created to smite the Syrians and to crush the
                                        Sand-crossers.
How this land rejoices now that he is come to rule!

Send to him, cause him to know your name as an inquirer far
from His Majesty. He will not cease to make happy a land which
will be loyal to him!"

Then he said to me, "Well, assuredly then, Egypt is happy, knowing that he flourishes. Behold, you are here, and you shall stay with
me. I will treat you well."

He placed me at the head of his children, and he married me to
his eldest daughter. He let me choose for myself from his land,
from the choicest that he had, on his boundary adjoining another
territory. It was a good land, and Yaa was its name. There were
figs in it, together with grapes. It had more wine than water; great

was its honey and abundant its olives. Every fruit was on its trees. There was barley there, and emmer wheat, and all kinds of cattle without limit.

And much, indeed, accrued to me as a result of the love of me. He appointed me as ruler of a tribe of the choicest of his country. Provisions were assigned for me daily, and wine for each day's needs; cooked meat and roasted fowl besides desert game. They used to snare for me and set aside game for me over and above what my hounds caught. Much wine was made for me, and milk was used in every kind of cooking.

Thus I spent many years. My children became strong men, each man in control of a tribe. The couriers who went north or south to the Palace would tarry because of me, and I made all travelers tarry. I gave water to the thirsty; I put on the road those who had become lost, and I rescued those who were plundered.

When the Bedouin became so bold as to oppose the "Chiefs of the Foreign Lands,"[14] I advised them how to proceed. This ruler of the Syrians[15] caused me to spend many years as commander of his army. Every foreign territory against which I went forth, I attacked and it was driven away from its pasturage and its wells. I plundered its cattle, I carried away its inhabitants, and seized their food. I slew people thereof with my strong arm, and by my movements and my excellent devices, I found favor in the ruler's heart, and he loved me. He recognized my valor, and placed me even before his children, since he saw that my arms flourished.

There came a powerful man of the Syrians to taunt me with challenges in my tent. He was a hero without peer, and he had beaten all the Syrians. He said he would fight with me. He expected to despoil me and plunder my cattle, being so counseled by his tribe.

[14] By this name the Egyptians denoted a loose confederation of North Syrian tribes, composed of various ethnic and linguistic groups. The phrase, in Egyptian, is *Hekau Khasut,* "Rulers of Foreign Lands," rendered into Greek almost two millennia later as *Hyksos.* During the decline of the Middle Kingdom, the Hyksos penetrated into Egypt and eventually seized control of most of the kingdom. After ruling almost two centuries, they were expelled under the first kings of the Eighteenth Dynasty (beginning about 1580 B.C.).
[15] That is, Amu-nenshi.

294

The ruler discussed the matter with me, and I said, "I do not know him, and I certainly am not an associate of his going about in his camp. Is it that I have opened his gate, or thrown down his fence? It is envy, because he sees me carrying out your orders. Assuredly, I am like a bull who has wandered into the herd, and whom the long-horned steer of the herd attacks. Is there any man of humble origin who is loved when he becomes a superior? Well, if he wants to fight, let him speak out what he has in mind. Is a god ignorant of the fact that the nature of whatever he has ordained will eventually be known?"[16]

During the night I strung my bow and practised my shooting. I made my dagger loose and free and polished my weapons. At dawn all Syria came, its tribes stirred up and half its peoples assembled; this fight had been planned.

Then he came toward me as I waited, and I placed myself in position near him. Every heart burned for me, and the women and even the men were murmuring. Every heart was sick for me as they said, "Is there another strong enough to fight him?"

But I escaped his missiles and made his arrows pass me by until none remained, and his shield, his ax, and his armful of spears fell down before me. Then he charged at me. I shot him; my arrow stuck in his neck. He shrieked and fell on his nose. I killed him with his own battle-ax. I gave forth my shout of victory on his back while every Syrian roared. I gave jubilant praise to Montu[17] while his partisans mourned him.

This ruler Amu-nenshi took me in his embrace. Then I carried away my enemy's goods, and I plundered his cattle. What he had planned to do to me, this I did to him. I seized all that was in his tent, and stripped his encampment. Thus I widened my possessions and became numerous in cattle. I became great there. Thus has the god done, in being gracious unto one against whom he had been angered, and whom he had sent astray into another land. Today is his heart appeased.

[16] The precise meaning of this phrase is obscure.
[17] An Egyptian war god, originally a local deity of Thebes.

A fugitive has fled in his straitened moment;[18]
   now my good report is in the Palace.
A lingerer lingered because of hunger;
   now I give bread to my neighbor.
A man left his land because of nakedness;
   now I am bright of raiment and of linen.
A man ran for lack of someone to send;
   now I am rich in slaves.
My house is beautiful, and broad is my abode.
   The memory of me is in the Palace.

O whichever God ordained this flight, show mercy and return me to the Palace! Surely you will grant that I see the place where dwells my heart!

What is more important than that my body be buried in Egypt, the land where I was born? O come to my aid!

That which has occurred is a fortunate event—the god has shown mercy. May he do the like to bring to a good end him whom he has afflicted!

May his heart be sick for him whom he has cast out to live in a foreign land. Is it true that today he is appeased? Then let him hear the prayer of one who is afar! Let him turn his hand toward him who trod the earth, leading him back to the place whence he drew him forth!

May the King of Egypt be gracious unto me, who lives in his grace! May I hail the Lady of the Land,[19] who is in his Palace, and may I hear word of his children! Then might my limbs flourish, since old age has befallen me, and infirmity has overtaken me.

My arms are weak, and my legs have slackened. My heart is weary; I am near to departure, and they will take me away to the City of Eternity![20]

Might I once more serve the Lady of All! Then will she tell

[18] Sinuhe is of course referring to himself.
[19] Namely, the queen.
[20] His great fear was that he would be buried by the Syrians in a foreign land and without the requisite magical funeral rites, and consequently would not enter into eternal life with Osiris.

me that it is well with her children! May she spend eternity over me![21]

Now, it was told to the Majesty of the King of Upper and Lower Egypt, Kheper-Ka-Ra [Senusret I], regarding the circumstances under which I was living. And His Majesty kept sending to me bearers of gifts of the royal bounty, that he might gladden the heart of this his servant like the ruler of any foreign land. And the children of the King, who were in the Palace, let me hear word from them.

[Here Sinuhe inserts the text of the message sent by King Senusret inviting him to return to Egypt:]

Copy of the decree brought to this servant about bringing him back to Egypt:

"The Horus Living-of-Births, the Two Ladies Living-of-Births, the King of Upper and Lower Egypt, Kheper-Ka-Ra, Son of Ra, Senusret, Living forever unto eternity![22]

"A decree of the King to the Retainer Sinuhe:

"Behold, this decree of the King is brought to you to advise you as follows: You have wandered about foreign lands—you have gone from Kedem to Tenu. Under the counsel of your own heart, land gave you to land! What have you done, that anything should be done against you? You have not blasphemed, that your words should be reproved. Your words have not been evil in the Council of the Nobles, that your utterances should be opposed. This plan of yours carried away your heart. It was not in my heart against you.

"This your 'Heaven,'[23] who is in the Palace, today prospers and flourishes. Her head is covered with the royalty of the land. Her children are in the Residence; you shall heap up precious things of what they will give you, and you shall live by their largesse.

---

[21] That is, like heaven. The sky-goddess Nut is often represented as enfolding the deceased in her wings. Later on, the queen is referred to as Sinuhe's "heaven."
[22] The official titulary of the king consisted of five names: the king as (1) the living Horus, (2) The Two Ladies—the vulture-goddess Nekhbet and the cobra-goddess Buto, protectresses of Upper and Lower Egypt respectively, (3) the Horus of Gold, which is not given here, (4) King of Upper and Lower Egypt, and (5) Son of Ra. The last two names were written in cartouches.
[23] The queen, as in note 21.

"Do you return to Egypt, that you may see the Residence wherein you grew up. You shall kiss the earth at the Great Double Door, and you shall join the courtiers.

"For today indeed you have begun to grow old, and have lost your virile powers. Be mindful of the day of burial, of passing to a revered state! A night will be assigned for you for oils and wrappings from the hands of Tayit.[24] A funeral cortege will be made for you on the day of interment—a mummy case of gold with a headpiece of lapis lazuli, and a heaven canopy above you. You will be placed upon a bier, with oxen drawing you and singers going before you, and the mortuary dances will be performed at the door of your tomb. The lists of the offering-table shall be invoked for you, sacrifices shall be made before your tomb stelae, and your tomb columns shall be built of white limestone amidst the tombs of the royal children.

"You must not die in a foreign land! The Asiatics shall not escort you to burial. You shall not be put in a sheepskin and a mound made over you!

"This is too long to tread the earth. Be mindful of illness, and come back!"

This decree reached me as I was standing in the midst of my tribe. It was recited to me; I placed myself on my belly. I touched the earth and scattered it upon my hair. I went about my camp rejoicing and saying, "How can such things be done to a servant whom his heart led astray to foreign and barbarous lands? Good indeed is the clemency which rescued me from the hand of death! Your Divine Essence will allow me to make my end with my body in the Residence!"

[Sinuhe now gives the text of his reply:]

Copy of the answer to this decree:
"The Servant of the Palace, Sinuhe, says:

"In very good peace! It is known to your Divine Essence, this flight made by your servant in his ignorance, O good God, Lord of the Two Lands, Beloved of Ra, Favored of Montu, Lord of Thebes!

"Amen, Lord of the Thrones of the Two Lands, Sebek, Ra,

[24] Goddess of textile weaving.

298

Horus, Hathor, Atum with his Ennead, Soped, Nefer-Bau, Semseru, the Eastern Horus, the Lady of Yemet—The Serpent-goddess, may she continue to enfold your head—the Council over the Nile waters, Min-Horus amidst the foreign lands, Wereret Lady of Punt, Nut, Ra-Horus the Elder, and all the Gods of Egypt and the Islands of the Sea, may they give life and strength to your nostrils, may they endow you with their bounty, may they give you eternity without bound and everlasting without limit! May the fear of you be repeated in the lowlands and the highlands, when you have subdued all that the sun encircles! This is the prayer of your servant for his Lord, who saves from the West!

"The lord of perception who perceives his people, he perceives in the Majesty of his Palace that which your servant feared to say, and which is a grave thing to repeat. O great God, likeness of Ra, make prudent one who is laboring on his own behalf! Your servant is in the hand of one who takes counsel concerning him, and verily am I placed under his guidance. Your Majesty is Horus the Conqueror; your arms are mighty over all lands.

"Lo, this flight your servant made, I did not plan it; it was not in my heart, I did not devise it. I do not know what separated me from my place. It was like some sort of dream, as when a man of the Delta marshes sees himself in Elephantine, or a man of the northern swamps in Nubia. I did not take fright, no one was pursuing me, I had heard no reviling word. My name had not been heard in the mouth of the herald.

"However, my limbs began to quiver, and my legs began to tremble. My heart led me away. The god who ordained this flight drew me, although I had not been rebellious.

"Any man who knows his land stands in awe, for Ra has set the fear of you throughout the earth, and the dread of you in every foreign land. Whether I am at the Palace or whether I am in this place, it is you, indeed, who clothes this horizon. The sun shines at your pleasure; the water in the rivers, it is drunk at your desire; the air in the heaven, it is breathed when you so say.

"This your servant will resign the viziership which he has exercised in this place; it was a function they had requested your servant to perform. Your Majesty will act as he pleases; one lives by the breath which you bestow. Ra, Horus, and Hathor love this thy noble nose, which Montu, Lord of Thebes, desires shall live for ever!"

They came for me. I was allowed to spend a day in Yaa for transferring my possessions to my children, my eldest son having charge of my tribe—my tribe and all my property in his hands, my serfs and all my cattle, my stores of fruit and every pleasant tree of mine.

Then this servant went southward. I halted at the Roads of Horus. The commander there who was in charge of the frontier patrol sent a message to the Palace to make it known. Then His Majesty sent a capable overseer of the peasants who belonged to the Palace, followed by ships laden with gifts of the King for the Syrians who had come escorting me to the Roads of Horus. I introduced each of them by his name. Every servant was at his task when I set out and hoisted sail. They kneaded and strained before me,[25] until I reached the vicinity of Yetchet-Tawy.[26]

And when it dawned, very early, they came to call me, ten men coming and ten men going, to conduct me to the Palace. I touched my forehead to the ground beneath the sphinxes. The King's children were standing in the gateway to meet me. The courtiers who had been led into the Great Hall took me on the way to the royal chambers.

I found His Majesty on a great throne in a gilded niche. Then when I was stretched out on my belly, I lost consciousness before him. This god addressed me joyfully, but I was like a man overcome by dusk. My soul departed; my limbs were powerless, my heart, it was not in my body, that I should know life from death.

Then His Majesty said to one of the courtiers, "Raise him, and let him speak to me."

And His Majesty said, "Behold, you have returned! You have trodden foreign lands; you fled away. Now infirmity has seized you, and you have reached old age. It is of no little importance for your body to be buried, that you should not be interred by the Bedouin. Come, do not behave thus, not to speak when your name is pronounced!"

[25] That is, prepared fresh bread and beer during the entire journey.
[26] Literally, "the (city which) holds the Two Lands," a town south of Memphis, the residence of the first kings of the Twelfth Dynasty.

But I still feared punishment, and I answered with the response of
one afraid, "What does my Lord say to me? I should answer, but
I can do nothing. It is indeed the hand of a god. There is a terror
in my belly, like that which brought about that destined flight. Behold me before you; life is yours; may Your Majesty do as he
desires!"

Then they had the King's children brought in, and His Majesty
said to the Queen, "Behold Sinuhe, come as a Bedouin, as if born
a Syrian!"

She uttered a very great cry, and the King's children all shouted
together. And they said to His Majesty, "Is it not he, in truth, O
King, My Lord?"

And His Majesty said, "It is he, in truth!"

Now they had brought with them their *menit* collars and their
rattles and sistra of Hathor, and they presented them before His
Majesty, saying:

"Put forth your hands to these beautiful things. O enduring King,
    the adornments of the Lady of Heaven!
May the Golden One give life to your nostrils;
    may she join with you, the Lady of the Stars![27]
May the Crown-goddess of Upper Egypt sail northward
    and the Crown-goddess of Lower Egypt sail southward,
    joined and united by the utterance of Your Majesty!
The Cobra-goddess is set upon your brow,
    and you have removed your subjects from evil.
May Ra, Lord of the Two Lands, be gracious unto you;
    hail to you, as to the Lady of All!
Slacken your bow, make loose your arrow,
    give breath to him who is stifling!
Give us as a good festal gift this sheik, son of the North,
    a barbarian born in Egypt!
He made flight through fear of you,
    he left the land through dread of you!
May the face of him who has seen your face not be afraid;
    may the eye which has looked at you not be terrified!"

[27] These are various epithets of Hathor.

Then said His Majesty, "Let him not fear, and let him not fall into dread. He shall be a courtier among the nobles, and he shall be placed in the midst of the courtiers. Proceed you to the Morning-chamber, and wait upon him!"

And so I went forth from the royal chambers, the King's children giving me their hands. We proceeded afterward to the Great Double Door. I was placed in the house of a son of the King, which had fine things in it; there was a cooling room in it, and landscape decoration. There were valuables of the Treasury in it, and in every room was clothing of royal linen, and myrrh, and the best oil of the King, and of the courtiers, whom he loves. Every servingman was at his task.

The years were made to pass away from my limbs as I was shaved and my hair was combed. A load of dirt was given back to the desert, and their clothes to the sand farers. I was clothed in fine linen, and anointed with fine oil. I slept upon a bed. I gave back the sand to those who live in it, and tree oil to those who rub themselves with it.

There was given to me a house with grounds, which had belonged to a courtier. Many craftsmen restored it, and all its trees made to flourish anew. Meals from the Palace were brought to me three or four times a day besides what the King's children kept on giving me.

There was built for me a pyramid-tomb of stone, in the midst of the pyramids. The chief pyramid mason took charge of its ground, the chief draftsman designed it, the chief sculptor carved in it, and the chief builders of the necropolis concerned themselves with it. All the equipment which is placed in a tomb, those were supplied therein. Ka-priests were assigned to me. A funerary domain was made for me with fields in it, as is done for a foremost courtier. My statue was overlaid with gold, its kilt with fine gold.

By His Majesty was it caused to be done. There is no commoner for whom the like has been done. I was bestowed the favors of the King until there came the day of mooring.[28]

IT HAS COME FROM ITS BEGINNING TO ITS END, AS WAS FOUND IN THE WRITING.

[28] That is, the end of his life.

302

Appendix: How to
Become an Amateur Egyptologist

The word "amateur" literally means "lover," and when one is an amateur of anything, he is cultivating it out of sheer love, and without any thought of material gain. There are very few professional Egyptologists, and these few are teaching at universities (usually teaching subjects other than just Egyptology) or serving as museum curators. Staff members of archaeological expeditions are for the most part either university or museum people, and their professional salaries usually leave much to be desired. Most of the professional Egyptologists have been persons of independent means, but all are in the field because they love it, and if they have been favored by the opportunity of working in it professionally, they are still "amateurs" in the true sense of the word.

Anyone with love to give can become a lover of our dark and "mysterious" lady. But as we have mentioned in our Foreword, one has to take the trouble to get to know her. Fortunately, the means of acquiring this knowledge are readily available. Even an introductory bibliography with any pretensions to thoroughness would be beyond the scope of this book, but the works we will mention will supply many further leads for exploration to the lover of ancient Egypt.

Firstly, one should acquire a general working knowledge of the history and culture of Egypt, and the best book for an introductory survey is *The Culture of Ancient Egypt,* by Professor John A. Wilson of the Oriental Institute of the University of Chicago, and conveniently available as a Phoenix paperback (1956). This might be supplemented by *The Splendour of Ancient Egypt,* by Margaret A. Murray.

The interested (one almost said "hooked") reader could then proceed to such a standard history as James H. Breasted's *History of Egypt,* (New York, Charles Scribner's Sons, 1909), still in print; also available in paperback (New American Library). The best up-to-date history of Egypt, with excellent bibliography, is in French: *L'Égypte,* by Étienne Drioton and Jacques Vandier, (Paris, Presses Universitaires de France, 1952). This has not as yet been translated.

Two excellent works are available, published by museums and discussing the art of Egypt against the background of its history. Less expensive, and available in paperback, is *Ancient Egypt,* by William Stevenson Smith, curator of Egyptian art at the Boston Museum of Fine Arts and published by the museum in 1960. The second, much more elaborate and in two large volumes, with full bibliography, is *The Scepter of Egypt,* by William C. Hayes, late curator of Egyptian art at the Metropolitan Museum in New York and published for the museum by Harvard University Press in 1959 and 1960. A work well illustrated from the Boston Museum's excellent collection, and which will give the reader a good idea of the methods and results of Egyptian archaeology, is *The Egyptian Department and Its Excavations,* by Dows Dunham, curator emeritus of Egyptian art (Boston, Museum of Fine Arts, 1958), and it is available in paperback. The standard work on the pyramids, with a wealth of solid scientific information and no nonsense, and also well illustrated, is *The Pyramids of Egypt,* by I. E. S. Edwards, now curator of the great collection at the British Museum, revised Pelican paperback, 1961. Another excellent work, made up of separate chapters dealing with various aspects of ancient Egyptian culture, such as art, literature, medicine, and so on, each written by an authority

304

in the field, is *The Legacy of Egypt,* edited by S. R. K. Glanville, (New York, Oxford University Press, 1942).

The best group of modern, scholarly translations of the literature are those of John A. Wilson in the large volume of *Ancient Near Eastern Texts,* edited by John B. Pritchard, (Princeton, N.J., Princeton University Press, 1950, 1955). The interested reader will find there bibliographical references to the various publications, translations, and criticisms of the texts. The good but rather outdated *Literature of the Ancient Egyptians,* by the great German scholar Adolf Erman with translations by A. M. Blackman, long out of print, has been reissued in paperback with an excellent new introduction, an up-to-date bibliography, and much new information, by William Kelly Simpson, under the title of *The Ancient Egyptians, A Sourcebook of Their Writings,* (New York, Harper Torchbooks, 1966). The best translations of the tales, with excellent introductions and notes by a renowned scholar, is again in French: *Romans et Contes Égyptiens de l'Époque Pharaonique,* by Gustave Lefebvre, (Paris, Adrien-Maisonneuve, 1949).